Treasury Markets and Operations

Treasury Markets
and Operations

The Hong Kong Institute
of Bankers

WILEY

Cover Design: Wiley
Cover Images: Fountain © iStock.com/Giorgio Fochesato;
techno background © iStockphoto.com/Polygraphus;
Marble © iStockphoto.com/Rusm

Copyright © 2014 by John Wiley & Sons Singapore Pte. Ltd.

Published by John Wiley & Sons Singapore Pte. Ltd.

1 Fusionopolis Walk, #07-01, Solaris South Tower, Singapore 138628

Other Wiley Editorial Offices
John Wiley & Sons, 111 River Street, Hoboken, NJ 07030, USA
John Wiley & Sons, The Atrium, Southern Gate, Chichester, West Sussex, P019 8SQ, United Kingdom
John Wiley & Sons (Canada) Ltd., 5353 Dundas Street West, Suite 400, Toronto, Ontario, M9B 6HB,
Canada
John Wiley & Sons Australia Ltd., 42 McDougall Street, Milton, Queensland 4064, Australia
Wiley-VCH, Boschstrasse 12, D-69469 Weinheim, Germany

Library of Congress Cataloging-in-Publication Data
ISBN 978-0-470-82757-4 (Paperback)
ISBN 978-0-470-82759-8 (ePDF)
ISBN 978-0-470-82760-4 (ePub)

Typeset in 11/14 pt, Arno Pro Regular
Printed in Singapore by C.O.S. Printers Pte. Ltd.

10 9 8 7 6 5 4 3 2 1

Contents

Preface

Treasury Markets and Operations (TMO) and *Bank Asset and Liability Management* (ALM) are the two modules within the Hong Kong Institute of Bankers' (HKIB) curriculum of Treasury Management. As part of the Associate of the Hong Kong Institute of Bankers (AHKIB) Qualifications structure, the syllabuses are tailor made for learning and development of a banking career in Hong Kong and Mainland China. Therefore, the two modules—TMO and ALM—are closely related with one focusing on treasury market knowledge and tools for strategic execution and the other on how the overall composition of assets and liabilities should be formulated and managed to support the bank business model.

Why is the role of bank treasury important? Bank treasury needs to have the capability to understand the complexity of market conditions and the usage of treasury market products to implement the ALM strategy set by the asset and liability management committee (ALCO) and bank management. It is also closely involved in the control of a number of key risks including market risk, interest rate risk and liquidity risk, which are among the eight inherent risks under constant vigilance at banks and financial institutions.

This book *Treasury Markets and Operations* aims to equip bank treasury professionals with the necessary knowledge and tools to understand the complexity of changing market conditions and to apply their learning to manage risks and take advantage of emerging opportunities. The launch of this book on treasury markets and operations is very timely given recent developments in 2013–14, including:

• Increased market volatility in both the currency and money market, such as the further liberalization of the CNY foreign exchange rate mechanisms, the Bank of Japan policy on the JPY exchange rate, and the tapering of the third iteration of the Federal Reserve program of quantitative easing and the effect on the interest rate cycle.

- The beginning of the rollout of Basel III, which will take effect through 2013–2019 and will have significant effects on the future of bank business models in particular the size of balance sheets through the leverage ratio, the decision on the holdings of high quality liquid assets against the composition of bank liabilities, the complexity of internal transfer pricing on both liquidity and capital costs, and the complexity of collateral management for ver the counter (OTC) derivatives contracts.

In his 2013–14 Budget Speech, the Financial Secretary of Hong Kong mentioned the importance of financial services as one of the four pillar industries for the territory.

There are several areas that the industry will depend upon to develop a strong bank treasury sector:

a. Strengthening RMB-denominated financial products in promoting Hong Kong as an offshore RMB business centre;
b. Enhancing services for multinational enterprises to manage their global or regional treasury functions in Hong Kong; and
c. Increasing the depth of the bond market with the growing adoption of bonds (post-2015) as eligible high quality liquid assets for bank liquidity risk management.

The Hong Kong economy has been resilient against international financial crisis and has earned the highest AAA sovereign credit rating from Standard & Poor's since 2010, thanks in part to the strong standard of governance and a well-regulated and capitalized banking sector. Due to the cross border nature and the growing size of financial intermediation activities vis-à-vis the size of our economy, the banking sector must remain vigilant against future financial shocks. A strong bank treasury operations are critical to the timely and sound execution, especially during times of crisis.

Strong treasury management operations are key to the safe and successful operation of a bank or financial institution.

This book is divided into three parts and nine chapters that delve deeply into the subject matter. Every effort has been made to ensure that policies and regulations discussed are up to date and current as of early 2014. Students are advised to keep themselves up-to-date on evolving TMO issues available through the web sites of the Institute, the Hong Kong Monetary Authority (HKMA), and the Bank for International Settlements (BIS).

The first part of this book starts with a background discussion of bank treasury management. Chapter 1 considers treasury management in financial institutions and the issues the bank treasury has to deal with. Chapter 2 looks at the foreign exchange market, a significant part of bank treasury operations given that Hong Kong was ranked in the 2013 BIS survey as the world's fifth largest centre for foreign exchange trading. Chapter 3 looks at the money and capital markets with a particular focus on how these markets operate in Hong Kong. Chapter 4 then looks in depth at the bond market—and an appendix provides a more detailed discussion of the quantitative aspects of bond valuation. The discussion then moves on to derivative products in Chapter 5.

The second part of this book starts with Chapter 6, with a discussion of the various operations associated with the treasury. Because much of what the treasury does involves considerations of risk, that is exactly what Chapter 7 starts to consider with a discussion of the various types of risk, in particular market risk and how to assess their potential impact. Chapter 8 then moves on to a discussion of RMB payment and settlement systems as part of the development of Hong Kong as an offshore RMB centre, which are critical to managing treasury operational risks.

The final chapter in this book brings the discussion to a practical conclusion by considering a series of case studies to illustrate how weaknesses in treasury control can result in significant financial loss to financial institutions.

This book includes detailed explanations, summaries, tables, and charts to help industry professionals develop a sound theoretical framework for their work in the field. Both students and working professionals can benefit from this detailed work, produced in collaboration with some of Hong Kong's most prominent professionals. Aimed at banking practitioners and designed as an essential tool to achieve learning outcomes, this book includes recommendations for additional readings. This textbook should be used in conjunction with related regulatory documents published by the BIS, HKMA and other institutions, some of which are referenced in the text. A list of further readings at the end of each chapter will help readers expand their knowledge of each subject while supplementary readings can help readers dig deeper into specific areas. Essential readings will occasionally be highlighted and these are important for students preparing for the examinations leading to the Associate of the Hong Kong Institute of Bankers designation (AHKIB).

The information resources in the collection of Hong Kong Monetary Authority publications provided essential references in developing much of the book. The preparation of this work would not have been possible without the support and assistance of a number of subject expert advisors. We would like to extend our sincere thanks to Mr. Peter Wong Wai Man for his valuable insight and review on the syllabus and content of this book. Mr. Wong is also the Executive Board Member of the Treasury Markets Association. There are many others whose generous advice, support and encouragement have contributed to the development of the book. The Hong Kong Institute of Bankers and future banking professionals are indebted to all of them.

The Hong Kong Institute of Bankers

PART 1

TREASURY MANAGEMENT

1

Treasury Management of Financial Institutions

Learning objectives

After studying this chapter, you should be able to:

1 Understand the role the treasury plays in financial institutions including those of the front office, middle office, and back office.

2 Discuss treasury issues such as management of the balance sheet, liquidity risk, settlement and pre-settlement credit risk, interest rate risk, and foreign exchange exposure.

3 Understand the implications of the Basel III accords on asset and liability management.

4 Describe the controls and measures in treasury management to protect against overexposure, errors, and fraud, manage conflicts of interest, and other issues.

Introduction

Among companies in general, the corporate treasury department makes sure there is sufficient cash at all times to meet the operational needs of the business. Treasury also takes charge of cash forecasting, working capital management, cash management, investment management, treasury risk management, and fund-raising.

Treasury in financial institutions functions the same way—with one important addition. In institutions where investment banking is a key activity, treasury also participates in the foreign exchange, loans and deposits, debt securities, commodity products, and their derivative instruments on behalf of the bank and the bank's clients.

As such, it is important for banking professional, not only to master the intricacies of managing the treasury function, but also to gain a deep knowledge of how financial markets work. The banking professional needs to know the products that are traded there, and the controls and code of ethics that are designed to help protect the organisation against fraud, errors, over-exposure, conflicts of interest, and other risks.

In this chapter, we discuss the general facets of treasury management in financial institutions to establish a broad framework for the succeeding chapters, which deal in more detail with the financial markets, risk considerations and controls, and model codes of conduct and best market practices.

Issues in Treasury Operations

Some people might think that treasury operations exist only to generate profits for the bank, but they would be wrong. In fact, treasury operations are integral to the proper functioning of a financial institution, including the areas of balance sheet management, liquidity risk management, management of settlement and pre-settlement credit risk, management of interest-rate risk, and management of foreign exchange exposure. Banking professionals in Hong Kong should, at the bare minimum, be intimately familiar with these processes.

In banks and financial institutions, treasury departments are typically split into front, middle, and back offices with different functions. These functions will be explored in greater detail later in the book.

There is an important relationship between the management of capital and the management of risk, a relationship that has to be fine-tuned. On the one hand, treasuries at banks and financial institutions are expected to manage capital to ensure there is always enough liquidity to "fund increases in assets or meet obligations as they fall due without incurring unacceptable losses," notes the Hong Kong Monetary Authority (HKMA) in its Supervisory Policy Manual.[1]

---

[1]"Supervisory Policy Manual: Liquidity Risk Management (LM-1)." Hong Kong Monetary Authority, V.1A, 1 April 2011. Web. 7 Mar 2014.

Managing this relationship has long required treasuries to walk a fine line but the job has become more complicated in the past decade as a result of changing regulations and new liquidity requirements. Relatively recent changes in the way institutions fund their liquidity include increases in the use of wholesale and capital market sources that are more sensitive to credit and price risks, more frequent use of off-balance sheet activities and advances in electronic technologies like internet banking and smart cards that allow for faster withdrawal of funds. It is up to the treasury to balance out all these changes and ensure there is enough liquidity at all times.

At the same time, the treasury has to keep risks within boundaries that are acceptable both to regulators and their institutions. There are multiple types of risk such as liquidity risk, liability risk, exchange rate risk, credit risk, regulatory risk, and so on.

Managing liquidity risk is central to the treasury's operations. This requires the treasury to stay on top of the institution's liquidity position at any given time, balance that against the liquidity needs of the institution, track off-balance sheet activities—such as trading in derivatives or options—to make sure the institution is not caught off guard by a sudden need to cover a position, and correlate the liquidity risk with other types of risk. A sudden and unaccounted-for change in interest rates could, for example, drain away some liquidity from the institution and cause a chain reaction with potentially serious consequences.

All these activities are spread throughout the treasury. Often unseen from the outside, treasury operations have grown in size and complexity over the past few years. The treasury is now involved in most operations of the bank in one way or another, as we explore in this section.

Balance Sheet Management

The term "balance sheet management" refers to the process of determining the size and composition of the bank's assets and liabilities to achieve (or exceed) capital adequacy requirements and other desired financial ratios. It is a complicated process that involves balancing the often-conflicting goals of making a profit, staying liquid, and reducing risk.

As a key member of the Asset-Liability Management Committee (ALCO), treasury contributes to balance sheet management through its fund-raising and proprietary trading activities.

Treasury's success or failure to raise loan capital, for example, has a direct impact on the bank's liquidity position on the balance sheet.

Treasury also plays a role in creating new instruments for trading on the external markets, which may include the bank's securitized assets. Securitization involves packaging and pooling assets on the balance sheet such as mortgages, car loans, and credit card loans into financial instruments, effectively taking them off the balance sheet and thus reducing capital requirements.[2]

---

[2] The role of the treasury and its instruments are discussed in greater detail in "Asset and Liability Management", another book in this series.

Basel III

Over the last few decades, there has been a visible process of consolidation among financial institutions. Fewer banks meant stronger banks, so the theory went, but it also meant a greater concentration of risk among fewer institutions. As a result, starting in the 1990s, the Basel Committee on Banking Supervision[3] (BCBS) of the Bank for International Settlements (BIS) started paying greater attention to issues associated with balance sheet management and the regulatory recommendations put forth in the Basel Accords, which many regulators use as the basis for domestic regulatory structures.[4]

Basel II, the second iteration of the accords, first introduced capital adequacy requirements in the mid-1990s to create an international standard for capital convergence and risk management. Basel II was finally approved in 2004. Capital requirements are the minimum amount of capital that a bank must maintain in relation to each of its activities—and different activities have different capital adequacy ratios. It became the job of the treasury to ensure these requirements are constantly met. These capital adequacy requirements created stronger banks but at a cost, particular in terms of opportunities. Taking capital out of operations and locking it away as an umbrella for a rainy days means banks have less capital to lend or invest. Since lending and investment are the lifeblood of banks, less capital in these activities invariably means less profit.

The third iteration of the accords, known as Basel III, started being introduced in phases starting in Jan. 1 2013. These are a series of capital and liquidity rules for banks to, in the words of the BCBS, "strengthen the regulation, supervision and risk management of the banking sector." In broad strokes, Basel III has three broad goals. The first is to improve the ability of the banking sector to absorb the shocks of financial and economic stress, a lesson hard learned in the aftermath of the Global Financial Crisis. The second is to continue to improve risk management and governance. The third is to strengthen transparency and disclosures of banks. To accomplish these three goals, the reforms target bank regulation to raise the strength of individual banks, as opposed to the banking sector in general, while also creating systems to tackle system-wide risks that can build up and be amplified by weak economic cycles.

The Basel III capital accords were introduced in 2010 and updated in mid-2011. The liquidity rules were introduced in 2013. Known as the Liquidity Coverage Ratio (LCR), these liquidity rules were endorsed by the Group of Central Bank Governors and Heads of

---

[3] The Basel Committee on Banking Supervision (BCBS) is an international standard-setting body that promotes sound standards of banking supervision globally. Its members come from Argentina, Australia, Belgium, Brazil, Canada, China, France, Germany, Hong Kong, India, Indonesia, Italy, Japan, Korea, Luxembourg, Mexico, the Netherlands, Russia, Saudi Arabia, Singapore, South Africa, Spain, Sweden, Switzerland, Turkey, the United Kingdom and the United States.

[4] Horcher, Karen A. "Essentials of Managing Treasury". New Jersey: John Wiley & Sons, 2005. Print. Pg 197.

Supervision (GHOS) in January 2013. A key revision introduced by the LCR is an amendment to the definition of high-quality liquid assets and net cash outflows. When the LCR is fully implemented, sometime around 2019, the minimum LCR requirement should be around 100%, up from 60% upon its introduction in 2015. The phase in of the various Basel III requirements started in 2013. (See Table 1.1.)

The HKIB book *Operational Risk Management* offers more in-depth discussions of the Basel accords. For our purposes, it is sufficient to point out that Basel II linked capital requirements with risk management and did so by basing banking regulations on three pillars[5]:

- **Pillar 1:** Minimum capital requirements;
- **Pillar 2:** Supervisory review and processes;
- **Pillar 3:** Market discipline.

As it turned out, however, the capital adequacy requirements introduced in Basel II proved to be insufficient to avert the crisis of 2008. So, the BCBS revisited the issue in Basel III, the third iteration of the accords (without counting Basel 2.5). Basel III is being implemented in stages in different markets. Basel III is designed to further enhance the resilience of banks and banking systems and address weaknesses observed in the recent Global Financial Crisis. G20 leaders endorsed Basel III in 2010. Details of the reforms are included in Table 1.2. Hong Kong plans to implement this latest version of the Basel accords in phases over several years starting in 2013. Implementation should be completed by January 2019.

While Basel II put much of its focus on risk management (including introducing entire sections on operational risk management that were previously overlooked), Basel III is basically divided into two areas:

- Additional regulatory capital;
- Asset and liability management that addresses leverage and liquidity risks.

In terms of regulatory capital, Basel III sets a series of new minimums and limits that banks should be intimately familiar with and maintain. (See Table 1.2). It is the second area, the focus on asset and liability management, that is most relevant to our discussion here.

Following the adoption of Basel III, banks will have to adopt two new ratios for liquidity standards.

The first is the Liquidity Coverage Ratio (LCR) and the second is a Net Stable Funding Ratio (NSFR).

The LCR was first published in December 2010 and was revised over the next couple of years to fine-tune the definitions of high-quality liquid assets (HQLA) and net cash outflows. By 2019, when the LCR is fully implemented, it will have a 100% threshold as a

---

[5] Horcher, Karen A. "Essentials of Managing Treasury". New Jersey: John Wiley & Sons, 2005. Print. Pg 200.

TABLE 1.1 Basel III phase in arrangements

Basel III phase-in arrangements
(All dates are as of 1 January)

Basel Committee on Banking Supervision

 BANK FOR INTERNATIONAL SETTLEMENTS

	Phases	2013	2014	2015	2016	2017	2018	2019
Capital	Leverage Ratio	Parallel run 1 Jan 2013 – 1 Jan 2017 Disclosure starts 1 Jan 2015					Migration to Pillar 1	
	Minimum Common Equity Capital Ratio	3.5%	4.0%	4.5%				4.5%
	Capital Conservation Buffer				0.625%	1.25%	1.875%	2.5%
	Minimum common equity plus capital conservation buffer	3.5%	4.0%	4.5%	5.125%	5.75%	6.375%	7.0%
	Phase-in of deductions from CET1*		20%	40%	60%	80%	100%	100%
	Minimum Tier 1 Capital	4.5%	5.5%	6.0%				6.0%
	Minimum Total Capital			8.0%				8.0%
	Minimum Total Capital plus conservation buffer	8.0%	8.0%	8.0%	8.625%	9.25%	9.875%	10.5%
	Capital instruments that no longer qualify as non-core Tier 1 capital or Tier 2 capital	Phased out over 10 year horizon beginning 2013						
Liquidity	Liquidity coverage ratio – minimum requirement			60%	70%	80%	90%	100%
	Net stable funding ratio						Introduce minimum standard	

* Including amounts exceeding the limit for deferred tax assets (DTAs), mortgage servicing rights (MSRs) and financials.

- - transition periods

Source: BCBS

TABLE 1.2 Basel III reforms

Basel Committee on Banking Supervision reforms - Basel III

Strengthens microprudential regulation and supervision, and adds a macroprudential overlay that includes capital buffers.

	Capital					Liquidity
	Pillar 1			Pillar 2	Pillar 3	Global liquidity standard and supervisory monitoring
	Capital	Risk coverage	Containing leverage	Risk management and supervision	Market discipline	
All Banks	**Quality and level of capital** Greater focus on common equity. The minimum will be raised to 4.5% of risk-weighted assets, after deductions. **Capital loss absorption at the point of non-viability** Contractual terms of capital instruments will include a clause that allows – at the discretion of the relevant authority – write-off or conversion to common shares if the bank is judged to be non-viable. This principle increases the contribution of the private sector to resolving future banking crises and thereby reduces moral hazard. **Capital conservation buffer** Comprising common equity of 2.5% of risk-weighted assets, bringing the total common equity standard to 7%. Constraint on a bank's discretionary distributions will be imposed when banks fall into the buffer range. **Countercyclical buffer** Imposed within a range of 0-2.5% comprising common equity, when authorities judge credit growth is resulting in an unacceptable build up of systematic risk.	**Securitisations** Strengthens the capital treatment for certain complex securitisations. Requires banks to conduct more rigorous credit analyses of externally rated securitisation exposures. **Trading book** Significantly higher capital for trading and derivatives activities, as well as complex securitisations held in the trading book. Introduction of a stressed value-at-risk framework to help mitigate procyclicality. A capital charge for incremental risk that estimates the default and migration risks of unsecuritised credit products and takes liquidity into account. **Counterparty credit risk** Substantial strengthening of the counterparty credit risk framework. Includes: more stringent requirements for measuring exposure; capital incentives for banks to use central counterparties for derivatives; and higher capital for inter-financial sector exposures. **Bank exposures to central counterparties (CCPs)** The Committee has proposed that trade exposures to a qualifying CCP will receive a 2% risk weight and default fund exposures to a qualifying CCP will be capitalised according to a risk-based method that consistently and simply estimates risk arising from such default fund.	**Leverage ratio** A non-risk-based leverage ratio that includes off-balance sheet exposures will serve as a backstop to the risk-based capital requirement. Also helps contain system wide build up of leverage.	**Supplemental Pillar 2 requirements.** Address firm-wide governance and risk management; capturing the risk of off-balance sheet exposures and securitisation activities; managing risk concentrations; providing incentives for banks to better manage risk and returns over the long term; sound compensation practices; valuation practices; stress testing; accounting standards for financial instruments; corporate governance; and supervisory colleges.	**Revised Pillar 3 disclosures requirements** The requirements introduced relate to securitisation exposures and sponsorship of off-balance sheet vehicles. Enhanced disclosures on the detail of the components of regulatory capital and their reconciliation to the reported accounts will be required, including a comprehensive explanation of how a bank calculates its regulatory capital ratios.	**Liquidity coverage ratio** The liquidity coverage ratio (LCR) will require banks to have sufficient high-quality liquid assets to withstand a 30-day stressed funding scenario that is specified by supervisors. **Net stable funding ratio** The net stable funding ratio (NSFR) is a longer-term structural ratio designed to address liquidity mismatches. It covers the entire balance sheet and provides incentives for banks to use stable sources of funding. **Principles for Sound Liquidity Risk Management and Supervision** The Committee's 2008 guidance *Principles for Sound Liquidity Risk Management and Supervision* takes account of lessons learned during the crisis and is based on a fundamental review of sound practices for managing liquidity risk in banking organisations. **Supervisory monitoring** The liquidity framework includes a common set of monitoring metrics to assist supervisors in identifying and analysing liquidity risk trends at both the bank and system-wide level.
SIFIs	In addition to meeting the Basel III requirements, global systemically important financial institutions (SIFIs) must have higher loss absorbency capacity to reflect the greater risks that they pose to the financial system. The Committee has developed a methodology that includes both quantitative indicators and qualitative elements to identify global systemically important banks (SIBs). The additional loss absorbency requirements are to be met with a progressive Common Equity Tier 1 (CET1) capital requirement ranging from 1% to 2.5%, depending on a bank's systemic importance. For banks facing the highest SIB surcharge, an additional loss absorbency of 1% could be applied as a disincentive to increase materially their global systemic importance in the future. A consultative document was published in cooperation with the Financial Stability Board, which is coordinating the overall set of measures to reduce the moral hazard posed by global SIFIs.					

Source: BCBS

minimum requirement in normal times. The LCR will be first introduced with a threshold of 60% in 2015.[6]

The NSFR acts as a supplement to the LCR and has a one year time horizon. The goal of the NSFR is to provide a "sustainable maturity structure of assets and liabilities".[7] At the time of writing, the NSFR was still undergoing a period of review, but the BCBS intended to adopt any necessary revisions and introduce it fully by January 2018.

Both ratios are significant for treasury operations because it is up to this particular function of a bank to ensure the ratios are met on a daily basis. A short examination of the LCR makes it clear that its impact on treasury operations is significant.

---

[6] "Basel III: The Liquidity Coverage Ratio and liquidity risk monitoring tools". Bank for International Settlements. January 2013. Web: www.bis.org/publ/bcbs238.htm. 17 April 2013.

[7] "Basel III: The Liquidity Coverage Ratio and liquidity risk monitoring tools". Bank for International Settlements. January 2013. Pg. 1–8.

The LCR is based on the stock of HQLA to cover net cash outflows over a 30-day period under a prescribed stress scenario. HQLA are assets that can be "easily and immediately converted into cash at little or no loss of value," meaning that they are typically low risk, easy to valuate, have little correlation with risky assets, and are listed on recognized exchanges, have low volatility, and are typically shelters in times of systemic crisis.

Significantly, the BCBS notes that these assets should be "under the control of the function charged with managing liquidity of the bank," meaning the treasurer and the treasury function. What's more, LCR assets should be kept in a separate pool and used solely as contingent funds. In other words, it is up to the treasury function to ensure LCR is met at all times and that the funds are appropriately managed.

Much like the LCR, the NSFR also requires access to a minimum amount of stable funding. This amount is linked to the liquidity profile of the assets of the bank as well as any needs for liquidity that the bank may face from its off-balance sheet commitments over a one-year period. The idea behind the NSFR is to limit reliance on short-term wholesale funding during times of too much liquidity and encourage better liquidity risk management.[8]

Liquidity Risk Management

The bank's ALCO also oversees liquidity risk management, which is concerned with the risk of having insufficient funds available to meet a sudden large-scale demand for funds from depositors or sudden draw downs from clients. As noted, liquidity is a factor in balance sheet management—the drive to maximize the value of assets must be balanced with the need to keep enough cash and cash equivalents on hand to service expected (and unexpected) demands on the liabilities side. Proprietary trading gains from treasury operations help enhance the bank's profitability, but these must be strictly separated from the bank book. This underscores the need for internal controls and monitoring to ensure that fraud and errors do not occur in treasury operations.

It is difficult to overestimate the importance of appropriately managing liquidity so as to ensure the bank is always in a position to meet its obligations while, whenever possible, deriving a benefit from its liquid reserves. Risks associated with liquidity are major and can be life threatening to an organization if not managed properly.[9]

Asset Quality Classification

A key aspect of managing liquidity risk is knowing what an organization does with its reserves. While it makes sense to invest as much as possible so as to generate a return, it is also important that the bank or financial institution have regular and rapid access to its liquid reserves. Asset quality classification is an important activity.

---

[8] "Basel III: A global regulatory framework for more resilient banks and banking systems". Bank For International Settlements. June 2011. Pg. 9.
[9] Horcher, Karen A. "Essentials of Managing Treasury". New Jersey: John Wiley & Sons, 2005. Print. Pg. 197.

It is up to the treasurer to consider the safety of the principal should the bank move to invest its liquid reserves. Author Steven Bragg notes: "It would not do to invest company funds in a risky investment in order to earn extraordinarily high returns if there is a chance that any portion of the principal will be lost."[10] Just as important, however, are considerations of maturity and marketability. Even the safest investment on the planet may pose a liquidity risk if it is not liquid, regardless of how much return it might generate.

For treasury managers, this means that the best investments are not only safe but also easily accessible through a strong liquid secondary market that guarantees immediate resale should the need arise.

When viewed through this lens, the yield that a particular investment might generate is the last consideration. After all, the goal of liquid reserves is not so much to generate profit but to guarantee the continuity of the operations of the bank or financial institution: "Within the boundaries of appropriate levels of risk, maturity, and marketability, the treasurer can then pick the investment with the highest yield. Since these criteria tend to limit one to very low-risk investments, the yield is also likely to be very low," notes Bragg.

Nevertheless, within these boundaries of low risk levels, short maturity, and high marketability there are a number of investment options such as bonds (preferably near their maturity dates), commercial paper, or treasury issuances.

Off-Balance Sheet Activities

Off-balance sheet (OBS) activities are assets or debt financing activities that are not included in a bank's balance sheet. An example may be asset management or brokerage services involving securities that belong to the client but are held by the bank in trust. Often, these assets are reported as "off-balance sheet."

Banks tend to have large sums in their off-balance sheet accounts. When a bank takes a deposit of, for example, HK$10 million, it has a corresponding liability. If the client then moves that money into a fund or buys a stock, the bank may hold the investment and have some fiduciary duties but it no longer has a liability. If the client then chooses to sell the investment, the liability would reappear.

Each of these transactions has an impact on the liquidity of a bank and its treasury operations and, since the Global Financial Crisis, a number of OBS operations have come under greater regulatory scrutiny. Collateralized debt obligations, subprime-mortgage securities (in the United States), and credit default swaps all have been used to move debt out of bank balance sheets. Often, the sale of these products is recorded as proceeds but the liability is rarely recorded on the company's balance sheet. Another example is securitized loans. A loan is generally kept in a bank's books as an asset but when loans are securitized and sold off as investments the debt, for which the bank is liable in case of a default, is moved off the books.

---

[10] Bragg, Steven M. "Treasury Management: The Practitioner's Guide". New Jersey: John Wiley & Sons, 2010. Pg. 165.

Under Hong Kong accounting standards banks are expected to disclose contingent liabilities and commitments associated with OBS items related to a number of areas, such as direct credit substitutes like bank acceptance guarantees and standby letters of credit, some transaction-related liabilities like performance bonds, and short-term self-liquidating trade-related contingent liabilities that arise from the movement of goods and others.[11]

Counterparty Exposures and Capital Requirements

Counterparty risk considerations are also key to effective liquidity management. Banks typically consider counterparty risk as part of their credit risk management strategies. After all, one definition of credit risk is "the probability of loss as a result of the failure or unwillingness of a counterparty or borrower to fulfill a financial obligation."[12]

Ratings and reviews can help choose appropriate counterparties and minimize risk. Banks often set up counterparty limits and alter those limits depending on their short or long-term liquidity needs and the nature of the transaction in which the counterparty may be involved.

Something similar happens with capital requirements that banks must meet at all times. It is up to the treasury function to ensure short and long-term requirements are constantly met or they may put the bank in a precarious position. As Basel III is introduced, these capital requirements will shift and, most likely, grow larger. It will be up to the treasury to make the necessary action to ensure the bank stays within its regulatory comfort zone.

Management of Settlement/ Pre-Settlement Credit Risk

Settlement credit risk refers to the risk of a counterparty failing to settle a transaction as expected through a transfer system, which can happen if one party defaults on its clearing obligations to one or more counterparties. Pre-settlement credit risk is the risk of a party failing to meet the terms of a contract before that contract's settlement date, thus terminating the contract and causing the bank to replace it with another one, incurring replacement costs in the process.

Settlement and pre-settlement credit risk is an issue in treasury operations, including in areas such as proprietary trading. Treasury should make sure it knows the identity of the counterparties it deals with. According to *The Model Code: The International Code of Conduct and Practice for the Financial Markets*, which is issued by ACI—The Financial Markets Association, "it is good practice for the Compliance, Legal and Credit functions within a firm to have full knowledge of the end principal's identity, prior to the execution

---

[11] Hong Kong Institute of Certified Public Accountants. "Hong Kong Accounting Standard 30". 2005. Available online at http://app1.hkicpa.org.hk/professionaltechnical/accounting/exposuredraft/HKAS30cl.pdf.
[12] Karen A. Horcher; "Essentials of Managing Treasury"; John Wiley & Sons; New Jersey; 2005; p 153.

of a transaction, in order that credit, 'Know Your Customer,' anti-money laundering and potential fraud issues can be addressed."[13]

Treasury should determine there is sufficient credit limit available for the counterparty before entering into any contract, in cases where the bank is dealing over the counter (OTC) and not through an exchange.

Treasury should be careful in dealing with overly complicated and large transactions, which could place a greater strain on the counterparties and thus heighten settlement risk. It should be extra vigilant during times of economic and financial crisis, which intensifies the risk of liquidity problems and even bankruptcy among counterparties. Finally, it should make sure to use payment systems that are based on internationally accepted standards and practices, and which have a track record for safety and efficiency.

Management of Interest-Rate Risk

Interest-rate risk is defined as the potential impact on the net asset value of a bank's balance sheet and earnings from a change in interest rates. Fixed-rate assets will fall in value when rates go up, for example, while funding costs will increase. Interest-rate risk typically arises when there is a maturity date mismatch between assets and liabilities.

Even more important is the shape of the yield curve and the changes to the shape. For example, a book with a combination of short-term and long-term asset- or liability maturity structures is at risk from a yield curve inversion. The bank will need to change the structure of the book to take into account its views on the yield curve.

We will discuss this topic in more detail in Chapter 3 but, for the moment, it is important to understand that treasury is a key player in managing interest-rate risk through the trading book or banking book. Based on the bank's interest-rate scenarios and views on the yield curve and the likely impact on the balance sheet and earnings, treasury can devise trading strategies that can be put into effect at the appropriate time, involving financial instruments such as interest rate swaps. Provided these strategies are well designed and executed, they should help the bank mitigate the negative effects of interest rate changes and the yield curve, and maximise their positive impact.

Management of Foreign Exchange Exposure

Few banks deal only in a single currency. Most have assets and liabilities in their home currencies, U.S. dollar, euro, yen, renminbi, and other currencies accrued in the normal course

---

[13] The Financial Markets Association; *The Model Code: The International Code of Conduct and Practice for the Financial Markets*; January 2013, pg 17.

of lending, raising capital, issuing letters of credit, and other activities. This mix exposes the bank to foreign exchange risk, particularly if a currency experiences a steep fall in value. The bank's assets denominated in that currency then lose value against its home currency, although its liabilities in that devalued currency will also shrink.

Treasury operations have a role to play in managing foreign exchange exposure in response to the currency position of the bank and the currency movements, as well as the determination of whether the foreign exchange risk should be hedged. There are a number of foreign exchange exposures, such as economic exposure, accounting exposure, and transaction exposures. One may decide to hedge economic and transaction exposures, which reduce the future volatility of cash flows that are subject to foreign exchange rate movement, but not accounting exposures, which result only in unrealized gain and loss arisen from period-to-period balance sheet re-measurement.

Treasury Controls and Measures

The Nick Leeson case outlined in Chapter 9 shows how dangerous out-of-control treasury operations can be to a financial institution. How can a bank make sure it does not suffer the same tragic fate as Barings Bank?

The answer lies in well-designed and implemented oversight and management systems within and outside the treasury function. These include internal controls, trading limits, monitoring and control of the dealing operation, audit and compliance issues, management of conflicts of interest, and internalisation of the best-practice recommendations of *The Model Code*.

Managing the treasury is a very practical, pragmatic, and hands on exercise but one that leaves plenty of room for more theoretical considerations that extend beyond spreadsheet rows, columns and balances. Ethical issues linked to treasury management are of increasing consideration for regulators, in not small measure because treasury decisions and trading actions can influence the size of the unsquared open position with risk consequences for a financial institution.

Hong Kong's Treasury Markets Association (TMA) has developed a comprehensive *Code of Conduct and Practice*. The Global Financial Crisis of 2008 "highlighted the dangers of unchecked financial innovation and insufficiently regulated market behaviour," notes the TMA. "At the same time, however, it is perhaps neither adequate nor desirable for regulations to be the sole curb moderating the actions of market participants."

The TMA was established in 2006 to promote professionalism and competitiveness within Hong Kong's treasury markets and develop codes and standards for the industry. Populated by active market participants, the TMA is not a regulator but it does set standards for the industry to follow. The code of conduct published in 2011 and updated in 2014 covers a range of financial products including foreign exchange, money market instruments, debt securities, over-the-counter (OTC) derivatives, repurchase agreements (repo), commodities and credit derivatives, and structured products.

The Code covers a wide range of ethical considerations including the need for confidentiality within and without the institution, the importance of legal and regulatory compliance, requirements for training for staff, how to handle conflicts of interest, the role of diligence in dealing with clients and executing mandates, and the importance of honesty and fairness. These broad considerations come into play when dealing with the myriad issues that treasuries confront every day such as money laundering, fraud, criminal activities, segregation of duties, personal data, and complaints.[14]

Internal Controls

One lesson from the collapse of Barings is the importance of internal controls. Leeson was able to falsely claim huge profits and hide his true losses because there was no segregation of duties at Barings Securities (Singapore). He was in effect judge, jury, prosecutor, and defence attorney all in one.

The essence of internal controls is to make sure that persons initiating and completing transactions do not control or account for the results of that deal. For example, trading should always be separated from confirmations. This will help ensure that someone who is making unauthorised trades will not be able to hide confirmations from the counterparty that would alert supervisors of the fraud. Similarly, a senior treasury officer should approve all trades, but another official outside of treasury, such as a specialist in the accounting department, should reconcile the total transactions.

Part of a good internal control system is a clear definition of responsibilities and authorisations within the treasury function. The content of which must be comprehensive and regularly updated. The bank's list of authorised dealers and authorised signatures should also be periodically updated and distributed to all concerned. There should be a written notification whenever a responsible person is dropped or added to the list.

It is also important to fully document all transactions and assign custody of records to persons other than those directly involved in trading and confirmation. Securities are commonly stored by a third-party custodian, but if they are kept on site, those responsible for them must not be assigned the accounting task.

There should be procedures in place to regulate the documentation and recording of transactions, including taping of telephone conversations and recording electronic text messages. Who can access these records and for how long they should be kept should also be made clear. The length of time for keeping records varies, depending on the product. For example, if the transaction is related to a 10-year interest rate swap, the records must be maintained over 10 years. The same logic applies to taped phone records. However, the financial institution should comply with the legal requirements related to these issues in the country where it operates.

---

[14] Code of Conduct and Practice, Treasury Markets Association. Hong Kong, April 2011. Accessed at https://www.tma.org.hk/PubFile/tmacode.pdf.

The segregation of duties and other control measures are meant not only to discourage fraud. They can also help avert honest errors because there are different sets of eyes that look at the same transaction. Despite the automatic systems in place in modern trading, the front office can still commit inadvertent mistakes. The typical treasury structure of front office, middle office, and back office is useful in this regard, as long as those units are properly segregated and fully informed about various responsibilities and authorisations.

Trading Limits

There are various types of trading limits. The most common limits are:

- Position limit or open position limit;
- Stop loss limits; and
- Value-at-Risk (VaR) limits.

The limits should be measurable in order to clearly segregate trading positions taken by individual traders, business units, and the entire financial institution that make them. In addition, these limits should be also clearly defined and communicable, thereby allowing strict monitoring and enforcement by an independent third party on all trading activities.

The objective is to make sure that the bank is not exposed to specific market risks at levels that exceed what the board and senior management have authorized. In setting those limits, the bank should be guided by value-at-risk (VaR), which is a methodology that computes the probabilistic bounds of market losses over a given period of time expressed in terms of a specified degree of certainty, known as the confidence interval. VaR limit is also a compulsory requirement as stipulated in the Basel II agreement to measure overall market risk, if the financial institution is using internal models.

Basel III introduces further checks on trading activities to limit exposures. A key requirement is for banks to reduce trading capital to a significant portion of Tier 1 capital, for which banks have to have enough capital reserves in place to cover adequacy requirements. At the same time, Basel III increases requirements for supervisory focus on proprietary trading activities—these requirements have already pushed banks to reorganize their operations to separate banking and trading.

Markets and the instruments that trade on them constantly change and evolve, as do the experience, expertise, and track record of the bank's individual traders and the bank's own tolerance for market risk. There must be a system to deal with exceptions that breach trading limits. This typically involves case-by-case decisions by senior treasury managers who may act on their own or elevate the case to ALCO, the chief executive, or the board.

Monitoring and Control of Dealing Operations

The bank should strike the right balance between allowing traders the freedom to do what they must do and keeping track of their activities, to make sure fraud is not being committed and that the bank is not being overexposed to market risk. Fortunately, electronic trading and sophisticated management software are making it easier for trading floor activities to be monitored without unduly hampering trading flexibility.

The back office should take full advantage of these advances to examine, verify, and reconcile trades in real or near-real time. The middle office should use them to monitor the risk exposure of dealers, business units and the financial institution as a whole. For their part, senior managers should obtain and use technologies to track mistakes and omissions in deals, identify possible settlement errors, and detect any possible fraud. All these will help the bank detect red flags and pick up warning signs, and address fraud, overexposure, and errors before they become intractable problems.

The fact that these monitoring and control procedures are in place and that they are strictly practiced by the back office and senior managers should serve as deterrent to those contemplating fraud on the trading floor.

Audit and Compliance

Internal audits can detect problems only after they have occurred, but they remain an important part of treasury controls and measures. Unlike the back office and senior managers who conduct day-to-day monitoring of dealing operations, auditors are able to see the broader picture and can spend more time analysing procedures and transactions towards the goal of verifying compliance with bank policies and determining efficiency and effectiveness.

The internal audit function is independent of the business function of the financial institution and reports directly to the board of directors. Because they are outside the treasury function, internal auditors bring a fresh perspective to treasury operations and are not subject to personal relationships that may have developed among dealers, supervisors, managers, and the middle and back offices. They are more likely to spot gaps and inefficiencies in treasury operations that the practitioners may be too close to notice or too comfortable with the way things are done to want to change.

Among the specific tasks that internal auditors can do are to compare brokerage fees or commissions with reported transactions to detect unauthorised and unrecorded trades for which the bank is paying fees, and to examine spreadsheet calculations and contents, including formula ranges and totals. It is possible that wrong or incomplete formulas and macros have been inputted, causing inadvertent errors.

Another example of internal audit's task is to choose at random a number of executed deals and then, using the manual of policies and procedures of the treasury function, go through the process of execution, settlement, controls, and reporting again to make sure these transactions were handled properly.

Conflicts of Interest

In treasury operations, a conflict of interest may arise if traders are allowed to deal for their own personal accounts. *The Model Code* recommends: "Where dealing for personal account is allowed, management should ensure that adequate safeguards are established to prevent abuse of insider dealing in any form.... Written procedures should be put in place by management to cover personal transactions of staff as well as those on behalf of the dealer's family and other members of personnel, management included ... There should be a full disclosure and transparency requirement."[15]

The Model Code singles out the undesirable practice of "front-running" or "parallel-running," which refers to a dealer making a personal trade ahead of a large order by the bank in anticipation of a sharp movement in the market price. These trades would not have been executed without prior information obtained as a result of the trader's position and "hence this is a form of insider trading and should be banned accordingly," according to the Code.[16]

Another source of conflict of interest is the use of a connected broker, that is, there is a shareholding or material connection between the broker and the principals, including the trader and the bank itself. "In order to avoid any potential conflict of interest and safeguard the independence of the broker, it is important that all the relevant information is disclosed and that the principals are fully aware of the situation," says *The Model Code*.[17]

Code of Conduct

There are various codes of conduct and practices available for banks and financial institutions to follow. The importance of establishing and following a code was highlighted by the Global Financial Crisis in 2007–8.

In Hong Kong, the TMA developed ts code which it published in 2011. Its focus is a "wide range of financial products."[18] The TMA is established and chaired by the HKMA, the ultimate industry regulator.

---

[15] *The Model Code*, pg 12–13.
[16] *The Model Code*, pg 13.
[17] *The Model Code*, pg 59.
[18] Treasury Markets Association; *Code of Conduct and Practice*; July 2011; pg 5.

An internationally recognized code is the ACI's *The Model Code*. This code of conduct and practice was compiled with inputs from the central banks of the various Organization for Economic Cooperation and Development (OECD) countries, the UK's Financial Services Authority, the Foreign Exchange Committees in New York, Tokyo and Singapore, and ACI representatives and market participants in the 66 countries where ACI—The Financial Markets Association has a presence. As such, it is a comprehensive document that has been adopted by regulators in 17 jurisdictions, with 35 others considering adoption.

Last revised in January 2013, *The Model Code* is published and updated electronically and can be downloaded from the ACI website.[19] It is recommendatory in nature, although all candidates for the ACI Dealing Certificate are required, to study the Code and pass an examination on it.

Some financial institutions require their traders and dealers to study *The Model Code*, which has sections on best practice dealing procedures and practices, risk management principles, and personal conduct issues such as the use of drugs, acceptance of entertainment and gifts, misinformation and rumours, and use of confidential information. The intent is that treasury practitioners will internalise the recommendations.

Some countries have their own model codes, like the one issued by the TMA in Hong Kong. Singapore has had "The Singapore Guide to Conduct & Market Practices for Treasury Activities" since 2003. In finalising its model code, ACI took the Singapore guide into account, along with the London Code of Conduct, the French Code of Conduct, and the Code of Conduct of the Tokyo Foreign Exchange Market Committee.

Summary

- Treasury operations in financial institutions include cash forecasting, working capital management, cash management, investment management, treasury risk management and fund-raising—and trading in the foreign exchange, money and capital, debt security, and other external markets on behalf of the bank and the bank's clients.
- Important issues in treasury operations include balance sheet management, liquidity risk management, management of settlement and pre-settlement credit risk, management of interest-rate risk, and management of foreign exchange exposure.
- Balance sheet management is the process of determining the size and composition of a bank's assets and liabilities to achieve (or exceed) capital adequacy requirements and other ratios.
- Basel III is the third version of a series of rules issued by the BIS through the Basel Committee on Banking Supervision (BCBS). Two important ratios considered in Basel III are the Liquidity Coverage Ratio (LCR) and the Net Stable Funding Ratio (NSFR).

---

[19] (see "*Further Reading*" at the end of this chapter).

- Liquidity risk management is a key operational activity of the Asset and Liability Management Committee (ALCO). Managing liquidity risk requires taking into consideration a number of factors such as the quality of a bank's assets, off-balance sheet activities, counterparty exposures, and capital requirements.
- Managing interest rate risk and foreign exchange exposures are two key functions of the treasury.
- Internal controls ensure that persons initiating or completing a transaction do not control the results of the deal. This ensures that anyone making unauthorized trades will not be able to hide the transactions, as Nick Leeson of Barings Bank did in bringing down that venerable institution. Other controls include trading limits, monitoring, internal audits, and conflict of interest rules.
- Treasury control measures are needed to avert fraud, overexposure to market risks, and errors. These include internal controls, position and dealer limits, monitoring and control of the dealing operation, audit and compliance issues, management of conflicts of interest, and internalisation of the best-practice recommendations of *The Model Code*.

Key Terms

Asset-Liability Management Committee
    (ALCO)
Asset quality
Audit
Back office
Balance sheet management
Bank for International
    Settlements (BIS)
Basel Committee on Banking
    Supervision
Basel II
Basel III
Capital requirements
Compliance
Conflict of interest
Counterparty exposure
Dealer limit
Foreign exchange exposure
Front office

High Quality Liquid Assets
    (HQLA)
Hong Kong Monetary Authority
    (HKMA)
Internal audit
Internal controls
Interest rate risk
Liquidity Coverage Ratio (LCR)
Liquidity risk management
Middle office
Net Stable Funding Ratio (NSFR)
Off-balance sheet
Position limit
Securitisation
Settlement/pre-settlement risk
The Model Code
Trading limits
Treasury Markets Association
    (TMA)

Study Guide

1. Why do treasury departments typically have a front office, a middle office, and a back office? Would it not be simpler and more efficient to have just one integrated unit that conducts trading, confirmation, analysis, accounting, and other treasury activities?
2. You are an internal auditor tasked with making a surprise examination of treasury operations. Create a general checklist of the areas and specific activities you will focus on to avert fraud, overexposure to market risks, and errors.
3. Give two examples of how conflict of interest may arise in treasury operations. How may these conflicts be avoided?
4. How important is a highly developed sense of personal ethics among traders in the proper functioning of the treasury department? Do you think a trader who is highly ethical will not earn as much money for the bank as someone else who is more flexible and willing to cut corners in pursuit of the most lucrative deals?

Further Reading

ACI—The Financial Markets Association. *The Model Code: The International Code of Conduct and Practice for the Financial Markets*. Updated Electronic Version, January 2013. Web. 07 April 2010. http://www.aciforex.org/docs/misc/20130222_ACI_The_New_Model_Code_Feb_2013.pdf.

Bragg, Steven M. *Treasury Management: The Practitioner's Guide*. New Jersey: John Wiley & Sons, Inc., 2010. Print.

Choudhry, Moorad. *Bank Asset and Liability Management: Strategy, Trading, Analysis*. Singapore: John Wiley & Sons (Asia) Pte Ltd, 2007. Print.

Hong Kong Institute of Certified Public Accountants. *Hong Kong Accounting Standard 30*. 2005. Available online at http://app1.hkicpa.org.hk/professionaltechnical/accounting/exposuredraft/HKAS30cl.pdf.

Hong Kong Monetary Authority. *Supervisory Policy Manual: Liquidity Risk Management* (LM-1 and LM-2). Web.http://www.hkma.gov.hk/media/eng/doc/key-functions/banking-stability/supervisory-policy-manual/LM-1.pdf.

The Singapore Foreign Exchange Market Committee. *The Singapore Guide to Conduct & Market Practices for Treasury Activities*. Web. 07 April 2010. http://acisin.com/bluebook_as_of_nov_2003.pdf.

Treasury Markets Association of Hong Kong. *Code of Conduct and Practice*. Available online at https://www.tma.org.hk/PubFile/tmacode.pdf.

CHAPTER 2

The Foreign Exchange Market

Learning objectives

After studying this chapter, you should be able to:

1 Explain the structure of the global foreign exchange market, its participants, and how it operates.

2 Understand how exchange rates are set, the impact of interest rates, capital flows, and international investment.

3 Understand the method of quotation, including two-way quotation, sell/buy spread, and cross-rate quotation.

4 Describe the forward market, including various types of outright contracts and the pros and cons of each.

5 Analyse the ways to hedge foreign exchange exposure, measure such exposure, and use hedging tools.

Introduction

Banks are among the key players in the foreign exchange market as they trade on their own account and for their clients to hedge risks and make trading profits. In this chapter, we discuss the structure, operations, and various products on the foreign exchange market.

Although banks everywhere are active participants in the foreign exchange (forex) market, Hong Kong banks place particular emphasis on foreign exchange for two reasons. One is the ease with which multiple currencies flow through the city's banking system. Another reason that is related to the first is the fact that Hong Kong is one of the world's key foreign currency trading centres along with London, New York, Tokyo, and Singapore.

Understanding the functioning of the foreign exchange market is of great importance. A wrong bet or a failed hedging strategy can cost the bank or its clients millions or even billions. Massive changes in the value of foreign currency were key drivers behind the Asian Financial Crisis in 1997, which was kick-started by massive imbalances in the Thai Baht.

Trading in foreign exchange markets has risen steadily over the last few decades. The latest Triennial Central Bank Survey by the BIS, which provides information on the size and structure of the global foreign exchange markets, suggest that trading averaged USD5.3 trillion per day as of April 2013. That was up by USD300 million per day from three years earlier. Smaller banks accounted for about a quarter (24%) of this turnover. The US dollar is still the most traded currency by far, sitting on one side of 87% of all trades. The Euro, the second most traded currency, was part of 33% of all trades. Most of the trading was concentrated in sales desks in the UK, US, Singapore, and Japan. In the three years to 2013, the RMB also saw increased trading, from the equivalent of USD34 billion per day to USD120 billion to become the ninth most actively trade currency in the world, accounting for 2.2% of global forex volumes thanks to the expansion of offshore RMB trading.

Basic Operation of Forex Market

Global foreign exchange activities are conducted mainly in loosely regulated over-the-counter (OTC) markets and a small portion of trades are done on exchanges.

By OTC, we mean a decentralised market for securities (underlying assets) that are not listed on an exchange. In the OTC foreign exchange market, participants trade over the telephone or on electronic networks.

In general, OTC trades are flexible and can be tailored for specific requirements such as tenure, contract size, and strike price (in the case of option), but carry counterparty risk. On the other hand, exchange-traded transactions are standardized, have low transaction costs, and have much lower no counterparty risks due to the collateral margining requirement.

Market Participants

The participants of the foreign exchange market include financial institutions engaged in the interbank market, commercial companies that need foreign exchange for trade and capital market activities, investment management firms with international equity portfolios, central banks that both regulate and invest in the foreign exchange market, and hedge funds that aggressively exploit currency movements to make trading profits. Participants have their own unique characteristics and goals for participating in the market. They include:

- **Banks:** The interbank market, which comprises transactions between and among banks, accounts for the majority of commercial turnover and large amounts of speculative trading every day. A large bank may trade billions of dollars daily. Some of this trading is undertaken on behalf of customers, but much is conducted by proprietary desks that trade for the bank's own account.

- **Commercial companies:** The financial activities of companies seeking foreign exchange to pay for goods or services comprise an important part of the FX market. Commercial companies often trade fairly small amounts compared with those of banks or speculators, but the volume can become fairly large when they take part in capital market activities, such as mergers and acquisitions, bond issuance, or initial public offerings.

  Trade flows are an important factor in the long-term direction of a currency's exchange rate. Some multinational companies can have an unpredictable impact when very large positions are covered due to exposures that are not widely known by other market participants.

- **Investment management firms:** Investment management firms, which typically manage large amounts of cash on behalf of customers, use the foreign exchange market to facilitate transactions in foreign securities. For example, an investment manager with an international equity portfolio will need to buy and sell foreign currencies on the spot market in order to pay for purchases of foreign equities. Since the FX transactions are secondary to the actual investment decision, they are not seen as speculative or aimed at profit maximization.

  Some investment management firms do have more speculative specialist currency-overlay operations, which manage clients' currency exposures with the aim of generating profits as well as limiting risk. Whilst the number of this type of specialist firms is quite small, many have a large value of assets under management and hence can generate sizeable foreign exchange trades. In Hong Kong, these firms often rely on cross-currency swaps, which are very liquid. Because of the ample liquidity of this type of instrument in Hong Kong and the fact that companies can issue instruments denominated in USD and convert them to local currency with ease, the use of HKD denominated bonds is limited.

- **Central banks:** National central banks play an important role in the foreign exchange markets, both as regulator and investor. Some central banks are particularly active in the FX market, among them the Bank of Japan, People's Bank of China, Bank of England, European Central Bank, and the U.S. Federal Reserve.

Central banks usually set monetary policy to achieve certain economic goals. On top of this, some of them will implement a publicly announced exchange rate policy. For example, the U.S. Federal Reserve sets the nation's monetary policy towards the objectives of promoting maximum employment, stable prices, and moderate long-term interest rates.

The HKMA, for its part, participates in the market to maintain a peg between the Hong Kong and U.S. dollar. The HKD trades in a narrow band between HKD7.75 and HKD7.85 to the USD.[1]

AN AGGRESSIVE TRADER

One of the best known and most aggressive currency speculators in the world is the Quantum Fund owned by billionaire investor George Soros. The fund earned its reputation as an aggressive investor in the 1990s.

Soros is best known as the man who broke the Bank of England. His bear raid on the British pound (GBP) in 1992 precipitated the collapse of the European Monetary System. The Bank of England was trying to defend GBP against the German mark (before the Euro took hold in Western Europe) as part of its obligations under the decades-old Bretton Woods agreements.

Soros took the very public position that the post-Cold War world had changed, thanks to the inflationary effects of Germany's reunification, and that the traditional currency relationships would have to change, too.

On Black Wednesday, September 16, 1992, Soros sold sterling valued at more than USD10 billion, a move followed by a chain reaction of speculators who piled on after him.

The assault on the British currency was so massive that the Bank of England was forced to withdraw it from the European Exchange Rate Mechanism and to devalue it. This resulted in the transfer of billions of pounds from Her Majesty's Treasury to Soros's coffers, earning the hedge fund investor USD1.1 billion in the process.

- **Hedge funds:** There is no official definition of what a hedge fund is even in the U.S. In practice, it is usually a fund that is allowed to use strategies normally not available to mutual funds. These strategies include selling short, leverage, program trading, swaps, arbitrage, and derivatives. Hedge funds are not covered at this time from many of the

---

[1]Li, Susan and Li, Fion. "Ackman Won't Realize Bet on Hong Kong's Peg, K.C. Chan Says". Bloomberg. 14 January 2013. Web.

rules and regulations governing mutual funds, which allow them to accomplish aggressive investing goals. Hedge funds typically use banks to do much of their trading and there is a fair amount of business sourcing by banks from hedge funds.

Operations

The major markets for foreign currency trading are in London, New York, Tokyo, Hong Kong and Singapore. However, since the FX business operates 24 hours a day given that one market is always open somewhere in the world, traders all around the world effectively participate in the same market.

For example, the night desk of a commercial bank in Asia can deal with the morning shift of its counterpart in New York, in the same way that the night desk in London can deal with the day desk in Hong Kong and Singapore.

London has a geographical advantage over the other financial centres because the European time zone straddles the normal working hours in both North America and Asia. Traders can thus keep in touch with their clients all around the world during the normal trading hours in London.

Official Trading Hours

The official trading hours of the global foreign exchange market starts at 5:00 Sydney Time on Monday morning and ends at 5:00 New York Time on Friday afternoon all year-round, except during public holidays.

As mentioned, FX deals are loosely regulated, being traded mostly over the counter. A foreign exchange deal is a binding agreement between a buyer and a seller only. However, these trading hours have been adopted as best practice and standard market practice by global market practitioners, related organisations such as the TMA, and regulators.

There are implications in disregarding official trading hours:

- **High-low of trading range:** If the trade is made outside the official hours, the trade record will not be considered in the daily trading range, which may thus fail to be fully reflective of the market.
- **Order execution:** Practitioners do not execute customer orders outside official hours, even though the actual market level had reached the desired execution level.

For example, a practitioner has an order to buy the euro at US$1.31, the level it had reached before the official opening in Australia. But after the opening, the euro never hit that level again. Should the limit order at USD1.31 be honoured? The answer is no, since trade records before official hours do not count in the daily trading range.

But if a bank has agreed to a transaction on Saturday evening, the deal is binding between the two parties. This is because FX is an over-the-counter product. As long as the buyer has agreed to the terms and conditions of a deal with the seller, the deal is binding despite being done outside of official hours.

Market Transparency

The well-developed global infrastructure of the FX market means that participants can easily find an executable or indicative quotation. Market participants can access executable quotations offered by investment banks over the Internet and indicative quotations compiled by information services providers like Thomson Reuters.

- **Executable quotation** is a price offered by a market maker to a market user or a group of users. The market user, such as the customer over the counter, can execute a transaction with an executable quotation. The subscriber to the FX service can input a trade amount into the blank box of the currency and then click or double-click to execute a trade.
- **Indicative quotation** is the price contributed by liquidity providers such as investment banks and commercial banks to various financial information service providers like Thomson Reuters and Bloomberg, websites, and individual commercial banks. The user cannot execute a deal with the provider of the indicative quotes, only with the market maker that provides executable quotations.

Transaction Costs

The foreign exchange market generally has lower transaction costs than do equities and futures. That's because, in the interbank market, participants seldom charge a commission on the trade. Trader quotes are an "all-in" price for the user.

The major transaction cost is the spread of the quote, the brokerage cost, which is subject to negotiation between the bank and the broker, the overhead of the operation, and the settlement cost, which typically accounts for the largest portion of the total cost. Figure 2.1 illustrates the normal transaction costs of an FX deal. In practice, the actual figure depends on the transaction amount, the trade relationship, and the market condition.

Dealing Methods

There are three ways that participants in the foreign exchange markets conduct transactions: through direct dealing, brokers dealing and prime broker.

- **Direct dealing** is broadly defined as a dealing method in which a market user requests a quote from a market maker or liquidity provider. The traditional direct dealing platform includes Thomson Reuters dealing, FX trader of Bloomberg, and the respective internet dealing portal of Deutsche Bank, UBS, Barclays, and other banks. Trading over the phone is popular only with corporate clients. The use of telex, the most important platform in the past, is now obsolete.

FIGURE 2.1 Illustrative foreign exchange transaction costs

Source of transaction cost	Range of cost
Spread	Major currency: 1–2 pips
	Minor currency: 3–5 pips
	Exotic currency: 5 and more pips
Brokerage	Electronic broker: USD20–25/US mio
	Human broker: USD5–15/US mio
	Prime broker: USD3–12/US mio
Commission	Interbank: 0
	Customer: 0.1 pip

"Pip" stands for price interest point and refers to the smallest move possible in the price of a unit of currency against another; "mio" in FX trading is shorthand for million. Source: HKIB

- **Brokers dealing** entails the presence of a middle person to consolidate all the interests of players. The middle person (the broker) may be human or a machine. The business turnover of human brokers has contracted significantly since 1992, when services like EBS and Reuters matching were launched. Internet dealing portals featuring multiple liquidity providers have also become popular.
- **Prime broker** is a variant of brokers dealing. The market user signs a prime contract with a major investment bank that allows the market user to trade FX in the name of the investment bank. The service provider of the market user will sign a "give-up" contract with the prime broker. The market user pays a prime brokerage fee on top of the original brokerage fee. Prime broker services are available on the Thomson Reuters matching system, EBS, and other electronic trading platforms.

Settlement Cycle

The settlement procedure for an FX transaction varies from bank to bank. The flowchart in Figure 2.2 shows an illustrative example of how it works in general terms. Thus:

- Bank A enters into an FX deal with Bank B (middle of the picture)
- The front offices of Bank A and Bank B inform their respective back offices of the deal
- The back office of Bank A instructs its agent in Country X to transfer the agreed amount of foreign currency to the agent in Country X of Bank B. Bank B does the same thing for the other leg of the currency pair, that is, inform its agent in Country Y to make payment to Bank A's agent in Country Y
- On the day following the settlement, the agent in Country Y informs Bank A of the account balance so the back office of Bank A can reconcile and verify the trade with Bank B.

FIGURE 2.2 Illustrative example of the settlement process

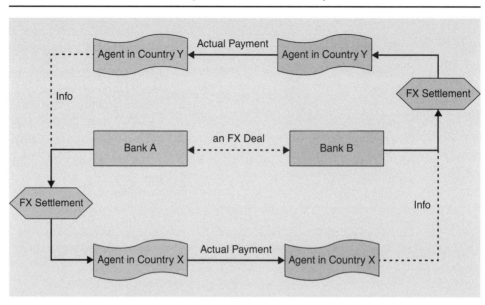

Source: HKIB

This is discussed at greater length in Chapter 7 but it is important to remember the following three points when considering the settlement process:

- It is risky to execute a transaction that is to be settled on the same transaction day because the agent bank (another bank that is responsible for the funds settlement in other country) may not be able to process the request on time.
- The settlement procedure involves counterparty risk because it is possible that the outflow of funds does not match the inflow. The banks are actually extending an intraday credit facility to the counterparty. If Bank A defaults on the payment, Bank B will suffer a total loss of the trade.
- In practice, interbank transactions between counterparties are based on clean facility. No collateral is required to secure the FX trade.

Forex Risk Management

The HKMA considers the importance of managing foreign exchange risk in its Supervisory Policy Manual.[2] Risk associated with foreign exchange is present in both the trading book

[2] Hong Kong Monetary Authority. Supervisory Policy Manual: Foreign Exchange Risk Management (TA-2). 14 January, 2009.

and the banking book and excessive foreign exchange risk can pose a significant threat to the earnings and capital adequacy of a bank.

The three main ways to address this risk are to maintain an effective system of internal controls to identify, measure, monitor, and control FX risks; set appropriate limits on risk exposures to avoid risk concentrations; and to hold enough capital against possible losses.

In broad strokes, foreign exchange risk exposures can be either structural or from trading. The former emerge from imbalances between assets and liabilities. There are a number of structural exposures that may arise from forex activities including, for example:

- Investments in fixed assets and premises;
- Equity investments in overseas subsidiaries and related companies;
- Capital endowed to overseas branches;
- The issue of capital instruments such as subordinated debt and preference shares;
- Booking of unremitted profits or remittance of profits from overseas.

The HKMA monitors and reviews the soundness of the forex risk management plans of banks in Hong Kong as a matter of course. As part of this role, it considers a number of factors such as the complexity and level of forex risk in a bank's balance sheet, the strength of the bank's forex risk management framework, the management's knowledge of foreign exchange, and a number of others.

Quotation

In the foreign exchange market, the "base currency" is the first currency in a currency pair. The second currency is termed the "quote currency," or alternatively, the "counter currency" or "terms currency." Exchange rates are quoted per unit of the base currency. Note that FX market convention is the reverse of mathematical convention. The "reciprocal rate" is the opposite rate in a foreign exchange relationship.

Quotations are divided into three groups: direct quotation, indirect quotation, and cross-rate quotation.

Direct Quotation

In direct quotation, the value of a U.S. dollar is denominated in a non-USD currency (that is, a foreign currency). For example, USD/JPY is quoted at 108.30. This means that one U.S. dollar can buy 108.30 Japanese yen. In this direct quotation, the USD is the base currency and JPY is the quote currency.

Here's another example. USD/CHF is quoted at 1.0550. What does this mean? It means that one U.S. dollar can buy 1.0550 Swiss francs. USD is the base currency and CHF is the quote currency.

The following are some direct quotation currency pairs:

- USD/JPY (referred to by traders as "dollar-yen" or simply "yen")
- USD/CHF (referred to as "dollar-Swiss" or simply "Swiss")
- USD/CAD (referred to as "dollar CAD" or simply "CAD")
- USD/HKD (referred to as "dollar-Honki" or simply "Honki")

Note that some academics sometimes use the term JPY/USD instead of the correct market notation USD/JPY. This is probably because, from the mathematician's perspective, the currency pair refers to the number of yen per one USD, and so yen should come first. To avoid confusion, you should always use the market convention.

Indirect Quotation

Indirect quotation is the opposite of direct quotation: it is the non-USD currency (foreign currency) that is the base currency. As such, the currency pair is denominated in USD. For example, GBP/USD is quoted at 2.0370. This means that one pound sterling can buy USD2.0370. Another example: EUR/USD is quoted at 1.5480. This means one euro can buy USD1.5480.

The following are some indirectly quoted currency pairs:

- EUR/USD (referred to by traders as "euro-dollar" or simply "euro")
- GBP/USD (referred to as "Cable")
- AUD/USD (referred to as "Aussie-dollar" or simply "Aussie")
- NZD/USD (referred to as "Kiwi-dollar" or simply "Kiwi")

Cross Rate Quotation

In a cross rate quotation, neither the base currency nor the quote currency is in USD. For example, EUR/JPY is quoted at 167.70. This means that one euro can buy 167.70 yen. EUR is the base currency and JPY is the quote currency.

The following are some examples of cross rate quotations:

- EUR/GBP (referred to by traders as "euro-pound")
- EUR/JPY (referred to as "euro-yen")
- AUD/JPY (referred to as "Aussie-yen")

Two-Way Quotation

A professional trader (that is, a market maker) quotes a two-way price to a market user. The user has an option to sell the bid or buy the offer from the maker. The option is not free of charge. The maker usually charges a spread. The size of the bid-offer spread depends on the liquidity and volatility of the currency pair in the market.

For example, you may come across the notation "USD/JPY I quote 33/35 for ten" in a trading environment. What does this mean? Put simply, it means that "the market maker (I) is willing to buy USD10mio [million] at 117.33 or sell USD10mio at 117.35." Professional traders seldom mention the full number (or so-called big figures), just the cents that come after it (not 117.33/117.35, just 33/35) in dealing with other professionals. This does not apply in the retail market, however.

What happens if the trade is wrongly confirmed? In the professional market, it is unethical to hold another trader to the mistake in the confirmation of the trade. You must void the deal or adjust the execution rate to a reasonable level (both parties should always refer to *The Model Code* of Conduct and Practice of the Treasury Markets Association).

Value Date of FX Deals

Foreign exchange deals are valued depending on the agreement between the two parties. Participants may decide to do a spot deal, value tom (tomorrow), or value today, depending on the currency pair, regulation, and other factors.

Spot Deal

This is a foreign exchange transaction in which the amounts of two freely convertible currencies are immediately exchanged at an agreed rate between the two counterparties at the spot rate. The value date of the trade is the settlement date, which is normally two business days after the transaction date, referred to as T + 2. Figure 2.3 illustrates the relationship between the transaction date and the spot date.

Note that participants in the retail market sometimes mistake a T + 2 transaction with a forward deal. Be aware of this tendency to avoid confusion, particularly when dealing in the interbank market.

FIGURE 2.3   Relationship between transaction date and spot date

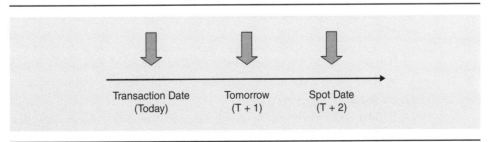

Transaction Date (Today) — Tomorrow (T + 1) — Spot Date (T + 2)

Source: HKIB

For example, suppose a calendar month has the following dates as set out below:

Mon	Tue	Wed	Thu	Fri	Sat	Sun
1	2	3	4	5	6	7
8	9	10	11	12	13	14

- If today is the 1st date of the month, the spot date (settlement date) of an FX trade will be on the 3rd day of the month (Wednesday). The settlement day is two business days after the transaction day.
- If today is the 4th date of the month, the spot date of the trade will be the 8th day of the month, Monday. This is because both the 6th and 7th days are not business days. The settlement date is four days after the transaction day.
- If today is the 1st day of the month and the 2nd day of the month is a public holiday, the spot date of the trade will be the 4th instead of the 3rd. The settlement day is three days after the transaction day.

Value Tom or Today Deal

A tom deal means an FX trade is settled one day after the transaction day. A today deal means the FX trade is settled on the same day of the transaction date. Below are some issues to keep in mind:

- **Currency pair:** The value date of the FX deal depends on the currency pair. For example, USD/CAD is normally settled on T + 1 or value tom. That's why USD/CAD is sometimes called "Tom Fund."
- **Cut off time:** The cut off time of the settlement agent will affect the selection of the settlement date. For example, if it is 5 pm Hong Kong time, you will not be able to settle your NZ dollar transaction today because the settlement agent in NZ has ended the business day there.
- **Regulation:** Not all currencies are freely tradable in the market. For example, you cannot execute a today or a tom deal for USD/THB because the Bank of Thailand does not allow Thai banks to quote in this way. USD/THB is thus always a spot deal.

Let us use the calendar month above to look at how a tom or today deal works in practice.

- If today is the 1st day of the month, the tom date (settlement date) of an FX trade will be the 2nd day of the month, Tuesday. The settlement day is one business day after the transaction day.
- If today is the 5th day of the month, the tom date of the trade will be the 8th day of the month because both 6th and 7th days are not business days. The settlement date is three days after the transaction day.

- If today is the 1st day of the month, the settlement date of a value today FX trade will be the 1st day of the month. The settlement day is the same as the transaction date.

How to Quote a Value Tom or Today Deal

The spot deal is the default value date in the interbank market. If you want to quote the transaction value at other than the standard spot day, you will need to adjust the quote according to the cost-of-carry (that is, the transaction cost).

For example, the objective is to quote a value tom and a value today for USD/HKD. The market data is as follows.

- Calendar month:

Mon	Tue	Wed	Thu
1	2	3	4

- **Spot USD/HK is 7.8280/85:** The current spot USD/HKD is quoting at 7.8280/85. The normal spot transaction day is the 3rd day of the month (if the transaction day is the 1st day of the month)
- **Overnight swap is (5/4):** The swap point between the 1st and 2nd days of the month is trading at a discount of 5/4 pips.
- **Tom next swap is (2/1):** The swap point between the 2nd and 3rd days of the month is trading at a discount of 2/1 pips.
- Note: "Pip" usually (but not always) stands for the fifth significant figure of a quotation. For example, if Euro/USD is 1.2431, one pip of this pair is 0.0001 or so-called 1 pip. If USD/JPY is 91.21, one pip of this pair is 0.01 (this is an exception to the rule).

Value Tom

1. Reverse the numbers of the Tom next (T/N) swap: $(2/1) \Rightarrow (1/2)$
2. Combine with the spot rate: $(1/2)$ and $(7.8280/85)$
3. Tom TT $= (7.8280 + 0.0001, 7.8285 + 0.0002) = (7.8281/87)$

Value Today

1. Combine the O/N and T/N swap: $(5/4) + (2/1) = (7/5)$
2. Reverse the numbers of the swap: $(7/5) \Rightarrow (5/7)$

3. Combine the swap with the spot rate: $(5/7) + (7.8280/85)$
4. Today TT $= (7.8280 + 0.0005, 7.8285 + 0.0007) = (7.8285/92)$

Arbitrage in the FX Market

Arbitrage is defined as a dealing activity that captures slight differences in market value when there is disparity in the price of the same instrument in two different markets. A trader simultaneously buys at the lower price and sells at the higher price of the underlying asset in the two markets or within the same market.

Arbitrage is virtually risk-free to the trader. It also has short life, in theory, when the market is efficient. If the market is inefficient or is being distorted by something else, such as legal matters, government subsidies, or foreign exchange restriction, the arbitrage opportunity may persist for a long time.

An arbitrage opportunity may suddenly appear. For example:

- **Execution of a big order:** In this situation, a trader offers at a lower rate or bids at a higher price to liquidate his huge position, which may run into billions, even though he has a full idea of the market. This is because he knows the limit order will seriously affect the market. The flow may temporarily affect the balance of supply and demand and result in an arbitrage opportunity.
- **Credit limit issue:** Sometimes, a counterparty with a poor credit history is forced to bid at a higher price or offer to sell at a lower price to execute a transaction. This is because no one is willing to transact with that counterparty unless the trade offers a higher-than-normal return to cover the higher risk. As an aside, this is one weakness of small names in the execution of FX deals.
- **Asymmetry of information:** A counterparty may not have as much information as others in the market, causing **t** to offer at a lower price or bid at a higher price. If one counterpart is offering USD through a particular broker, the price he offers may be lower than the current bid of another broker. This situation happens almost everyday.

Theoretical Value of Cross Pair

The arbitrage relationship is critical in determining the theoretical price of a financial instrument. A cross rate can be replicated by a pair of related currency pairs.

For a EUR/JPY deal, for example, traders can also quote EUR/USD, USD/JPY, and EUR/JPY at the same time. These currency pairs are being traded independently in the market. In economic terms, they have their own demand-supply curve. Others may have various limit orders at both sides of the market. As a result, the quotation of these three currency pairs might result in arbitrage opportunities due to a temporary and sudden imbalance in demand and supply.

FIGURE 2.4   Trading in related currency pairs

Trade	Euro	USD	JPY
Buy EUR/USD 1mio	+1,000,000	– 1,549,500	
Sell USD/JPY 1.5495mio		+1,549,500	–167,888,325

Source: HKIB

For example, we may have the following conditions:

USD/JPY = (108.30/35)
EUR/USD = (1.5490/95)

If you want to buy EUR against JPY, you may:

- Buy EUR from the quote 1.5495 (EUR/USD), and
- Sell JPY from the quote 108.35 (USD/JPY)
- In effect, you have bought EUR/JPY 1mio at 167.888325
- The transactions are summarised in Figure 2.4.

Mathematically:

EUR/JPY = (1.5490 * 108.30, 1.5495 * 108.35)
EUR/JPY = (167.76, 167.89)

The two-way quotation for the synthetic cross rate is 167.76/89.

Least-Cost and Arbitrage Condition

What happen if a trader quotes EUR/JPY at (167.75/80) or (167.90/95)?

- **Least-cost:** In the former case (167.75/80), if you want to buy EUR/JPY, you will buy it from this trader. On the other hand, if you want to sell EUR/JPY, you will sell USD/JPY at 108.30 and EUR/USD at 1.5490 to replicate EUR/JPY at 167.76.
- **Arbitrage:** In the later case (167.90/95), you should buy EUR/JPY synthetically at 167.89 and sell at the market rate at 167.90 to lock in the arbitrage profit. Figure 2.5 illustrates the mechanism (the three trades) to capture the arbitrage profit.

The existence of arbitrage opportunity happens for a very short time in an efficient market. Market forces soon drive the currency pairs to its theoretical price.

FIGURE 2.5　Three trades to capture arbitrage profit

Trade	Euro	USD	JPY
Buy EUR/USD 1mio	+1,000,000	−1,549,500	
Sell USD/JPY 1.5495mio		+1,549,500	−167,888,325
Sell EUR/JPY 1mio	−1,000,000		+167,900,000
Net	0	0	+11,675

Source: HKIB

Calculation of Cross Rate

Basically, it is a separate market from dollar majors[3] but all the risk free opportunity should be removed in a split second unless there is significant information asymmetry.

In arbitrage free condition:

Given: USD/JPY 117.25/30 (Direct quote) EUR/USD 1.1880/85 (Indirect quote)		
The quote for EUR/JPY is:		
USD/JPY 117.25/30	USD1 = JPY117.25	USD1 = JPY117.30
EUR/USD 1.1880/85	EUR1 = USD1.1880	EUR1 = USD1.1885
	Maker buys EUR	Maker sells EUR
EUR/JPY	EUR1= 1.1880×117.25	EUR1 = 1.1885 × 117.30
	EUR1= JPY139.29	EUR1 = JPY139.41

Given: USD/JPY 117.25/30 (Direct quote) USD/HKD 7.7990/95 (Direct quote)		
The quote for JPY/HKD is:		
USD/JPY 117.25/30	USD1 = JPY117.25	USD1 = JPY117.30
USD/HKD7.7990/95	USD1 = HKD7.7990	USD1 = HKD7.7995
	Maker buys JPY	Maker sells JPY
JPY/HKD	JPY1 = 7.7990/117.30	JPY1 = 7.7995/117.25
	JPY1 = HKD0.066488	JPY1 = HKD0.066520

---

[3] Dollar majors are the currency pairs of G7 countries: EUR/USD, GBP/USD, USD/CHF, USD/JPY, AUD/USD, NZD/USD and USD/CAD.

Given: GBP/USD 1.6740/45 (Indirect quote) EUR/USD 1.1880/85 (Indirect quote)		
The quote for EUR/GBP is:		
GBP/USD 1.6740/45	GBP1 = USD1.6740	GBP1 = USD1.6745
EUR/USD 1.1880/85	EUR1 = USD1.1880	EUR1 = USD1.1885
	Maker buys EUR	Maker sells EUR
EUR/GBP	EUR1 = 1.1880/1.6745	EUR1 = 1.1885/1.6740
	EUR1 = GBP0.7095	EUR1 = GBP0.7100

Note that the value date of currency pairs do affect the calculation of the theoretical value of a cross pair.

For example, if the spot value date of USD/HKD is 12 Feb 20xx but the spot value date of USD/JPY is 8 Feb 20xx, the spot value date of JPY/HKD will be 12 Feb 20xx (not 8 Feb 20xx).

In this case, you must adjust the spot price of USD/JPY to an outright price value on 12 Feb 20xx before you construct the JPY/HKD quotation.

Determining Exchange Rates

As we have discussed, the exchange rate is an expression of the value of one currency relative to another. Dealing in foreign exchanges and multiple currencies is often necessary for organizations involved in multinational transactions. This is almost always true of banks and, particularly in Hong Kong, often true of bank clients as well.

With freely traded currencies such as the U.S. dollar or the euro, the exchange rate is set on international markets and affected by a number of factors such as interest rates, the rate of inflation, demand for a particular currency, monetary policy, fiscal policy, and more. Other currencies may have less flexibility. The Hong Kong dollar, for example, is tied to the U.S. dollar and allowed to trade in a very narrow band. This peg gives Hong Kong's currency a degree of stability but it restricts the ability of Hong Kong to set its own monetary policy. The RMB is under strict control by the government in Mainland China, which decides its own monetary policy, so the currency cannot be allowed to be freely converted—although at the time of writing China was in the midst of a major currency reform.

One of the basic principles of international economics is that a country may pursue only two of the three policy directions known as the Unholy Trinity: free movement of capital, an independent monetary policy, and a pegged exchange rate policy. Hong Kong pegs its currency to the dollar and allows for free movement of capital, so it cannot set an independent monetary policy without risking massive imbalances if the U.S. were to move in a different direction. Mainland China, on the other hand, has a fixed exchange rate and an independent monetary policy, so it cannot allow for the free movement of capital without allowing for imbalances that stem out of its fixed exchange rate.

These principles have an impact on treasury management. The different policies of different countries can translate into different interest rates and different rates of inflation. Both of these may, in turn, have an impact on balances of trade and payments and also on investment and capital flows.

Interest Rate Parity and Inflation

A situation in which the interest rates on deposits available in two different currencies is equivalent is known as interest rate parity. More specifically, interest rate parity occurs when the differential in the interest rate in two countries is equivalent to the differential between the forward exchange rate and the spot exchange rate, thus eliminating opportunities for arbitrage. However, parity rarely holds for long.

There are two main forms of interest rate parity. The first is uncovered interest rate parity, which has full exposure to foreign exchange risk. If interest rates between two currencies change suddenly, the balance in the interest rates is affected immediately. For example, if the interest rate between currency X and currency Y is on par but the value of currency Y suddenly drops, then the interest rate would have to rise proportionally to the drop so as to maintain the parity. The second form is covered interest rate parity, used to eliminate exposure to foreign exchange risk. The most common way to cover interest rate parity is to use forward contracts to eliminate foreign exchange risk.

There are a number of factors that impact interest rate parity. For starters, capital has to be mobile, allowing investors to easily exchange one currency for another. Parity also assumes that the assets held in one currency are perfectly substitutable with assets in another currency.

Inflation is another factor to consider when determining how to best leverage interest rates. Inflation is the percentage increase in prices, generally measured using tools such as the Consumer Price Index. The *Routledge Dictionary of Economics* describes inflation as "a general sustained rise in the price level that reduces the purchasing power of the country's currency."[4] The value of the currency of a country with high inflation drops over time in relation to the value of a currency of a country with lower inflation. So, inflation plays a significant role in determining how best to manage foreign exchange.

The currencies of countries with lower inflation tend to rise in value over time. This is because the purchasing power of that currency rises in relation to the purchasing power of a currency in a country with high inflation. The opposite is also true. The currencies of countries with high inflation, often less developed countries, lose value faster. At times of low interest rates, the holdings a bank might have denominated in these

---

[4] Rutherford, Donald. "Routledge Dictionary of Economics". Second Edition; Routledge: London; 2005.

high-inflation currencies might lose value faster than the income generated through loans denominated in that currency.

Balance of Trade and Payments

Two other important factors to consider when dealing in a particular foreign currency are the balance of trade and the balance of payments of the country whose currency may be in question. Both these factors are often used to determine the terms of trade of a particular country, which is a ratio that compares export and import prices. The exchange rate of a currency is key to setting up the terms of trade.

A part of a country's current account, the balance of trade is the difference between the value of a country's exports and its imports. When a country has a trade surplus, the value of its exports is larger than the value of its imports. A trade deficit occurs when the value of imports is larger than the value of exports. The United States, for example, typically runs a trade deficit which in 2013 was USD472 billion, according to the U.S. Census Bureau. Much of that was with China, with which the US had a trade deficit of USD315 billion on total trade of USD4.93 trillion. Conversely, China recorded a trade surplus of USD231.1 billion that year on total trade worth USD3.867 trillion, according to the General Administration of Customs.

The balance of payments is a wider figure. It is a record of how much a country trades in goods, services, and assets with other countries. A country's net exports are equal to the sum of the balance of trade and the balance of services. The latter is the difference between the value of the services a country exports and the value of the services it imports during a period of time.

There are three areas to consider when examining a country's balance of payments.

The first is the current account, which records short-term flows in and out of a particular economy. The current account includes imports and exports of goods and services, income from investments abroad and the difference between transfers out of the country and those coming in. To simplify, a payment made by a Hong Kong-based person or company to one outside of Hong Kong is a negative number in the current account while a payment made into Hong Kong is a positive.

The second is the capital account, which is a record of purchases a country has made abroad and foreign purchases made within the country in question. When someone in a place like Hong Kong makes a purchase of, for example, a U.S. bond there is a resulting outflow of capital from Hong Kong to the U.S. and, necessarily, a foreign exchange transaction at some point. Conversely, when a foreign investor buys a Hong Kong dollar-denominated treasury, there is a capital inflow.

The third and smallest component of the balance of payments is the capital account, a record of minor transactions like transfers made by migrant workers or sales of nonproduced and nonfinancial assets like copyrights, patents, trademarks, or rights.[5]

---

[5] R. Glenn Hubband and Anthony Patrick O'Brian; "Economics"; Third Edition; Prentice Hall; Boston, 2010.

International Investments and Capital Flow

There are several ways to move capital across borders, not all of them practical. In theory, funds can be moved in the form of hard currency notes, cheques or drafts, cards, bills and negotiable instruments, or electronic funds transfers. In this day and age, however, most capital moves electronically using an international network and passing through the clearing and settlement systems of each country.

The term "clearing" refers to the "entire end-to-end process of receipt, transmission, reconciliation, and confirmation of requests or orders for payments," explains Rajiv Rajendra. "Settlement" is the "provisional or final completion or discharging of payment obligations for transfer of fund from one party to another."[6] When capital flows across international borders it usually passes through some kind of central bank clearing system. High value payments around the world are typically done through real-time gross settlement (RTGS) systems. A key user of these systems is the Continuous Link Settlement (CLS) bank launched in 2002, which aims to enhance financial stability by mitigating forex market risk. The largest financial institutions in the world jointly own CLS, which handles transactions in 17 currencies. A key role of CLS is operating payment vs. payment (PvP) protocols. PvP ensures both parties in a foreign exchange transaction follow through on their settlement duties. PvP ensures payments to both sides of a transaction are settled before payment to either side is released.

The common standard of international capital flows is generally handled by the Society for Worldwide Interbank Financial Telecommunication (SWIFT), a worldwide cooperative. The SWIFT network has been in operation since 1973. Banks, broker-dealers, investment companies, and corporations are all part of the SWIFT network, which has the necessary infrastructure to handle payments, securities, trades, treasuries, and account information. Every participant in the network has a SWIFT code, a unique combination of between 8 and 11 alphanumeric characters. The SWIFT network allows participants to send safe, secure, and authentic messages to each other to process a wide range of operations, from funds transfers to foreign exchange and derivatives information and commodities trades. The use of the SWIFT network is now virtually universal.[7]

Trend Forecasting

One of the most challenging aspects of dealing in foreign exchange is forecasting trends. Accurate forecasts are key to successful forex management. There are a number of different approaches to forecasting forex trends but they boil down to two basic methods: technical analysis and fundamental analysis. In both cases, the goal is to predict the price or

---

[6] Rajiv Rajendra; "The Handbook of Global Corporate Treasury"; John Wiley & Sons; Singapore; 2013; p 76.
[7] Ibid; p 94. For more information see Chapter 8.

movement of foreign currency. In actual practice, rarely is one method used on its own. Rather, practitioners tend to combine technical and fundamental analysis in different ways.

Technical analysis seeks to predict price movements and market trends based on past behavior of the markets. There are three basic principles involved in technical analysis. The first is that actual prices reflect everything that is happening on the market, from supply and demand to politics and market sentiment. The second is that there are trends in all price movements and technical analysis can identify patterns that are recognized and significant. The third principle is that history repeats itself.

Technical analysts rely on charts and graphs of what happened before to predict what will happen in the future. They take into account myriad factors like the volume of trading or the price of a particular currency at various points in time to create charts. They rely on five general categories of factors: indicators, number theory, waves, gaps and trends. Among the most common technical tools are the Coppock Curve, which is used to predict bear market lows, and the Directional Movement Indicator used to determine if there are trends in a currency pair.

In analyzing these various factors, technical analysis relies on a series of tools. The major tools include:

- **Relative Strength Index (RSI):** A measure of the ratio of up-moves to down-moves expressed in an index that ranges from 0 to 100. When the index is above 70, a particular instrument is considered overbought.
- **Stochastic oscillator:** Based on the theory that on an upward trend prices tend to close high and in a downward trend prices tend to close low; this is an indicator of whether an instrument is overbought or oversold.
- **Moving average convergence divergence (MACD):** Plots two momentum lines to determine when a trend might change.
- **Number theory:** Uses various number sequences, such as Fibonacci numbers, to consider trends.
- **Gann numbers:** Used by W.D. Gann, a trader in the 1950s who made a fortune in the markets by considering angles in charts to analyse price movements.
- **Elliott wave theory:** Considers repetitive wave patterns and Fibonaccin numbers.
- **Gaps:** The spaces left on a bar chart when no trading takes place is also useful information. A down gap, for example, emerges when the highest price of an instrument in a given day is lower than the lowest price the day earlier.
- **Trends:** The peaks and troughs make up trends on their own. Changes in the peaks and troughs can indicate significant changes.

Fundamental analysis is more subjective as it considers factors such as economics, politics, and the environment along with any other relevant factor or statistic that could affect the supply and demand of an instrument. A key difference is that fundamental analysis seeks to predict what is likely to happen in a particular market based on an assessment of all these factors. Whereas technical analysts look at actual past market movements regardless of cause, fundamental analysts seek to understand why a market might move in one direction or another. This is often more art than science but the reality is that many of the best trades are made just before or just after big economic or policy announcements.

Forward Markets

A forward contract is a binding agreement between two parties to exchange two different cash flows at the forward rate at/or within a particular time in future. There are three variants of forward contracts:

- Normal forward (outright) contract;
- Time options (optional outright) contract;
- Non-deliverable forward contract.

Value of a Forward Contract

The value of a forward contract is zero at inception. Afterwards, it may be either positive or negative, depending on the market situation, such as:

- The spot rate of the pair (exchange risk);
- The interest rate of currency of both legs (interest rate risk).

The value of a long position (say long EUR outright) of a forward contract on the maturity date (time T) is illustrated in Figure 2.6. If the underlying asset price at the maturity (T) is higher than the forward contract rate, the contract has a positive value (in the money). Otherwise, it will have a negative value (out of the money). Note that the payoff diagram of a forward contract is linear.

FIGURE 2.6   Value of forward contract at maturity

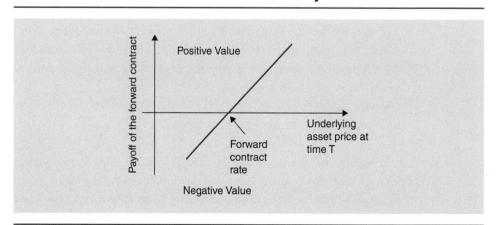

Source: HKIB

Hedging with a Forward Contract

You may hedge your exchange exposure with a forward contract so that the value of your exposure is locked at a particular rate. However, you have to weigh the disadvantages of a forward contract against the advantages and judge whether the positives outweigh the negatives in a particular case. The advantages and disadvantages are shown in Figure 2.7.

Figure 2.8 shows two positions. The broken line is the payoff for a short position in an underlying asset at time T. The red line is a long position in a forward contract to hedge the exposure of the previous asset. If the exposure on the short position is certain:

- The future value of the exposure is locked at value K irrespective of the movement of the future price of the underlying asset.
- The forward price of the asset is locked at the forward contract rate.

FIGURE 2.7   Positives and negatives of forward contracts

Advantages	Disadvantages
• Low transaction cost • Simple to understand	• Requires a credit facility • Problem in handling uncertain exposure

Source: HKIB

FIGURE 2.8   Hedging with a forward contract

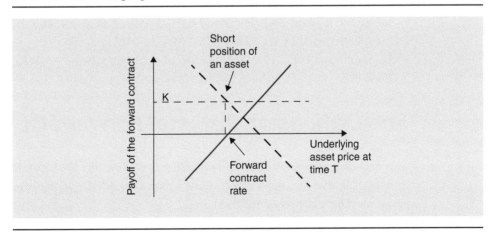

Source: HKIB

Normal FX Outright Rate

It is defined as a binding contract in which both parties agree to exchange one currency with another currency for a certain amount, in a transaction that will be settled only on a particular date as determined by the contract. The settlement date is usually longer than two business days. The general formula in a normal FX outright rate is:

$$\text{Outright rate} = \text{spot rate} + \text{forward swap (premium or discount)}$$

For example, the spot rate for USD/CHF is (1.4530/40) while one-month USD/CHF swap is (10/08). Assuming one-month swap of USD/CHF is quoting at a discount (10/08):

- One-month forward USD/CHF = (1.4530 − 0.0010, 1.4540-0.0008)
- One-month forward USD/CHF = (1.4520, 1.4532)

Let's take a second example. If spot USD/HKD is (7.7995/00) and one-month swap of USD/HKD is (320/330):

- One-month forward USD/HKD = (7.7995 + 0.0320, 7.8000 + 0.0330)
- One-month forward USD/HKD = (7.8315, 7.8330)

Given the above information, what is the one-month forward rate of CHF/HKD and its one-month swap? The answer:

- Spot USD/CHF is (1.4530/40)
- Spot USD/HKD is (7.7995/00)
- Spot CHF/HKD = (7.7995/1.4540,7.8000/1.4530)
- Spot CHF/HKD = (5.3642, 5.3682)
- One-month forward USD/CHF = (1.4520,1.4532)
- One-month forward USD/HKD = (7.8315, 7.8330)
- One-month forward CHF/HKD = (7.8315/1.4532, 7.8330/1.4520)
- One-month forward CHF/HKD = (5.38914, 5.39463)
- One-month swap of CHF/HKD = (5.38914 − 5.3642, 5.39463 − 5.3682)
- One-month swap of CHF/HKD = (0.02494, 0.02543) or (249.4/254.3)

Time Options or Optional Forward Contract

This is a binding agreement between two parties that allows the holder of the contract to fully or partially exercise (uplift) the contract within a period of time, say from t1 to t2. The contract must have been fully exercised on t2.

Figure 2.9 shows a timeline from now to future time t1 and t2. The contract offers the buyer flexibility to handle his exposure in future. It is more flexible than the normal

FIGURE 2.9 Timeline for an optional forward contract

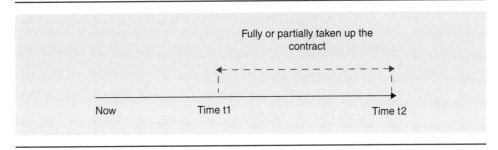

Source: HKIB

forward contract, but it comes at a cost. The spread of a time options contract is always higher than a normal forward contract of the same tenor.

For example, you would like to hedge your future exposure to a shipment. You know the ship will arrive roughly in one to two months. In this case, you may consider buying a 1×2 optional forward contract.

Theoretical Value of Optional Forward Contract

It is similar to the normal forward contract rate. On top of the original mechanism, you need to consider the normal forward rate at time t1 and t2. You then need to select the lowest value between the two outright bids and make it the bid. You also need to choose the highest value between the two outright offers and make it the offer, as shown in Figure 2.10.

FIGURE 2.10 Theoretical value of an optional forward contract

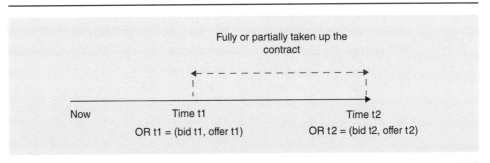

Source: HKIB

The formula is:

$$\text{Optional contract } (t1, t2) = \left(\text{Min}\left(\text{bid}_{t1}, \text{bid}_{t2}\right), \text{Max}\left(\text{offer}_{t1}, \text{offer}_{t2}\right)\right)$$

For example, if:

- Spot USD/HKD is 7.8280/85
- One-month swap is $(55/50)$
- Two-month swap is $(100/95)$
- The normal one-month forward $= (7.8280 - 0.0055, 7.8285 - 0.0050) = (7.8225, 7.8235)$
- The normal two-month forward $= (7.8280 - 0.0100, 7.8285 - 0.0095) = (7.8180, 7.8190)$
- The maker gives the user a right to exercise the contract starting from next month for one month:
- 1×2 optional forward $= (7.8180, 7.8235)$

Is there an alternative? Yes, there is. If you need to buy USD/HKD forward but don't know for sure when you will need to pay the money in the next two months, you can buy a one-month normal forward at 7.8235 and roll over the contract to match your cash flow.

Par Forward Contract

A par forward, also known as a flat rate forward, is an agreement to exchange a series of cash flows over time that is in one currency for a series of cash flows that is in another currency. All exchanges are carried out at the same exchange rate. The par forward is therefore a series of foreign exchange forward contracts at one agreed rate.

It is not necessary for the cash flow to be of the same notional amount. The par forward potentially has taxation and accounting implications for the user, and so independent advice should be sought before use.

How does a par forward work? Figure 2.11 shows an illustrative example. In this situation, a client would like to buy USD100,000 each month in the next 12 months. The first column is the number of months from the transaction day (tenor). The second column is the interest rate of HKD. The third column is the discount factor of HKD in the next 12 months. The fourth column is the normal forward rate of USD/HKD, showing the current spot USD/HKD at 7.8000.

The fifth and sixth columns show the cash flow of USD and HKD, respectively, if the client entered into 12 normal forward contracts to buy USD 100,000 each month. The seventh column is the cash flow of HKD for a par forward contract. The last two columns are the nominal difference and the present value of the difference of columns six and seven, respectively.

The present value of the 12 normal forward contracts must be identical to the 12 par forward contracts. Therefore:

$$\sum \text{Pi}\left(\text{ORi} - \text{Par}\right) * \text{DFi} = 0$$
$$\left(\sum \text{Pi} * \text{ORi} * \text{DFi}\right) / \left(\sum \text{Pi} * \text{DFi}\right) = \text{Par}$$

FIGURE 2.11 Illustrative example of a par forward contract

Tenor	HKD Interest rate	Discount Factors	Current Rate 7.8000	Normal Forward Contracts		Par Contract HKD*	Diff (HKD)	PV (Diff)
				USD	HKD			
1	1.50%	0.9988	7.7955	100,000	779,550.00	777,088.80	−2,461.20	−2458.13
2	1.64%	0.9973	7.7910	100,000	779,100.00	777,088.80	−2,011.20	−2005.73
3	1.77%	0.9956	7.7865	100,000	778,650.00	777,088.80	−1,561.20	−1554.31
4	1.91%	0.9937	7.7820	100,000	778,200.00	777,088.80	−1,111.20	−1104.17
5	2.05%	0.9915	7.7775	100,000	777,750.00	777,088.80	−661.20	−655.61
6	2.18%	0.9892	7.7730	100,000	777,300.00	777,088.80	−211.20	−208.92
7	2.32%	0.9867	7.7685	100,000	776,850.00	777,088.80	238.80	235.61
8	2.45%	0.9839	7.7640	100,000	776,400.00	777,088.80	688.80	677.71
9	2.59%	0.9809	7.7595	100,000	775,950.00	777,088.80	1,138.80	1117.09
10	2.73%	0.9778	7.7550	100,000	775,500.00	777,088.80	1,588.80	1553.49
11	2.86%	0.9744	7.7505	100,000	775,050.00	777,088.80	2,038.80	1986.65
12	3.00%	0.9709	7.7460	100,000	774,600.00	777,088.80	2,488.80	2416.31
							Sum (roughly)	0

Source: HKIB

P_i = principle amount of the contract in USD at time i
OR_i = normal outright rate of USD for time i
Par = constant outright rate for all forward contracts
DF_i = discount factor of the quote currency for time i
$DF_1 = 1/(1+1.5\%*1/12) = 0.9988,$
$DF_2 = 1/(1+1.64\%*2/12) = 0.9973$
$(\sum P_i * OR_i * DF_i)/(\sum P_i * DF_i) = 7.770888$

Covered Interest Rate Parity Relationship

As mentioned in the previous section about the risk of holding a forward contract, the theoretical value of a forward contract can be replicated with a portfolio comprising a spot transaction, a loan denominated in the home currency, and a bond in a foreign currency.

Figure 2.12 shows an illustrative example of a covered interest rate parity relationship, with the following conditions:

Spot USD/HKD = 7.8000
One-year HKD interest rate is 2% per annum
One-year USD interest rate is 1.5625% per annum

FIGURE 2.12   Replicating theoretical value of a forward contract

	Now		One-year
HKD (loan)	76,800	(1 + 2%)	78,336
HKD-USD (exchange)	76,800/7.8 = US9,846.15		
USD (deposit)	9,846.15	(1 + 1.5625%)	10,000

Source: HKIB

Using the information in Figure 2.12, you can replicate a forward rate by borrowing HKD76, 800 for one year, exchange the HKD into USD at 7.8000, and then deposit the USD proceeds for one year. By the end of the year, you repay the HKD loan and obtain USD10,000. The forward rate equals 7.8336 (synthetic forward rate).

If the one-year forward rate is quoted at (7.8340, 7.8355), you can make an arbitrage profit by selling the forward at 7.8340 and buying a replicated portfolio of above at 7.8336 to capture a risk-free profit of HKD0.0004 per U.S. dollar.

To generalise the USD-HKD forward equation:

$$\text{Spot rate} * (1+R_{hkd})/(1+R_{usd}) = \text{Forward rate} \tag{2.1}$$

$$7.8 * (1+0.02)/(1+0.015625) = 7.8336$$

The above equation is a simplified formula. In practice, you must take into consideration the money market convention.

$$\text{Spot rate} * (1+R_{hkd}*n/365)/(1+R_{usd}*n/360) = \text{Forward rate}$$

Here is another example involving the euro, yen and US dollar. Suppose:

- Spot EUR/USD = 1.0095
- One-year EUR/USD swap = −135
- One-year EUR deposit rate = 2.95%
- Spot USD/JPY = 120.95
- One-year USD/JPY swap = −149
- One-year JPY deposit rate = 0.12%
- Spot EUR/JPY = 1.0095 * 120.95 = 122.10

We will discuss two procedures in replicating the synthetic forward rate of EUR/JPY.

FIGURE 2.13 **Replicating theoretical value of a forward contract**

	Now		One-year
JPY (loan)	1,186,012	(1 + 0.12%)	1,187,435
EUR-JPY (exchange)	1,186,012/122.10 = EUR9713.45		
EUR (deposit)	9,713.45	(1 + 2.95%)	10,000

Source: HKIB

In Approach 1:

- One-year EUR/USD forward = 1.0095 − 0.0135 = 0.9960
- One-year USD/JPY forward = 120.95 − 1.49 = 119.46
- One-year EUR/JPY forward = 0.9960 * 119.46 = 118.98

Figure 2.13 utilises Approach 2, which is what was used in the previous example (Figure 2.12). Repeating the procedure in that previous example, the synthetic forward rate of EUR/JPY can be replicated at 118.74, which is lower than the result in Approach 1.

To generalise the euro-yen forward equation:

$$\text{Spot rate} * (1 + R_{jpy})/(1 + R_{eur}) = \text{Forward rate} \quad (2.2)$$

$$\text{Spot rate} * (1 + R_{jpy} * n/360)/(1 + R_{eur} * n/360) = \text{Forward rate}$$

A general formula in daily continuous compounding is:

$$\text{Spot rate} * e^{(Ry - Re)*t} = \text{Forward rate} \quad (2.3)$$

Ry = JPY deposit rate
Re = EUR deposit rate

Note that you may price your instrument using different models. However, you must actually structure a set of trades to lock in the theoretical price. Therefore, you must always take the market convention into consideration.

Meaning of the Forward Rate

The forward rate is an unbiased estimator of the future spot rate under risk-free conditions. This means that the difference between the spot rate and forward rate is mainly due to the cost-of-carry of the position. Therefore, a higher forward rate does not mean the underlying asset will rise in the future. A lower forward rate does not predict a fall in the value of the underlying asset either.

For example:

- Spot USD/HKD is 7.8000
- One-year forward USD/HKD is 7.7000
- The one-year forward rate does not imply the USD/HKD will rise from the current level of 7.8 to 7.7.

In reality, the forward rate may also be considered as the market consensus on the future spot rate of a currency, which is true particularly when the currency is of an unusual nature or is controlled by the government—that is, if it is an exotic currency.

For example, empirical evidence indicates that the RMB would appreciate more or less in a similar fashion as that currency's non-deliverable forward rate. However, note that you cannot replicate non-deliverable forwards (NDFs) or even deliverable forwards with a money portfolio because these forwards are restricted. Traders actually use NDF contracts to speculate on the movement of RMB, rather than to manage currency risk. As a result, sometimes you can derive backwards the NDF rate and come up with a negative interest rate on the RMB.

Bid and Offer for an Outright Quote

As with the spot quotation, traders quote two-way prices of different tenors. In theory, the trader should consider the bid and offer of the interest rates of the money market in the calculation of the forward rate. In practice, they usually refer to the swap market only, because the swap market is more efficient than the money market.

In addition, you may note that the spread of an outright quote is bigger than a spot quote. In the professional market, the trader may charge the user with only a single spread. Therefore, you may use the mid-rate of the swap point to calculate the forward rates.

For example:

- USD/JPY 118.00/05
- One-month swap (50/48)
- One-month forward rate $= (118.00 - 0.49, 118.05 - 0.49) = (117.51/56)$

Instead of:

- One-month forward rate $= (118.00 - 0.50, 118.05 - 0.48) = (117.50/57)$

Discounts and Premiums

However, in a professional dealer market, traders sometimes do not quote the sign of the swap point. The rule of thumb is:

- Premium: when LHS < RHS
- Discount: when LHS > RHS

For example:

- Spot EUR/USD is 1.2163/66
- EUR1M = 10.85/10.67

And:

- Spot USD/CAD is 1.3125/30
- CAD1M = 19.5/20.0

Exception:

- Spot USD/CAD 1.4695/00
- Swap CAD1M = 6/4 A/P[8]
- Forward outright = 1.4689/1.4704
- A/P means "Around Par"

Rollover of Forward Contracts

Generally, all transactions should be executed at current market rates.[9] Off-market or historical-rate rollover transactions should not normally be permitted, as these transactions may be used to hide a loss or extend a profit-or-loss position. Any such transactions should be subject to prior approval and stringent monitoring procedures.

There are two approaches to the rollover of forward contracts, namely market rate rollover and historical rate rollover. In principle, regulators do not recommend that financial institutions participate in the second approach. They should have a policy to manage the use of historical rate rollover.

For example, a client sold forward euro 1mio at 1.1250 due today. However, the client wants to extend the contract for one month.

- Spot EUR/USD is 1.2166/71
- EUR1M = 20/22
- Mid-rate is 1.2168 (roughly)
- The client needs to buy euro now and sell forward again at an outright price of (1.2168 + 0.0020) 1.2188.

---

[8] Steiner, Robert. "Mastering Financial Calculations: A Step- By- Step Guide to the Mathematics of Financial Market Instruments". FT Press: London, 2007. Pg. 161.

[9] Hong Kong Monetary Authority. "Foreign Exchange Risk Management: Guidance Note". 17 Sep 2004. Web. Sub-section 5.4.12.

FIGURE 2.14   Market rate rollover

	Now		One-month later	
	EUR	USD	EUR	USD
Previous contract	−1mio	+1.125mio	−1mio	+1.2188mio
Spot deal	+1mio	−1.2168mio		
Net		−91,800		

Source: HKIB

Market Rate Rollover

The client buys EUR/USD 1mio at 1.2168 to settle the previous forward contract. A loss of USD91,800 is realised. Then, the client sells one-month forward again at the current forward rate of 1.2188, shown in Figure 2.14.

Historical Rate Rollover

In this approach, the client does not realise the loss of the previous contract, but the new contract is set well away from the current market price, as shown in Figure 2.15.

Non-Deliverable Forward

A non-deliverable forward (NDF) contract is essentially an outright (forward) foreign exchange contract of a restricted or exotic currency where, on the settlement date, the

FIGURE 2.15   Historical rate rollover

	Now		One-month later	
	EUR	USD	EUR	USD
Previous contract	−1mio	+1.125mio	−1mio	+1.127mio
Spot deal	+1mio	−1.125mio		
Net		0		

Source: HKIB

profit and loss of the contract will be exchanged according to a reference rate or a benchmark as predetermined at inception.

NDFs are prevalent in some countries where forward FX trading is either restricted or illiquid, usually as a means to prevent exchange rate volatility. They once included the Philippine peso (PHP), Indian rupee (INR), New Taiwan Dollars (TWD), Korean won (KRW), Russian rouble (RUR), and Chinese renminbi (CNY). With the liberalization of the current account, the outright forward market for CNY/USD is now more liquid and the need for NDF decreases.

Fixing Date and Settlement

Every NDF has a fixing date and a settlement (delivery) date. The fixing date is the day and time when the comparison between the NDF rate and the prevailing spot rate is made. The settlement date is the day when the difference is paid or received.

Depending on the currencies dealt, there are variations in fixing and settlement. For some currencies, the fixing date is one good business day before the settlement date. For others, it is two good business days before the settlement date. Generally, the fixing of the spot rate is based on a reference page on Thomson Reuters and Bloomberg, with a fallback of calling four leading dealers in the relevant market for a quote.

Settlement of the NDF Contract

On the settlement date, if the fixing rate is higher than the contract rate, the buyer of the contract would receive compensation in terms of the base currency. For example, in an RMB NDF, the seller will pay the buyer if the Chinese currency depreciated more than (or appreciate less than) expected against the USD as stated in the contract rate, say from 6.2 to 6.3.

- Contract Rate > Fixing rate (on fixing date): The buyer pays and compensates the seller.
- Contract Rate < Fixing rate (on fixing date): The seller pays and compensates the buyer.

    For example:

- Today's spot date is 10 July 20xx
- The maturity of a one-week tenor is 17 July 20xx
- The current one-week NDF is 6.2776

If the client **bought** USD/CNY 1mio and the fixing rate is 6.2766 at 9:30 am on 15 July 20xx (two days prior to contract date), the cash settlement is:

Cash settlement (in USD)
$$= \text{Nominal amount} \times (\text{Fixing rate} - \text{Contract price})/\text{Fixing rate}$$

Cash settlement (in USD)
$$= +1,000,000 \times (6.2766 - 6.2776)/6.2766 = -US120.82$$

This means that the client must pay the bank USD120.82 on 17 July 20xx. But if the client *sold* USD/CNY 1mio, the client will get USD120.82 from the bank on 17 July 20xx.

Cash settlement (in USD)
$$= -1,000,000 \times (6.2766 - 6.2776)/6.2766 = +US120.82$$

Hedging the FX Exposure

When banks are seriously exposed to currency risk, which can be the case when they have very large positions or are dealing with volatile currencies, they may decide to lower the risk by hedging a portion of their positions.

Approaches to FX Hedging

Financial institutions should make sure to practice hedging using a well-thought-out and methodical strategy. Foreign exchange risk exposures can be broadly divided as structural and trading exposures. The HKMA says structural exposures arise from imbalances between assets and liabilities and are hard to change quickly. Examples include investments in fixed assets, equity investments overseas, or the issue of capital instruments. Trading exposures are almost all other kind of exposures other than structural and may arise from business needs, customer transactions that are not immediately covered, or from taking a view on currency movements.[10]

The following steps are useful in developing a good hedging strategy.

- **Identify the exposure:** The user should identify the nature of the exchange exposures. If it is translation exposure, the user should consider swaps and foreign currency borrowing to mitigate the risk. If it is economic exposure, the user may consider operational hedging (see Figure 2.16 for a list of hedging tools, of which operational hedging is one).
- **Assess the probability of the exposure:** The user should then assess the probability of the exposure. For example, if the exposure involves a lump sum of foreign currency that must be paid one week later, the probability of the exposure is certain. The user may use spot or forward to hedge the risk. If the exposure is contingent, the user will

---

[10] Hong Kong Monetary Authority. "Supervisory Policy Manual: Foreign Exchange Risk Management". TA-2. 14 January 2009. Web. 15 February 2014.

not be able to confirm the exact time and volume of risk. In this case, the user will pursue options or other tools to hedge the risk. Auctioning of a foreign project is one example of such other tools.

- **Determine the market view:** The ultimate objective of hedging is to create value for the firm. If the user firmly believes the market is moving in favour of his position, the user will have no economic incentive to hedge or reduce the exposure of the risk. For example, if the user is holding RMB assets, the user will not hedge in the face of the rising RMB.

- **Choose the hedging tool:** The user should match the nature of the payoff of the hedging tools with the underlying exposure. It is important to remember that the payoff of spot, outright, and futures contract are linear. These tools are perfect for hedging exposures with high certainty of occurrence. On the other hand, the payoff of an options contract is non-linear. It is good for hedging assets with a high uncertainty of occurrence. In addition, the user may use a combination of financial tools to reflect a particular view of the market.

- **Execute, maintain, and evaluate the hedge:** Hedging activity is not a one-off transaction. Sometimes the user must continue maintaining the hedge. For example, a futures contract to hedge risk will eventually expire. Depending on the circumstances, the user must rollover the futures contract from time to time. Another example is a non-perfect hedge—the correlation of the hedge and the underlying asset may vary from time to time. The user must monitor closely the market and make adjustments frequently.

Measuring Exposure

FX exposure can be defined as the sensitivity of the firm's financial situation to market rates. There are three types of FX exposure: transaction exposure, economic exposure and translation exposure. The choice of how to hedge a foreign currency exposure must take the type of exposure into account.

- **Transaction exposure** reflects risk to past contractual undertakings that have future cash flow implication (and effects on the current portfolio). For example, a company involved in international trade is vulnerable to a sudden and significant change in the currency exchange rate in signing a contract where it agrees to shoulder financial obligations. Such exposure to fluctuating exchange rates can lead to major losses.

- **Economic exposure** refers to the effects of changes in the exchange rate on the future cash flow of the firm, through the effect on future operational or strategic decisions (effect on future cash flow from operation). Exposure to fluctuating exchange rates affects a company's earnings, cash flow, and foreign investments. The extent to which a company is affected by economic exposure depends on the specific characteristics of the company and its industry.

- **Translation exposure** refers to the effect of unexpected changes in spot rates on the firm's consolidated balance sheet and income statement. This occurs when a firm denominates a portion of its equities, assets, liabilities or income in a foreign currency. It will not result in any actual cash flows for the firm.

Hedging Strategies

As mentioned, the ultimate objective of hedging is to increase the value of a firm. The goal of protecting against risk and limiting the downside of certain positions is certainly important and useful, but in the end, the hedging should end up enhancing the company's profitability. To do this, banks have to accurately measure their risk. This measurement should include evaluations of forex risk by maturity, employ accepted financial models, be comprehensive, be based on timely data, allow the bank to monitor exposures, and be well documented.[11]

The problem is in striking the right balance. Hedging can entail costs, particularly if the bank utilises options and currency swaps, and requires sophisticated infrastructure in terms of specialist skills and state-of-the-art technology. The hedging products employed can become very complicated as well, which raises the possibility that the very act of reducing risks could end up causing new risks and bring unintended consequences.

It is therefore important to consider the characteristics of the exposure before doing anything to hedge it, if in fact you need to hedge at all. It is also best practice to match the nature of the exposure and the hedging tools. Figure 2.16 summarises the typical hedging tools, their properties, and the situations in which each one is most applicable.[12]

In practice, forward contracts are more popular with parties that have actual demand in foreign currencies. This is because forward contracts do not require the user to provide home currency or any other funds immediately. However, only a user with a credit facility can execute a forward contract with a bank or another financial institution.

As discussed previously, the payoff from spot and forward contracts is linear, allowing the user to fix the cost of the underlying asset today. However, the user also effectively foregoes potential profit from any appreciation in the price of the underlying asset, if the market takes a bullish turn while the hedging tool is in force.

Futures contracts, which are bought and sold on an exchange, trade the underlying assets of March, June, September, and December contracts of each year. The liquidity of the contract for the first few contract months is usually abundant.

---

[11] Hong Kong Monetary Authority. "Supervisory Policy Manual: Foreign Exchange Risk Management". TA-2. 14 January 2009. Web. 15 February 2014. Sec. 5.3.2.
[12] See Chapter 4 for more detail.

FIGURE 2.16 Hedging financial and operational tools

Choice	Features
Spot	Liquid and efficient, but need to accompany the hedge with a loan and/or a deposit to match the future cash flow.
Outright	Tailor-made, low cost and hedge perfectly the future exposures. Good for known cash flows.
Futures	Liquid and efficient but need to be traded on the exchange and maintain a margin account. Cannot match cash flows perfectly.
Options	Illiquid and costly but good for non-linear and uncertain cash flows, and possible unlimited gain.
Currency Swaps	Tailor-made and costly but good for long term hedging complicated cash flows.
Operational Hedging	Shifting of production and sourcing abroad to match revenues in foreign currency, to reduce the exposure.

Source: HKIB

The merit of hedging with a futures contract is that the service is open to everyone as long as you can provide sufficient money to maintain the margin requirement. Moreover, users do not need to worry about counterparty risk. One of the problems, though, is that it is difficult to match the underlying exposure perfectly. The cost to rollover futures contract, is uncertain and therefore affects the success rate of the hedging strategy.

There are different types of operational hedging strategies, such as selecting low-cost production sites, flexible sourcing policy, market diversification, and product diversification. These operational matters are outside the scope of this discussion.

However, these operational hedging strategies can have foreign-currency implications that can pose a hedging dilemma. For example, if a Japanese carmaker decides to shift production to North American Free Trade Area (NAFTA) countries to be closer to its American customers, the issue of the relative strength of the yen against the U.S. dollar, the Canadian dollar, and the Mexican peso comes into play.

Summary

- The world's largest financial market, the foreign exchange market, is mainly a loosely regulated over-the-counter (OTC) market where transactions are done through the telephone, facsimile, and electronic networks, not in a physical trading floor as is the case with exchange trading. The participants include banks, commercial companies, investment management firms, central banks, and hedge funds.

- The major physical markets for foreign currency trading are in London, New York, Tokyo, Hong Kong, and Singapore. However, since FX operates 24 hours a day given that one market is always open somewhere in the world, traders all around the world effectively participate in the same market.

- The foreign exchange market generally has lower transaction costs than do equities and futures. In the interbank market, participants seldom charge a commission on the trade. The major transaction cost is the spread of the quote, the brokerage cost, which is subject to negotiation between the bank and the broker, the overhead of the operation, and the settlement cost, which typically accounts for the largest portion of the total cost.

- The base currency is the first currency in a currency pair. The second currency is termed the quote currency, or alternatively, the counter currency or terms currency. Exchange rates are quoted per unit of the base currency. The FX market convention is the reverse of mathematical convention.

- A market maker quotes a two-way price to the market user. The user has an option to sell the bid or buy the offer from the maker. The maker usually charges a bid-offer spread, whose size depends on the liquidity and volatility of the market.

- Foreign exchange deals are valued depending on the agreement between the two parties. Participants may decide to do a spot deal, value tom (tomorrow), or value today, depending on the currency pair, regulation, and other factors.

- Arbitrage is a dealing activity that captures slight differences in market value when there is disparity in the price of the same instrument in two different markets. The arbitrage relationship is critical in determining the theoretical price of a financial instrument. A cross rate of such theoretical price can be replicated by a pair of related currency pairs. The quotation of these currency pairs may result in arbitrage opportunities.

- Exchange rates are typically determined by the market, which takes into consideration a number of factors like demand for a particular currency or the available liquidity. It is also important to consider factors like the parity of interest rates affecting different currencies in a pair, inflation, the balance of trade, and the balance of payments of the currencies being traded.

- A forward contract is a binding agreement between two parties to exchange two different cash flows at the forward rate at/or within a particular time in the future. There are three variants: normal forward (outright) contract, time options (optional outright) contract, and non-deliverable forward contract.

- Generally, all forward transactions should be executed at current market rates. Off-market or historical-rate rollover transactions should not normally be permitted, as these transactions may be used to hide a loss or extend a profit-or-loss position.

- FX exposure can be defined as the sensitivity of the firm's financial situation to market rates. There are three types of FX exposure: transaction exposure, economic exposure, and translation exposure. The choice of how to hedge a foreign currency exposure must take the type of exposure into account.

Key Terms

Arbitrage

Balance of payments

Balance of trade

Base currency

Bid-offer spread

Brokers dealing

Counter currency

Cross pair

Cross-rate quotation

Currency pair

Currency swaps

Direct dealing

Direct quotation

Discount

Economic exposure

Exchange-traded market

Executable quotation

Forward contract

Hedging

Historical rate rollover

Indicative quotation

Indirect quotation

Inflation

Interest rate parity

Market rate rollover

Non-deliverable forward contract

Normal forward contract

Operational hedging

Over-the-counter (OTC) market

Par forward contract

Pip

Premium

Prime broker

Quote currency

Settlement process

Spot deal

Swap point

SWIFT network

Synthetic forward rate

T + 1

T + 2

Terms currency

Time options contract

Transaction exposure

Translation exposure

Two-way quotation

Value today

Value tom

Study Guide

1. "The settlement procedure involves counterparty risk because it is possible for the outflow of funds not to be matched by the inflow." What do you think a bank should do in order to mitigate or eliminate counterpart risk in foreign exchange trading? Include hedging in your answer.

2. For USD/JPY, the current quote is 99.26/31 while for EUR/USD, it is 1.3390/95. How would you go about buying the euro against the yen? What is the effective rate of your euro purchase? What is the two-way quotation for the synthetic cross rate?

3. In the situation presented in Question 2 above, the current market quote for EUR/JPY is 132.88/93. What should you do to lock in the arbitrage profit?

4. You spent RMB10 million to make toys that you then shipped to a client in the U.S., who will pay you USD1.6 million for the merchandise in six weeks' time. Using an NDF contract, how do you make sure you will lock in at least a 10% profit in Chinese yuan when you actually receive the payment? The USD/CNY rate is currently at 6.8179/84.

5. In the situation presented in Question 4, what hedging strategies other than NDFs can you use to achieve the same objective of locking in a 10% profit in Chinese yuan? Include operational hedging tools in your answer.

Further Reading

Rajendra, Rajiv. *The Handbook of Global Corporate Treasury*. Singapore: John Wiley & Sons (Asia), 2013. Print

Horcher, Karen A. *Essentials of Managing Treasury*. New Jersey: John Wiley & Sons, 2005. Print.

Choudhry, Moorad. *Bank Asset and Liability Management: Strategy, Trading, Analysis*. Singapore: John Wiley & Sons (Asia) Pte Ltd, 2007. Print.

Hong Kong Monetary Authority. *Foreign Exchange Risk Management. Supervisory Policy Manual*. Web. 24 April 2010. Available online at http://www.info.gov.hk/hkma/eng/bank/spma/attach/TA-2.pdf

Riehl, Heinz. *Managing Risk in Foreign Exchange, Money and Derivative Markets*. McGraw Hill, 1999. Print.

Steiner, Robert. *Mastering Financial Calculations: A Step- By- Step Guide to the Mathematics of Financial Market Instruments*. FT Press, 2007. Print.

3

Money and Capital Markets

Learning objectives

After studying this chapter, you should be able to:

1 Describe the structure, players, and instruments used in the Hong Kong dollar market.

2 Describe the functions of the international money market and the money market desk within organisations, including compliance with regulatory requirements.

3 Explain the properties of money market instruments such as government bills, certificates of deposit, commercial papers, and repurchase agreements.

Introduction

Money markets exist in every market economy, which is practically every country in the world. In every case, they comprise securities with maturities of up to 12 months. That's because the money market is designed for short-term borrowing and lending. Its main function is to transfer funds from lenders to borrowers through various financial instruments that have a tenor of a year or less.

The funding position of financial institutions varies day by day. To handle the short-term and long-term requirement for funds, the treasury manager must properly monitor the daily funding requirement and market situation so that he can: a) hold a minimum cash balance required for day-to-day transactions, and b) put surplus funds in money market instruments that are easily convertible to cash, that is, that are highly marketable. Moreover, the treasury manager participates actively in the interbank money market in order to maintain access to the money funds if required.

As with the foreign exchange market, which was discussed in Chapter 2, money market transactions are traded over the counter. The market participants are commercial banks, governments, corporations, government-sponsored agents, investment funds, brokers, and dealers.

Hong Kong Dollar Market

The Hong Kong dollar (HKD) is actively traded. In 2010, daily turnover of the global foreign exchange market was USD4 trillion. By 2013, the currency accounted for about 1.4% of all foreign exchange trades on a daily basis and ranked 13th around the world, according to a triennial survey of central banks by the BIS. The USD, the most heavily traded currency, accounted for 87% of daily trades through 2013. The euro, at number two, took 33.4%. The RMB was in ninth place with 2.2% of daily turnover.[1]

The HKMA regulates the Hong Kong dollar market. The HKMA is a regulatory body that is also responsible for achieving the monetary policy objectives set by the government of Hong Kong. The main policy objective of the Hong Kong government is currency stability and the monetary system is characterized by a Currency Board arrangement, which requires Hong Kong's monetary base to be backed by reserves of either foreign currency or a commodity equivalent to at least 100% of the monetary base.

---

[1] Bank for International Settlements. "Triennial Central Bank Survey." September 2013. P 6.

Peg System

Hong Kong uses the USD as the backing for the HKD through the Linked Exchang Rate System (LERS). Changes in the monetary base have to be matched by corresponding changes in the USD reserves. Since the main objective of Hong Kong's monetary policy is currency stability, Hong Kong maintains a link or peg to the USD, which is set within a band of HKD7.75 to 7.85 to USD1. The Currency Board system ensures the stability of the peg and the HKD.

In practical terms, the monetary base of the Hong Kong dollar is 100% backed by corresponding reserves in USD. It is up to the Exchange Fund to ensure that the reserves are adjusted daily to keep this 100% level.

Hong Kong's LERS was established in 1983. The HKMA explains that operations are essentially those of a Currency Board system, under which the stock and flow of the HKD monetary based is fully matched by changes in foreign reserves.

Hong Kong's monetary base includes:

- **Certificates of Indebtedness** that provide full backing to banknotes issued by the three note-issuing banks and in 2013 amounted to HKD329 billion. Three commercial banks in Hong Kong are licenced by the HKMA to issue notes—HSBC, Standard Chartered Bank, and Bank of China. Banks are required to submit to the Exchange Fund enough USD to cover the bills they issue.
- **Government-issued currency notes and coins** amounting to HKD11 billion in 2013.
- **Balances in the banking system** of HKD164 billion as of December 31, 2013.
- **Exchange Fund Bills and Notes (EFBN)** issued in the amount of HKD673 billion also as of December 31, 2013.

The HKMA operates using Currency Board system rules. The aggregate balance varies depending on the flows into and out of Hong Kong dollars. To maintain stability, the HKMA undertakes to buy USD from banks at a rate of HKD7.75 to USD1 and sell them at a rate of HKD7.85 to USD1. Any surplus or proceeds are switched into USD-denominated assets and new Exchange Fund paper is only issued when there is an inflow of capital, which ensures all new paper is backed by reserves of foreign currency.[2]

Operations of the Exchange Fund

The HKMA manages the Exchange Fund. The main objective of the HKMA's monetary policy is stability in the exchange rate. As discussed earlier, the main goal of Hong Kong's

---

[2] Hong Kong Monetary Authority. "Linked Exchange Rate System". 26 August 2011. Accessed online at http://www.hkma.gov.hk/eng/key-functions/monetary-stability/linked-exchange-rate-system.shtml.

monetary policy is stability of the currency. This is achieved through a peg to the USD that is maintained through foreign exchange reserves that amount to at least 100% of Hong Kong's monetary base. The Exchange Fund manages these reserves.

The main objective of the Exchange Fund is set out in the Exchange Fund Ordinance, which requires the Exchange Fund to maintain the value of the HKD either directly or indirectly.[3] The Exchange Fund holds the reserves submitted by the note issuing banks to cover the notes issued. As for the bills and coins issued by the government, the banks responsible for storing and distributing them are expected to settle their reserves in USD.

The Exchange Fund can also be used to maintain stability and integrity in Hong Kong's monetary and financial systems, "to help maintain Hong Kong as an international financial centre." The Exchange Fund Advisory Committee has set a series of investment objectives for the Exchange Fund. These include[4]:

- To preserve capital;
- Ensure that the monetary base is always backed by "highly liquid" USD assets;
- Ensure sufficient liquidity is available to maintain monetary and financial stability;
- Achieve and investment return that helps preserve the long-term purchasing power of the fund as long as the first three objectives are met.

The Exchange Fund is divided into two portfolios: a Backing Portfolio and an Investment Portfolio. The Backing Portfolio holds liquid USD assets to back the monetary base. The Investment Portfolio is invested in bond and equity markets of countries that are membes of the OECD. The Exchange Fund keeps a long-term target bond-to-equity ratio of 74:26 in the two portfolios and, as of 2013, 83% of the assets were allocated to the USD and HKD and the other 19% to other currencies.[5]

Setting the HIBOR

Under the currency board system in Hong Kong it is interest rates and not exchange rates that are affected by the movement of funds in and out of Hong Kong. The rate of interest for HKD loans made by banks on the interbank market is determined by the Hong Kong Interbank Offer Rate (HIBOR)—the more commonly used name for the HKD Interest Settlement Rate. HIBOR is similar to its UK cousin, the London Interbank Offer Rate (LIBOR), but they are not identical neither in their ultimate objectives nor in how information is gathered to set them.

---

[3] Hong Kong Monetary Authority. "Exchange Fund". 26 April 2013. Accessed online at http://www.hkma.gov.hk/eng/key-functions/exchange-fund.shtml.

[4] Hong Kong Monetary Authority. "Reserves Management". 2011. Accessed online at http://www.hkma.gov.hk/media/eng/publication-and-research/annual-report/2011/12_Reserves_Management.pdf.

[5] Hong Kong Monetary Authority. "Reserves Management". 2011. Accessed online at http://www.hkma.gov.hk/media/eng/publication-and-research/annual-report/2011/12_Reserves_Management.pdf.

In Hong Kong, interbank rates are set on interest rates that the different banks in Hong Kong set on a daily basis. Interbank lending rates are used as a benchmark to determine the interest rates used in a variety of products, from simple loans to mortgages and complex derivative products.

HIBOR has been in place for more than two decades. The TMA estimates that in September 2012, Hong Kong banks held more than HKD2 trillion in products that referenced HIBOR.

As of early 2013, HIBOR was published for 15 maturities. The rates are set every business day, from Monday to Friday, using references to market rates offered for HKD-denominated deposits on the Hong Kong interbank market. There are 20 banks designated as reference banks that provide estimated offer rates that are quoted as of 11 am every day. The Hong Kong Association of Banks (HKAB) selects the reference banks on recommendation from the TMA. The HKAB publishs the rate daily on its website and at least four information providers (Bloomberg, Thomson Reuters, Tullett Prebon, and Quick) publish the rates provided from each of the contributing banks. The Hong Kong Interbank Clearing Ltd, a company that the HKMA and HKAB own, calculates the actual rate based on the rates from each of the contributing banks.

As way of example, some of the rates (in %) set as of 24 April 2013 were:

- Overnight: 0.08143
- 1 Week: 0.09571
- 2 Weeks: 0.12571
- 1 Month: 0.20714
- 12 Months: 0.84857

The HKMA's Discount Window provides a cushion of liquidity to limit volatility in interest rates. Through the Discount Window, banks can access overnight liquidity from the HKMA with repurchase agreements using Exchange Fund paper or other eligible collateral.

The Base Rate of the Discount Window is the interest rate that sets the foundations for the discount rates for repurchase agreements (repo) transactions. The Base Rate is set using a formula that takes into account fund targets from the U.S. Federal Reserve and HIBOR.

Central Moneymarkets Unit

In 1990, the HKMA set up the Central Moneymarkets Unit (CMU). At first, the CMU offered computerized clearing and settlement for Exchange Fund Bills and Notes. Three years later the service was expanded to include other HKD debt securities. The CMU has been linked with other regional and international systems since 1994 as part of an effort to promote HKD debt securities to investors abroad. Over the years, the CMU has continued to expand the range of services on offer. CMU is now linked in real time to USD, EUR, and RMB RTGS systems, which allows for real time delivery-vs-payment (DvP) services to members.

Among the services available to CMU members are[6]:

- A Collateral Management System with an Automatic Repo Facility that covers both intraday and overnight repos in HKD, USD, and EUR.
- A Securities Lending Service for debt securities.
- A market making arrangement for EF bills and notes.
- An issuance programme for EF bills and notes.
- Arranger, custodian, agent, and operator services for notes issued by public corporations.
- Real time and end-of-day DvP for CMU securities set in HKD, USD, EUR, and RMB.
- Cross border DvP settlement through central securities depositories and international central securities depositories.
- Other custodial services like paying agent, securities lodgement, and allotment by tendering.
- Income distribution services.
- Bank-to-bank repo services.

CMU members (a complete list is included in Appendix A at the back of this book) may also take advantage of repo facilities in USD. This is done through the USD Clearing House Automated Transfer System (USD CHATS), a system that started operating on 21 August 2000 but has, since 2004, been operating under the Clearing and Settlement Systems Ordinance of Hong Kong (CSSO).

The effective operation of a USD payment system in Hong Kong makes it easier to settle USD transactions in Hong Kong in real time, thus eliminating settlement risk that emerges when there is a time lag in settlements in a currency pair in different time zones, an issue that arises when working across multiple time zones.

The Hongkong and Shanghai Banking Corporation (HSBC) is the designated settlement institution for USD CHATS. The Hong Kong Interbank Clearing Ltd operates the system, which operates from 8:30 am to 18:30 pm every day except Saturdays, Sundays, and January 1.[7] Key functions of USD CHATS are:

- Settlement and clearing of interbank payments in USD.
- Settlement and clearing of DvP transactions for USD against the HKD, EUR, RMB, Malaysian Ringgit, and Indonesian Rupiah.
- Settlement and clearing of DvP transactions of USD debt securities through the CMU in Hong Kong and RENTAS in Malaysia, as well as USD securities through the Central Clearing and Settlement System (CCASS), a book-entry clearing and settlement system for securities listed on the Hong Kong Stock Exchange.

---

[6] Hong Kong Monetary Authority. "Central Money Markets Unit". 12 March 2014. Accessed online at http:// www.hkma.gov.hk/eng/key-functions/international-financial-centre/infrastructure/cmu.shtml.

[7] Hong Kong Monetary Authority. "Assessment of the USD Payment System in Hong Kong Against the Ten Core Principles for Systematically Important Payment Systems." 2011. Accessed online at http://www.hkma .gov.hk/media/eng/doc/key-functions/banking-stability/oversight/USD_CHATS_assessment_2011.pdf.

Banks can be Direct Participants, Indirect Participants, or Indirect CHATS Users depending on their needs. In 2013, to put the size of the system in perspective, there were 18,220 transactions per day on average worth USD18.1 billion.

Since 2007, CMU members can access an Electronic Trading Platform, which provides the infrastructure for electronic trading of EF bills and notes and can be used for other financial instruments. The use of the common platform, which was one of the recommendations put forth by a *Review of Debt Market Development* done by the HKMA in 2006, increases transparency and makes the trading process easier. Although it is not the only way to trade bonds and funds, local and foreign market players are encouraged to use it.

Registered CMU members can also take advantage of intraday repo facilities provided by the HKMA. These facilities are based on EF bills and notes. The repo facilities can be discretionary or automatic but, in order to take care of automatic arrangements, banks need to have a Master Sale and Repurchase Agreement with the MA. This allows intraday repos to be triggered automatically if the bank's settlement account with the MA has insufficient funds to meet the next outgoing payment, but the banks have to have enough EF papers in the repo account with the CMU. An intraday repo that is not reversed by the close of business is converted into an overnight liquidity adjustment facility (LAF) repo.

Certificates of Deposit and Bonds

Among the more common instruments used by the treasury to manage funds in Hong Kong are certificates of deposit and bonds, denominated in HKD or RMB.

Certificates of Deposit (CDs) are fixed income investments with guaranteed interest paid either regularly or at redemption. Only banks or other authorized institutions (AIs) can issue them. They are available in most currencies, including RMB, and interest can be paid at different intervals, such as semi-annually, annually, or at redemption. Although banks issue CDs, they are negotiable instruments that are held outside of the banking sector. CDs can be denominated in multiple currencies in Hong Kong, with the most popular being HKD and USD.

Other popular instruments are corporate bonds, which are debt issued by corporations that pay a certain interest or coupon over a prescribed amount of time. Bonds can and often be traded.

Bonds are discussed in greater details later in this chapter and elsewhere in the book, but it is worth highlight the growth in the issuance of RMB-denominated corporate bonds, known as "dim-sum" bonds.

Dim-sum bonds have grown in popularity in recent years as a result of economic growth in Mainland China. Authorities in Mainland China have, since 2009, allowed corporations to use RMB to trade internationally. Hong Kong is at the center of the push to internationalize the RMB and has become one of the largest markets for RMB-denominated bonds, known as "dim-sum" bonds. From 2009 to 2013, the issuance of dim-sum bonds in Hong Kong grew from RMB16 billion to RMB109 billion.

International Market

Money market debt facilitates the smooth running of the banking industry, as well as provides working capital for industrial and commercial corporate institutions. The money market is characterised by a diverse range of products that can be traded within it.

Money market instruments allow issuers, including financial organizations and corporates, to raise funds for short-term periods at relatively low interest rates. These issuers include sovereign governments, which issue treasury bills or Exchange Fund bills (EF-bills) as they are known Hong Kong, companies that issue commercial paper, and banks that issue certificates of deposit. At the same time, investors are attracted to the market because the instruments are highly liquid and carry relatively low credit risk.

Government bills are the debt security of a country that carry the least credit risk, as compared with other corporate issues that are denominated in the currency of that country, and consequently carry the lowest yield. Indeed, the first market that develops in any country is usually the government bills market. Investors in the money market include banks, local authorities, corporations, money market investment funds and mutual funds, and individuals.

In addition to cash instruments, the money markets also consist of a wide range of exchange-traded and over-the-counter off-balance sheet derivative instruments. These instruments are used mainly to establish future borrowing and lending rates, and to hedge or change existing interest-rate exposure. Banks, central banks, and corporates undertake this activity.

Interest Rate Risk Management

Buying securities, as much as lending or taking deposits, exposes banks and financial institutions to interest rate risk. Most banks accept some kind of interest rate risk but are aware that this type of risk poses a danger to both earnings and capital adequacy. The HKMA suggests that the institutions it controls have some kind of process in place to identify, measure, monitor and manage interest rate risk.[8]

Interest rate risk can be divided into four categories:

- **Repricing or maturity mismatches:** The most obvious source of interest rate risk emerges from timing differences in rate changes and cash flows in the repricing and maturity of fixed and floating rate assets, liabilities, and other instruments. Banks can take this risk as part of their balance sheet, but it can affect both income and the value of a bank if rates flucturate.

---

[8] Hong Kong Monetary Authority. "Supervisory Policy Manual: Interest Rate Risk Management." 13 December 2002. Web.

- **Yield curve risk:** Mistmatches in repricing can expose a bank to risk associated with changes in the relative level of rates across the yield curve of an instrument. This yield curve risk emerges when unanticipated changes in the yield curve of instruments have a negative effect on the income of a bank.

- **Basis risk:** Arises from an imperfect correlation between changes in rates earned and paid on different instruments but with similar repricing characteristics. An example might be found in a bank's mortgage business, if the bank has priced loans at a rate that is different than the rate in its funding such as, in Hong Kong, the HIBOR rate. If HIBOR changes but the prime rate does not, basis risk may emerge.

- **Option risk:** This is interest rate risk associated with the options that are included in a bank's assets, liabilities, and OBS portfolios. Options my be standalone instruments and include bonds and notes with call or put provisions or some types of loans with prepayment rights.

There are different ways to manage interest rate risk, the HKMA says that the "policies, procedures and limits . . . should be properly documented, drawn up after careful consideration of interest rate risk associated with different types of lending, and reviewed and approved by management at the appropriate level."[9] An information system that is accurate and timely is key to managing this type of risk and the policies should be included in internal risk control manual.

Eurodollar and Euroyen

Money market instruments are denominated in the local currency of the country where the market operates, but some loans and deposits can be in U.S. dollars. These are referred to as Eurodollars, referring to loans and deposits denominated in U.S. dollars that are conducted with banks outside the United States. These offshore activities are not under the jurisdiction of the U.S. Federal Reserve. Consequently, such deposits are subject to much less regulation than similar deposits within the U.S., allowing banks in theory to reap higher margins.

It is believed that a bank owned by the Soviet Union that sometimes used the telex address "Eurbank" initiated the first transaction of this kind. Initially dubbed "Eurbank dollars," these loans and deposits eventually became known as "Eurodollars." The latter name became widespread because banks and financial institutions in Europe generally held these money market instruments.

These loans and deposits are now available in many countries worldwide, but they continue to be referred to as Eurodollars regardless of the location where they are transacted. Eurodollar money market instruments are particularly important to smaller banks that have no branches in the U.S. or limited access to that market.

---

[9] Hong Kong Monetary Authority. "Supervisory Policy Manual: Interest Rate Risk Management." 13 December 2012. Web. Pg 15.

A similar situation applies to the Japanese yen. "Euroyen" deposits are yen deposits which are held outside Japan (not in a domestic bank account in Japan). There are Euroyen markets in Hong Kong, New York, and Singapore, but it is London that has the biggest share of Euroyen instruments. Euroyen instruments are facilitated by the Japan Offshore Market (JOM), which is patterned after the International Banking Facility in the U.S.

Bond Market

The bond market, also known as the debt, credit, or fixed income market, is a financial market where participants buy and sell debt securities usually in the form of bonds. The size of the international bond market is estimated at more than USD45 trillion and the size of outstanding U.S. bond market debt exceeds USD25 trillion. A bond is a debt security, in which the authorised issuer owes the holders a debt and is obliged to repay the principal and interest at a later date, known as the maturity. Other stipulations may also be attached to the bond issue, such as the obligation of the issuer to provide certain information to the bond holder and limitations on the behaviour of the issuer.

A bond is simply a loan, but in the form of a security. However, the terminology used for bonds is different from that of a loan. The issuer of the bond is equivalent to the borrower of the loan, the bond holder to the lender, and the coupon to the interest. Bonds are generally issued for a fixed term (the maturity) of longer than ten years. For example, the U.S Treasury issues bonds with a life of ten years or more. New debt between one year and ten years is referred to as a note, and new debt with a tenor of less than a year is a bill. Bonds are a large and intricate part of the money and capital markets and are discussed in much greater detail in Chapter 4.

Participants

The debt capital markets exist because of the financing requirements of governments and corporates. The source of capital is varied, but the total supply of funds in a market is made up of personal or household savings, business savings, and increases in the overall money supply. Individuals save out of their current income for future consumption, while business savings represent retained earnings. The entire savings stock represents the capital available in a market.

Investment banks are the primary vehicle through which a corporate will borrow funds in the bond markets. It will also act as wholesaler in the bond markets, a function known as market-making. The bond-issuing function of an investment bank, by which the bank will issue bonds on behalf of a customer and pass the funds raised to this customer, is known as origination.

There is a large variety of players in the bond markets, each trading some or all of the different instruments available to suit their own purposes. We can group the main types of investors according to the time horizon of their investment activity.

- **Short-term institutional investors.** These include banks and building societies, money market fund managers, central banks, and the Treasury desks of some types of corporates. Such bodies are driven by short-term investment views, often subject to close guidelines, and will be driven by the total return available on their investments. Banks will have an additional requirement to maintain liquidity, often in fulfilment of regulatory authority rules, by holding a proportion of their assets in the form of easily tradeable short-term instruments.
- **Long-term institutional investors.** Typically, these types of investors include pension funds and life assurance companies. Their investment horizon is long-term, reflecting the nature of their liabilities; often they will seek to match these liabilities by holding long-dated bonds.
- **Mixed horizon institutional investors.** This is possibly the largest category of investors and will include general insurance companies and most corporate bodies.
- **Market professionals.** They include the proprietary trading desks of investment banks, as well as bond market makers in securities houses and banks who are providing a service to their customers. Proprietary traders will actively position themselves in the market in order to gain trading profit. These participants will trade directly with other market professionals and investors, or via brokers. Market-makers or traders (also called dealers) are wholesalers in the bond markets; they make two-way prices in selected bonds.
- **Private investors**. These are individuals and corporates that purchase bonds through the primary market or secondary market. They can place a competitive bid or non-competitive bid in the primary market and/or buy bonds from bond market dealers. Once the bond is purchased, the transaction is settled through a local or global clearing house and the bond is lodged with a custodian.

Markets

A new issue of bonds made by an investment bank on behalf of its client is made in the primary market. Such an issue can be a public offer, in which anyone can apply to buy the bonds, or a private offer, where the customers of the investment bank are offered the debt security. The secondary market is the market in which existing bonds and shares are subsequently traded.

Bonds may be traded over the telephone or electronically over computer links; these markets are known as over-the-counter (OTC) markets, as we learned in the previous chapters. There is a bond market in almost any country; they primarily deal in domestic bonds, issued by borrowers domiciled in the country of issue and in the currency of that country.

Bond markets can also trade international bonds (also known as Eurobonds) that are issued across national boundaries and can be in any currency. Some may deal as well in foreign bonds, which are domestic bonds issued by foreign borrowers. An example of a foreign bond is a Bulldog, which is a sterling bond issued for trading in the UK market by a foreign borrower. The equivalent foreign bonds in other countries include Yankee bonds (United States), Samurai bonds (Japan), Alpine bonds (Switzerland), and Matador bonds (Spain).

RMB Market

Renminbi markets are increasingly important to banks and financial institutions in Hong Kong. A push by the government of Mainland China to internationalize the RMB has opened up this market, particularly in Hong Kong, London, and Singapore. For the time being, Hong Kong remains the premier offshore RMB market in the world.

Although the onshore RMB market (known as the CNY market) has been active for several decades, trading in offshore RMB (or CNH) is relatively new. Investors include domestic and international funds that seek exposure through bonds and equities listed on the A-share market. A-shares are listed in Mainland China markets and denominated in RMB as opposed to the much smaller universe of foreign-currency denominated B-shares.

Foreign investors first got access to onshore RMB through the Registered Qualified Foreign Institutional Investor (RQFII) program in December 2011, but faced stringent rules that required them to invest as much as 80% of their funds in bonds. Those rules were relaxed somewhat in March 2013. Investment quotas are allocated by the China Securities Regulatory Commission (CSRC) and approved by the State Administration of Foreign Exchange (SAFE). For the time being, allocations are around RMB270 billion per year. Opportunities to invest in CNY are expanding as regulators expand access in steps. By mid-2013, all asset managers licensed by the Securities and Futures Commission (SFC) of Hong Kong that are incorporated and mainly operated there had some form of access.

The CNY market was further boosted by a push to encourage trade settlement in RMB. This push started in five cities as a pilot project in 2009, but expanded to 20 provincies and cities in 2010 and to the entire country by 2011. By mid-2013 there were 21 unlisted funds with RQFII quota.

The offshore RMB market, known as the CNH market, has also been evolving rapidly. Before 2009, the RMB could only be used inside China, with cross-border flows effectively prohibited. Since then, China has been working to expand the use and convertibility of its currency and has created a new and active market that is rapidly growing. The RMB is now used in foreign currency trading, trade settlement, and as the currency of dim-sum bonds.

The CNH Market

The development and evolution of the CNH market started in 2005, when China allowed the RMB to appreciate. Over the next three years, the RMB appreciated 21% against the USD but its rise was temporarily halted during the Global Financial Crisis. Since 2010, the RMB has been allowed to fluctuate in a narrow band that is determined based on the prior day's price and is linked to a weighted basket of currencies.

In 2009, the government launched a pilot program that allowed 359 Mainland Designated Enterprises (MDE) from five cities, Hong Kong, and Macau to trade in RMB. This cross-border settlement program was extended to 20 provinces and all foreign countries and expanded to also cover the trade in services. By December 2010, the list of MDEs had expanded to some 67,000 enterprises. In early 2012, the government announced it would soon eliminate the MDE list.

The first dim-bum bond was issued by China Development Bank in July 2007, but it was not until July 2010 that the first such bond was issued by a non-financial Chinese institution. The next month, fast food chain McDonald's became the first foreign non-financial enterprise to issue one. In April 2011, the first CHN-denominated IPO was issued in Hong Kong. In November 2012, China Construction Bank issued dim-sum bonds in London. Non-Chinese banks like ANZ, HSBC and Banco de Brasil also issued dim-sum bonds. In 2010, as much as RMB35.7 billion in dim-sum bonds was issued. The next year, issuances topped RMB131 billion.

As of the end of 2013, the total outstanding dim-sum bonds amounted to RMB310 billion, up 31% year-on-year. By December 2013, the total RMB-denominated deposits in Hong Kong amounted to RMB860 billion, according to the HKMA. Remittances for cross-border trade settlement amounted to RMB3841 billion.

Most banks and financial institutions in Hong Kong now offer a whole suite of services in RMB, from credit cards to deposits. While there are limits—individuals are limited from buying RMB20,000 per day, for example—there is little that cannot be done in Hong Kong, which has emerged as the premier CNH center in the world. Bank accounts denominated in CNH are common, and so are time deposits. Many ATMs allow for RMB withdrawals.

In general, dim-sum bonds are sought after and their volume and issuance are growing rapidly. In the last half-decade, RMB-denominated products have become important parts of treasury operations in Hong Kong. Along with new opportunities, these products bring risks. Aside from the risks associated with all foreign exchange and bond transactions, there are a series of regulatory, interest rate, and legal risks associated with the trade in CNH that treasury operations have to consider.

The Money Market Desk

The bank's money market desk, which is typically part of the treasury function, deals in money market operations primarily for liquidity ratio and cash flow management. It may also use the money market to achieve a reasonable return from the bank's surplus funds or even to serve as a key profit centre, but its first and foremost goal is to use the money market to make sure the bank's liquidity ratio and cash flow management meet (or even exceed) statutory requirements. The money market's liquidity, short-term nature, and diverse range of products are useful in achieving this primary objective.

Liquidity Ratio

As required by Section 102(1) of the Banking Ordinance, authorised institutions (AIs) in Hong Kong must maintain a liquidity ratio of not less than 25% in each calendar month as calculated in accordance with the provisions set out in the Fourth Schedule and Part XVIII (4.1.1-2s) of the Ordinance. The ratio will apply only to the institution's principal place of business in Hong Kong and its local branches, in a manner that treats the principal place of business and the local branches as collectively a separate authorised institution, excluding subsidiaries and overseas branches.

The HKMA encourages AIs to set a target ratio higher than the regulatory requirement in order for management to get an early warning before the ratio dips below 25%. It tracks each AI's liquidity ratio closely, requiring them to report what their lowest monthly liquidity ratio is as well as the average ratio for the month. The HKMA will hold discussions with AIs that have lowest daily liquidity ratios significantly or consistently below 25% to make sure they have adopted prudent liquidity policies on a day-to-day basis.

The HKMA does not only look at the actual liquidity ratio levels. It also examines the systems and processes that result in the authorised institution achieving that ratio. AIs must set up a sound and proper cash management system so that the bank's cash flow position in the next seven days and the near month can be monitored and remedial measures taken whenever necessary.

Cash Flow Management

The HKMA's requirements are comprehensive. The way authorised institutions execute them in the light of their particular circumstances determine the volume of their money market operations and the particular products and tenors they will engage in. Among these requirements are the following:

- **Construction of a maturity profile of future cash flows.** AIs should measure and monitor their net funding requirements going forward by constructing a maturity profile that projects future cash flows arising from assets, liabilities, and off-balance sheet transactions. All cash flows should be allocated into a series of time bands according to their expected maturity dates.

A net mismatch figure should be obtained by subtracting outflows from inflows in each time band. A cumulative net mismatch figure should be derived by accumulating the net mismatch figures in each successive time band.

The maturity profile should encompass adequate time bands so that AIs can monitor their short-term as well as medium- to longer-term liquidity needs. Short-term means five to seven days.

- **Maturity mismatch limits.** AIs should set internal limits to control the size of their cumulative net mismatch positions (i.e., where cumulative cash inflows are exceeded by cumulative cash outflows) for the short-term time bands up to one month (i.e., next day, seven days, and one month). Such limits should be realistic and commensurate with their normal capacity to fund the interbank market. Maturity mismatch limits should also be imposed for individual foreign currencies in which they have significant positions.

  AIs should aim to keep their negative cumulative net mismatches within the established limits. Any exceptions should be approved by senior management /ALCO and must be fully justified.

- **Assumptions and techniques.** As far as possible, AIs should incorporate in the maturity profile realistic assumptions underlying the behaviour of their assets, liabilities, and off-balance sheet activities, rather than relying simply on contractual maturities.

  AIs may use a number of techniques ranging from historical experience and static simulations based on current holdings to sophisticated modelling. There is no standard methodology for making the assumptions. What is important is the use of consistent and reasonable assumptions that are supported by sufficient historical evidence.

- **Stress-testing and scenario analysis.** AIs should conduct regular stress tests by applying various "what if" scenarios on their liquidity positions, for all currencies in aggregate, to ensure that they have adequate liquidity to withstand stressed conditions.

  At minimum, AIs should include the following scenarios in their stress-testing exercise:
  i.   an institution-specific crisis scenario; and
  ii. a general market crisis scenario (based on assumptions prescribed by the HKMA from time to time).

Money Market Instruments

The most common instrument is a **loan/deposit transaction**. A bank either accepts or borrows funds from a counterparty. Lenders in the market are very cautious about the creditworthiness of the borrower, as money market transactions are on a clean line basis[10] —the lender is exposed to the credit risk of the loan in the full amount. This is why the cash market usually concentrates on short tenors such as overnight, tom next (tomorrow next), or within three months.

The following are some of the most popular on-balance sheet products in the money market.

- **Government (Treasury) bill:** A short term financial instrument that matures in a year or less, this is issued by the government or quasi-sovereign bodies, as its name indicates. For example, U.S. Treasury bills are issued by the U.S. Government. The HKMA issues Exchange Fund bills and notes. These instruments do not bear any coupon and are always sold at a discount on the par value to create a positive yield to maturity at inception. Many regard treasury bills to be default-free investments, particularly those issued by the U.S.

- **Certificate of deposit:** A CD is a promissory note issued by a bank. It is a time deposit that restricts holders from withdrawing funds on demand. It bears a maturity date and a specified fixed interest rate and can be issued in any denomination. The term of a CD generally ranges from one month to five years.

- **Banker's acceptance:** A BA is a time draft drawn on and accepted by a bank. Before acceptance, the draft is not an obligation of the bank; it is merely an order by the drawer to the bank to pay a specified sum of money on a specified date to a named person or to the bearer of the draft. Upon acceptance, which occurs when an authorized bank accepts and signs it, the draft becomes a primary and unconditional liability of the bank. If the bank is well known and enjoys a good reputation, the accepted draft will be readily sold in an active market.

  A banker's acceptance is also a money market instrument—a short-term discount instrument that usually arises in the course of international trade. Maturities on accepted drafts generally range from 30 to 180 days; payment is due at maturity, which usually coincides with the delivery of goods to the buyer.

- **Commercial paper:** A CP is an unsecured, short-term debt instrument issued by a corporation, typically for the financing of accounts receivable, inventories, and meeting short-term liabilities. Maturities on commercial paper rarely range longer than 270 days. The debt is usually issued at a discount, although some papers are interest bearing, reflecting prevailing market interest rates.

  The interest rates on commercial papers are often lower than bank loan rates, which makes the commercial paper market attractive to companies. Issuers market their papers through dealers, or alternatively, through direct placement with an investor. A commercial paper is rated by debt rating agencies and is generally backed by a bank line of credit. Secondary market sales are limited, as issuers are able to closely match the maturity needs of investors.

---

[10] Clean line means the borrower does not place any collateral against the loan.

- **Repurchase agreement:** A repo is a financial instrument created when a party enters into a Sale and Repurchase Agreement of an underlying asset in exchange for cash flow from another party. The cash receiver (borrower/seller) sells securities to the cash provider (lender/buyer) and agrees to repurchase those securities back at a later date for a greater sum of cash; the difference constitutes the interest paid. The repo rate is the difference expressed as a percentage of the borrowing.

    A repo is similar to a secured loan, with the buyer receiving securities as collateral to protect against default. There is little that prevents any security from being used in a repo; Treasury or Government bills, corporate and Treasury or Government bonds, and even stocks/shares may all be used as securities.

    However, the legal title to the securities passes from the seller to the buyer, or "investor." Coupons (instalment payments that are payable to the owner of the securities), which are paid while the repo buyer owns the securities, usually passes directly to the repo seller, despite the fact that ownership of the collateral technically rests with the buyer.

    Most repos are overnight transactions. Long-term repos, or term repos, can extend for a month or more, usually for a fixed time period. For the party selling the security (and agreeing to repurchase it in the future) it is a repo; for the party on the other end of the transaction, (buying the security and agreeing to sell in the future), it is a reverse repurchase agreement.

Bond Repurchase Programs

One increasingly important variable at play in markets around the world is the extent and depth of bond repurchase programs by central banks. Increasingly in the news, asset purchase programs are also known as "quantitative easing" or "bond buyback" programs. Through these programs government buy bonds from banks in exchange for cash when they implement these programs. The end result is that banks have more money to lend. For customers, this translates into easier borrowing conditions as the size of the money supply increases while the supply of government bonds is reduced.

At times of weak economic performance, banks tend to step up their asset purchases. The rationale for this is that as central banks buy more bonds, bond prices go up. This means that bond yields and interest rates go down. When interest rates go down, customers have an incentive to borrow more and, hopefully, invest more. Following the 2008 crisis, central banks implemented record asset buyback programmes, which helped increase the money supply while keeping interest rates at record lows for extended periods of time.

Quantitative easing is not a conventional approach to monetary policy; rather, it is a tool central banks use to supplement the impact of monetary policy on the economy at times of unusual stress. During the financial crisis of 2007 to 2012, banks in the U.S., U.K., and the Eurozone all undertook quantitative easing because interest rates were close to zero and there was little the banks could do, from a monetary policy standpoint, to encourage more bank lending.

The size of these buyback programs swelled the balance sheets of central banks. Take the U.S. Federal Reserve as an example. As of April 2013, the U.S. Fed was buying assets at a rate of USD85 billion per month and its balance sheet had grown to USD3.2 trillion and rising. Prior to the crisis, the balance sheet ranged from USD800–900 billion.

Quantitative easing has also been a favorite policy tool of the Bank of Japan, which adopted a zero interest rate policy in 1999 and brought it back several times over the next decade and a half, always keeping a pledge to keep rates as low as possible. With an economy that stalled in the early 1990s, the BOJ first adopted a policy of quantitiative easing in 2001. In October 2010, it set up a JPY35 trillion (around USD430 billion at the time) asset buying and lending program and steadily increased it to JPY55 trillion by 2001. In April 2013, the BOJ announced a massive asset purchase program, worth USD1.4 trillion, that would double the country's money supply and seek to power the economy.

Money Market Operations

There are a number of things to take into account when dealing in the money market. They include the parameters that must be set in order to complete a transaction, among them tenor, two-way quotation, market convention, basis conversion, and pricing the forward rate.

Tenor

Tenor refers to a money market instrument's maturity date. As discussed earlier, the tenor of money market instruments can range from overnight to one year. The tenors are categorised into two groups: short-date and term money.

Short-Date

The following are the short-date tenors in the money market: overnight, tomorrow-next, spot-next, spot-one-week, and tenors within one month.

- **O/N** (overnight). An overnight loan commences today and terminates on the next business day. The duration of an o/n tenor is normally one day during the weekday and three days over the weekend, depending on the business day convention.

    For example, if today is Tuesday, 1 May, the value day will be 1 May and the maturity date will be Wednesday, 2 May. If today is Friday, 4 May, the maturity date of the o/n loan will be Monday, 7 May—the first business day after non-business days on Saturday and Sunday. The calendar shown on Figure 3.1 can help you visualise these examples, which are summarised in Figure 3.2.

FIGURE 3.1 Calendar months for tenor examples

	May 2007								June 2007					
S	M	T	W	T	F	S		S	M	T	W	T	F	S
29	30	1	2	3	4	5							1	2
6	7	8	9	10	11	12		3	4	5	6	7	8	9
13	14	15	16	17	18	19		10	11	12	13	14	15	16
20	21	22	23	24	25	26		17	18	19	20	21	22	23
27	28	29	30	31				24	25	26	27	28	29	30

	July 2007								August 2007					
S	M	T	W	T	F	S		S	M	T	W	T	F	S
1	2	3	4	5	6	7					1	2	3	4
8	9	10	11	12	13	14		5	6	7	8	9	10	11
15	16	17	18	19	20	21		12	13	14	15	16	17	18
22	23	24	25	26	27	28		19	20	21	22	23	24	25
29	30	31						26	27	28	29	30	31	1
								2	3	4	5	6	7	8

Source: HKIB

- **T/N** (tom-next, meaning tomorrow next). A T/N loan commences on the next business day and terminates on the day after, depending on the business date convention. Refer once again to Figure 3.1. If today is 1 May, the value date of the T/N loan is 2 May and the maturity date is 3 May. If today is 3 May, the value day of the T/N loan is 4 May and maturity day is 7 May (because 5 May and 6 May are non-business days).
- **S/N** (spot-next). An S/N loan commences on the spot date, meaning two business days from the transaction day, and terminates on the day after the spot date, depending on the business date convention. Refer to Figure 3.1. If today is 1 May, the value date of the S/N loan is 3 May and maturity date is 4 May.
- **S/W** (spot-one-week). An S/W loan commences in two business days (spot) and terminates one week later, depending on the business date convention. The normal practice is "week day of this week to the same week day of the following week."

FIGURE 3.2 Summary of short-date tenor examples

Today is 1 May

Tenor	Period	Number of days
O/N	1 May to 2 May*	1
T/N	2 May to 3 May*	1
S/N	3 May to 4 May*	1
S/1W	3 May to 10 May*	7

*Provided all the maturity dates are business days. Source: HKIB

Referring to Figure 3.1, if today is 1 May, the value day of the S/W loan is 3 May, which is Thursday of the same week. The maturity date is the next Thursday, 10 May. If 10 May is a public holiday, the maturity date is the following business day, 11 May, which is a Friday.

Term Money

Term money tenors are measured in months, not in days. Thus, an S/1M (spot-one-month) loan terminates one month later. An S/2M loan matures two months later while an S/3M loan ends in three months. The longest tenor in this series is S/12M (spot-twelve-months).

For example (refer to Figure 3.1), today is 1 May. The value day for an S/1M loan is 3 May and the maturity date is 4 June because 3 June is not a business day. See Figure 3.3 for a summary of examples of term money tenors.

Day Count Convention

The preceding discussion used the phrase "depending on the business date convention." We explain this qualifier below in terms of the business day convention, following business day convention, and preceding business day convention.

- **Business day convention.** All loans must be due on a good business day of the currency.
- **Following business day convention.** If the original maturity day of the term money loan falls on a non-business day, it will be set on the *following* business day, except when that day falls in a different month.
- **Preceding business day convention.** Further to the previous statement, if the following business day of a term money loan falls in the next month, the settlement day will be one day before the original day (the immediate preceding business day).

FIGURE 3.3   Summary of term money tenor examples

Today is 1 May		
Tenor	Period	Number of days
S/1m	3 May to 4 June	32
S/2m	3 May to 3 July	61
S/3m	3 May to 3 August	92

Source: HKIB

For example, for a one-month term loan starting on 29 April, the end day should be 29 May (next month). If 29 May is a bank holiday, the maturity day of the term loan will be on 30 May instead. If both 29 May and 30 May are bank holidays, the maturity day of the term loan will be on 31 May. If 31 May is a Saturday and since it is the last day of the month, the maturity day of the term loan is set back to 28 May.

The value day of HKD term loans in the morning session is usually today. But if the transaction is done in the afternoon session, it is typically valued tomorrow or spot. However, the value date of a term loan is adjustable, so other arrangements may apply depending on the counterparties involved.

Two-Way Quotation

Quotation of a loan in the inter-dealer market is in terms of annualised interest rates and is given in the form of "offer-bid." The terminology in the money market is different from foreign exchange (see Chapter 2). The smaller number on the right hand side (the bid side) is the acceptance rate. The bigger number on the left hand side (the offer side) is the placement rate.

For example, an overnight HKD loan (O/N HKD) is followed by the notation $4\,^3/_{16}\,/\,^1/_8$. This means that the overnight loan is quoted at 4.1875/4.125. A user of the quote (e.g., a customer) may either place overnight funds to the market maker (e.g. a bank) at 4.125% per annum or accept overnight funds from the market maker at 4.1875% per annum.

The above is the traditional UK style of quotation. Some transactions are denoted in the decimal point format. For example, you may see a bid-offer of "EUR spot one-month 5.45/5.55 for EUR 100mio."

Money Market Convention

The money market convention for calculating interest payment or accrual interest of a loan is either ACT/360 or ACT/365, and is in simple interest rate. "ACT" means the actual number of calendar days from the value day to the maturity day or a particular day. The base value for major currencies is usually 360 days.

Note, however, that the convention for domestic loans may differ from offshore loans. For example, the convention for the Australian dollar is ACT/360 for the offshore market, but ACT/365 for the onshore market.

The formula to compute interest payment is as follows:

$$\text{Interest payment} = \frac{\text{Principal} \times \text{Annual Rate} \times \text{Actual Days}}{100 \times (365 \text{ or } 360)}$$

The interest payment for a 63-day term loan of USD10m at 5 ½% is therefore:

$$\text{Interest payment} = \text{US\$10,000,000} \times 0.055 \times 63/360 = \text{US\$97,777.78}$$

Pricing an Odd Day Loan

Market practitioners quote only standard term loans in the inter-dealer market. A loan with a maturity day different from the standard term loan of the day is called an "odd day loan."

The market quote of broken day loans can be measured by different models. The most popular one is the linear (straight line) interpolation model.

For example, you want to price a 39-day loan. The market data for one-month and two-month standard term loans are given below:

- 1-month LIBOR is 8.0% (30 days)
- 2-month LIBOR is 8.5% (61 days)
- So 39-day loan = 8.0% + (8.5%–8.0%) × 9/31 = 8.15%

You may employ any model to price the broken day loan. If the quote is different from what you derive from the market rates, in theory you may construct a market portfolio to take the arbitrage opportunity. Your model, of course, gives you only a theoretical value. The actual market value may have already incorporated the credit risk of the counterparty, the liquidity premium, as well as the profit margin of the transaction at the time when it is offered to the user.

Leap Year

You should pay attention to the effect of a leap year in your calculation of interest payment. Suppose the market convention is ACT/360, but the actual number of days for a one-year loan in a leap year is 366. So, the calculation of the interest payment should be:

Interest payment for 1-year loan (leap year) = principal × interest rate × 366/360

Basis Conversion

The return of a financial instrument is affected by the market convention of the product. You must take into consideration the convention factor before making any comparison. For example, you cannot compare the yield of a one-year Treasury bill to a one-year U.S. interbank deposit.

If you pay AUD$9,900 today and receive AUD$10,000 30 days later, what is the annualised return? From Figure 3.4, you can see that the AUD loan in ACT/365 offers a higher return than the one in ACT/360. However, you get AUD10,000 in both cases.

The general equation for base conversion is as follows:

$$R_{360x} * {}^{D}\!/_{360} = R_{365} * {}^{D}\!/_{365}$$

$$R_{360} = R_{365} * {}^{360}\!/_{365}$$

FIGURE 3.4   Two cases of different returns

Case 1: ACT/360	Case 2: ACT/365
$10,000 = (1 + R * {}^{36}\!/_{360}) * 9,900$	$10,000 = (1 + R * {}^{36}\!/_{365}) * 9,900$
$R = 12.12\%$	$R = 12.29\%$

Source: HKIB

Most money markets assume a conventional year of 360 days. However, there are a few exceptions:

- Sterling;
- Greek drachma;
- Hong Kong dollar;
- Singapore dollar;
- Malaysian ringgit;
- New Taiwan Dollar;
- Thai baht;
- South African rand.

Pricing Forward Rate

Forward rate is the interest rate for a period of time that commences on a particular future time. For example, a one-month-against-four-months loan is a loan where the borrower will receive a three-month loan in one month's time, with the cost of that loan determined now.

Suppose a client asks 5% for a three-month deposit, despite the fact that the market rate for one-month, three-month, and four-month deposits are 4%, 4.5%, and 5%, respectively. What will you do?

You may accept the deposit at 5%, but with the condition that the funds should be transferred only one month later. Why? It's because you can actually structure a portfolio to lock in the profit immediately.

- You invest funds for four months at 5%.
- You borrow one-month funds to finance the investment at 4%.
- The expected return of your funds after one month is 5.32%, which is higher than your offer of 5%, as computed below.

$$\left(1 + 4\% * {}^{1}\!/_{12}\right)\left(1 + R_{1\times4} * {}^{3}\!/_{12}\right) = \left(1 + 5\% * {}^{4}\!/_{12}\right)$$

$$R_{1\times4} = 5.32\%$$

Relationship of Forward and Spot Rates

Figure 3.5 shows a forward rate curve and a spot rate curve. The Y-axis is the level of interest rate and the X-axis is the tenor of the instrument.

On the left-hand side of the chart, the forward rate curve (red line) is always higher than the spot rate curve. It is because the yield curve of this portion is positive ($R_{t2} > R_{t1}$, $t_2 > t_1$). On the right-hand side, the forward rate curve is always lower than the spot rate curve. It is because the yield curve is negative ($R_{t1} > R_{t2}$, $t_2 > t_1$). The forward rate equals the spot rate when the yield curve is flat.

The general equation of forward rates is as follows:

$$(1 + R_{0,1} * D_{0,1}/year)(1 + F_{1,2} * D_{1,2}/year) = (1 + R_{0,2} * D_{0,2}/year)$$

$D_{0,1}$ = number of days between 0,1
$D_{1,2}$ = number of days between 1,2
$D_{0,2}$ = number of days between 0,2

For example, a one-month loan is priced at 3% while a two-month loan is at 4%. What is the theoretical rate of a one-month against two-month loan?

$$(1 + 3\% * 1/12)(1 + R_{1,2} * 1/12) = (1 + 4\% * 2/12)$$

$$R_{1,2} = 4.9875\%$$

FIGURE 3.5   Forward rate and spot rate

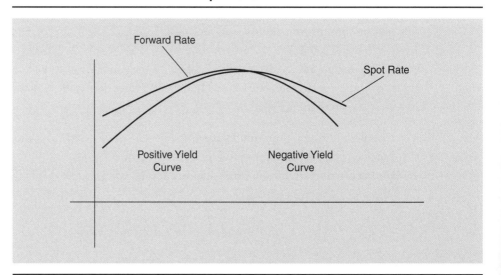

Treasury Bills

A treasury bill is a short-term debt obligation backed by a sovereign government such as that of the U.S. It has a maturity of less than one year (usually 13, 26, or 52 weeks). Treasury bills are the securities most frequently purchased or sold by the U.S. Federal Reserve when it carries out open market operations. Government/sovereign issues such as T-bill instruments carry the lowest default risk among the similar debt securities of the same country, and consequently carry the lowest yield among those debt instruments.

Government (T-) bills are issued through a competitive bidding process at a discount from par, which means that rather than paying fixed interest payments like conventional bonds, the appreciation of the bond provides the return to the holder.

The opposite of competitive bidding is non-competitive bidding, which is a process for the general public to participate in the bidding of government issues. For example, about 10% of the government issue will be assigned to the public. The return of the paper in the non-competitive bidding is determined by the average rate of the competitive bidding. Investors of this sector do not need to propose a bid in the bidding process.

In Hong Kong, the analogous instrument is the Exchange Fund bill, but this is slightly different from T-bills because the HKMA is not a central bank. Because its currency is pegged to the U.S. dollar, Hong Kong does not have an official monetary policy—it has to follow the monetary policy set by the United States.

Quotation of Discount Instrument

In the U.S. and UK, discount instruments are quoted in terms of the "discount rate" instead of the yield of the instrument. The formula for converting the discount rate into the actual settlement payment is giving below:

> Discount in dollars = Days to maturity/360 × Discount basis
> Quoted price = Face value × (1-Discount basis × Days to maturity/year)
> Settlement amount = Amount transaction × Quote price

For example, if a 180-day T-bill is selling at a discount rate of 7%, then:

$$\text{Discount in dollars} = \left(\tfrac{180}{360}\right) * 7\% \times 10{,}000 = \$350$$
$$\text{Quoted price} = 10{,}000 \left(1 - 7\% * \tfrac{180}{360}\right) = \$9{,}650 \text{ or simply } 96.50$$

True Yield

The bond equivalent yield of a 180-day Treasury bill is as follows:

$$10{,}000 = 9{,}650 \times \left(1 + R * \tfrac{180}{360}\right)$$
$$R = 7.26\%$$

You may compare the return (true yield) of the paper with another interest-bearing instrument using the formula below. Note that the calculation of true yield depends on the convention (365 or 360) of the instrument that you want to compare with.

$$\text{Discount/Purchase Price} \times {}^{360}\!/_{180} = 7.25\%$$

$$\left({}^{350}\!/_{9,650}\right) * {}^{360}\!/_{180} = 7.25\%$$

For example, if you buy a discount sterling bill (convention is 365) at a discount rate of 9.84% for 58 days, the actual amount you need to pay will be:

$$\text{Quoted price} = 100 \times (1 - 0.0984 * {}^{58}\!/_{365}) = 98.436\%$$

$$\text{Quoted price} = \text{Face value} / (1 + \text{true yield} \times \text{days}/\text{year}), \text{ or}$$

$$\text{True yield} = \text{Discount} / (1 - \text{Discount} \times \text{days}/\text{year})$$

Buy High, Sell Low

A trader in government bills should know when to buy high and when to sell low so as to generate a profit from the trading. In T-bills or any other discount instrument, the quotation is in terms of a discount rate. It means you will pay or receive less now if the discount rate is high.

For example:

$$\text{Discount in dollars} = \text{Discount Rate} \times \text{Notional Amount} \times \text{Days}/\text{Years}$$

Assume that the face value is USD10,000 and the tenor is 180 days

Discount Rate	Discount in dollars	Cash settlement
7%	10,000 * 7% * ${}^{180}\!/_{360}$ = 350	9,650
10%	10,000 * 10% * ${}^{180}\!/_{360}$ = 500	9,500

The cash settlement value of the 10% discount paper is cheaper than the 7%. If you buy the paper at 10% and sell the paper at 7%, you will gain a profit $150.

Another example is that of a 365-day T-bill that is quoted at 5.35% (the bid) and 5.25% (the ask). At first glance, the bid side seems to be higher than the ask side. But if you convert the bid and ask side (discount rate) into the dollar amounts of the prices, you will get $94.65 and $94.75 for a two-way quotation.

Exchange Fund Papers

Exchange Fund Bills and Exchange Fund Notes are Hong Kong dollar debt securities issued by the HKMA. They constitute direct, unsecured, unconditional, and general obligations of the Hong Kong SAR Government for the account of the Exchange Fund and have the same status as all other unsecured debt of the government. The bills and notes are for the account of, and payable from, the Exchange Fund, which holds the bulk of the government's financial assets.

Under the Exchange Fund Bills Programme, bills of 91-, 182-, and 364-day maturity are regularly auctioned by public tender. To facilitate the management of liquidity by banks participating in the Real Time Gross Settlement System (the interbank Hong Kong dollar payment system), 28-day Exchange Fund Bills have been issued since November 1996. But demand has tapered off as banks became more proficient in managing their intra-day liquidity. The HKMA is reducing the size of the tap issues of 28-day Exchange Fund Bills and replacing them with longer-term Exchange Fund Notes.

Bills are issued on a discount basis in denominations of HK$500,000 each, and higher integral multiples thereof. Settlement is effected on the first business day immediately following the relevant tender day. Appointed recognised dealers have undertaken to quote bid and offer yields for Bills during normal money market hours (9:00 a.m. to 12:00 noon and 2:00 p.m. to 4:00 p.m. Monday to Friday). The bills are exempt from profits tax and stamp duty in Hong Kong.

Application of Exchange Fund Instruments

Exchange Fund instruments are high quality debt paper that can be used for trading, investment, and hedging. Authorised institutions that maintain Hong Kong dollar clearing accounts with the HKMA may use their holdings of Exchange Fund papers to borrow Hong Kong dollars overnight from a discount window.

There are active primary and secondary markets for Exchange Fund bills and notes. The establishment of a reliable benchmark yield curve for up to ten years has facilitated the development of a sophisticated Hong Kong dollar debt market. The Hong Kong Futures Exchange also accepts Exchange Fund papers as margin collateral for trading in stock options and futures. Exchange Fund papers can be used as collateral in Hong Kong dollar repurchase transactions as well.

Capital Markets: Risk and Valuations

Credit risk can be defined as the potential that a bank borrower or counterparty will fail to meet its obligations in accordance with agreed terms. Generally, credit risk is greater for securities with a long maturity, as there is a longer period for the issuer potentially to default. For example, if a company issues ten-year bonds, investors cannot be certain that the company will still exist in ten years' time. It may failed and go into liquidation before the bonds' maturity date. There is also credit risk attached to short-dated debt securities. There have been instances of default by issuers of commercial papers, which as we learned in Chapter 3, is a very short-term instrument.

Banks need to manage the credit risk inherent in the entire portfolio as well as the risk in individual credits or transactions. Banks should also consider the relationships between credit risk and other risks. The effective management of credit risk is a critical component of a comprehensive approach to risk management and essential to the long-term success of any banking organisation.

There are two main types of credit risk that a portfolio of assets, or a position in a single asset, is exposed to. These are credit default risk and credit spread risk.

Credit Default Risk

This is the risk that an issuer of debt (obligor) is unable to meet its financial obligations, known as *default*. There is also the case of technical default, which is used to describe a company that has not honoured its interest payments on a loan for (typically) three months or more, but has not reached a stage of bankruptcy or administration. All portfolios with credit exposure exhibit credit default risk.

Credit Spread Risk

Credit spread is the excess premium, over and above government or risk-free risk, required by the market for taking on a certain assumed credit exposure. The benchmark is the on-the-run or active U.S. Treasury issue for the given maturity.

Credit spread risk is the risk of financial loss resulting from changes in the level of credit spreads, used in the marking-to-market of a product. It is exhibited by a portfolio for which the credit spread is traded and marked-to-market. Changes in observed credit spreads affect the value of the portfolio and can lead to losses for investors.

Measurement of Credit Risk Exposures

There are two ways to measure the credit risk exposure of banks to derivatives: the current exposure method and the original exposure method.

Current Exposure Method

International supervisory authorities believe that the best way to assess the credit risk exposure of banks is to ask them to calculate current replacement cost by marking contracts to

TABLE 3.1 Calculating potential future credit exposure

Residual maturity	Interest rate	Exchange rate and gold	Equity	Precious metals, except gold	Other commodities
One year or less	0.0%	1.0%	6.0%	7.0%	10.0%
Over one year to five years	0.5%	5.0%	8.0%	7.0%	12.0%
Over five years	1.5%	7.5%	10.0%	8.0%	15.0%

1. For contracts with multiple exchanges of principal, the factors are to be multiplied by the number of remaining payments in the contract.
2. For contracts that are structured to settle outstanding exposure following specified payment dates and where the terms are reset such that the market value of the contract is zero on these specified dates, the residual maturity would be set equal to the time until the next reset date. In the case of interest rate contracts with remaining maturities of more than one year that meet the above criteria, the add-on factor is subject to a floor of 0.5%.
3. Forwards, swaps, purchased options and similar derivative contracts not covered by any of the columns of this matrix are to be treated as "other commodities."
4. No potential future credit exposure would be calculated for single currency floating/floating interest rate swaps; the credit exposure on these contracts would be evaluated solely on the basis of their mark-to-market value.

market. This is thought to capture the current exposure without the need for estimation. A factor (the "add-on") is then added to reflect the potential future exposure over the remaining life of the contract.

In order to calculate the credit equivalent amount of these instruments under this current exposure method, a bank would add together:

- The total replacement cost (obtained by mark-to-market valuation) of all its contracts with positive value; and
- An amount for potential future credit exposure calculated on the basis of the total notional principal amount of its book, split by residual maturity. Table 3.1 shows the allocation of future credit exposure weights according to asset type and residual maturity. Note that credit derivatives are classified under "other commodities."

Regulators will take care to ensure that the add-ons are based on effective, rather than apparent, notional amounts. In the event that the stated notional amount is leveraged or enhanced by the structure of the transaction, banks must use the effective notional amount when determining potential future exposure.

Original Exposure Method

At the discretion of national regulators, banks may be allowed to use a simpler alternative method to determine credit exposure for interest rate and foreign exchange related contracts. The potential credit exposure is estimated against each type of contract and a notional capital weight assigned, regardless of what the market value of the contract might be at a particular reporting date. The original exposure method may be used until market risk-related capital requirements are implemented, at which time this exposure method will no longer be available.

TABLE 3.2   Calculating potential future credit exposure

Maturity	Interest rate contracts	Exchange rate contracts and gold
One year or less	0.5%	2.0%
Over one year to two years	1.0%	5.0% (i.e. 2% + 3%)
For each additional year	1.0%	3.0%

Source: HKIB

However, banks that engage in forwards, swaps, purchased options, or similar derivative contracts based on equities, precious metals except gold, or other commodities are required to apply the current exposure method.

In order to arrive at the credit equivalent amount using this original exposure method, a bank would apply one of two sets of conversion factors to the notional principal amounts of each instrument according to the nature of the instrument and its maturity, as shown in Table 3.2.

Potential Exposure of Credit Risks

When an asset is marked-to-market, the bank gets to know the current exposure. However, there is no way for it to know what the credit risk on that asset will be tomorrow. It therefore needs to have a cushion against the credit risk that may appear in the future. To do so, the bank needs to be aware of the potential exposure of its credit risks.

There are various models for measuring credit exposure, among them Monte Carlo or historical simulation studies and option valuation models. The analysis generally involves modelling the volatility of the underlying variables (such as interest rates and bond yield) and the effect of the changes on the value of the derivatives contract. These techniques typically generate two measures of potential exposure: expected exposure; and maximum or "worst case" exposure (see Figure 3.6).

The expected exposure of the contract at any point during its life is the mean of all possible replacement costs as probability-weighted, where the replacement cost is equal to the mark-to-market present value (if the contract has a positive value) and to zero (if negative). In general, expected exposure is the best estimate of the likely present value of the positive exposure and is therefore an important input in making capital-allocation and pricing decisions.

On the other hand, the maximum exposure is an estimate of the "worst case" exposure. The calculations are based on the most extreme adverse movements in the underlying variables. For example, if the maximum potential exposure is calculated as two standard deviations in a one-tail test, there is only a 2.5% statistical chance that the actual exposure will be greater than this worst case. The worst case exposure is important to estimate the maximum amount that could be at risk.

FIGURE 3.6   Measures of potential credit risk exposure

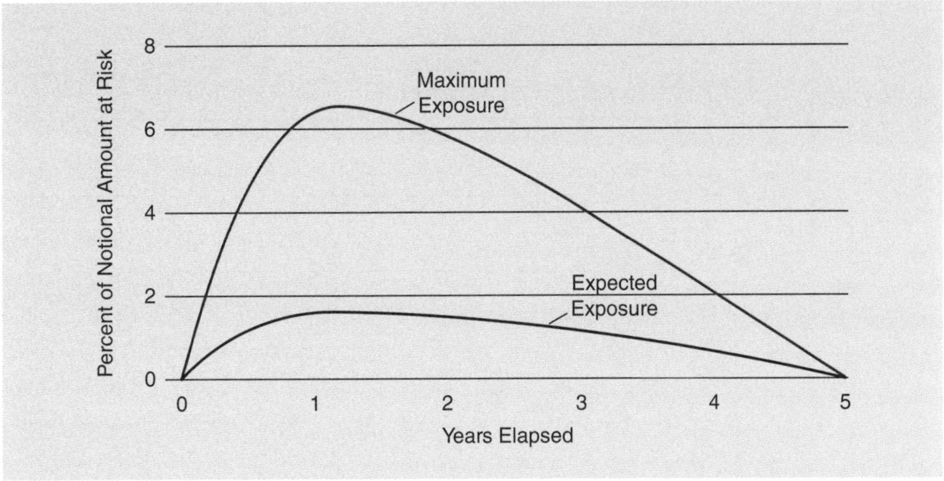

Source: HKIB

Figure 3.6 shows the profile of an interest rate swap's expected and maximum potential exposure. The "hump-back" shape is due to the offsetting effects of time on the magnitude of the potential movement in the underlying variables, and the number of cash flows to be replaced if there is a default.

One impact of the passage of time on potential exposure is an increase in the probability that the underlying variable will move significantly from the initial value. This "diffusion effect" is determined by the volatility and other stochastic characteristics of the underlying variable. The second effect, known as the "amortisation effect," is the reduction in the number of years of cash flows that must be replaced. The offsetting influences of the diffusion effect and the amortisation effect create the concave shape in Figure 3.6.

We can make several observations about the interest rate swap contract in Figure 3.6 by looking at the present value of the replacement cost if a default occurs immediately after the swap is executed. In this case, five years of cash flows will need to be replaced but it is unlikely that the swap rate will have moved very far from its initial level in such a brief period. Consequently, the expected and maximum potential exposures are low because the diffusion effect is low.

At the other end, if a default occurs just before the swap's last payment date, the market swap rate could be significantly different from its initial level. However, because only one semi-annual cash flow will need to be replaced, the expected and maximum potential exposures are also low.

The peak exposure (top of the hump) occurs at an intermediate point during the swap's life, when enough time has passed for the per-annum replacement cost to be high and sufficient time still remains to make the remaining accumulated per annum replacement cost significant in size.

FIGURE 3.7   Expected and maximum exposures, cross currency swap

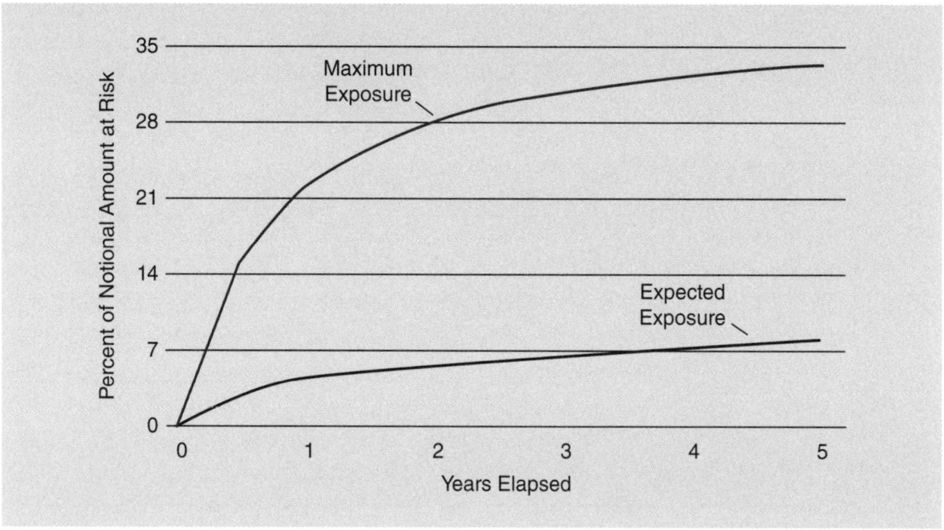

Source: HKIB

Unlike the interest rate swap, a cross currency swap shows a higher risk profile. The final exchange of principal increases the importance of the diffusion effect and reduces the amount by which the currency swap amortises, thus creating the upward slope of the exposure profile (see Figure 3.7).

Compared with the exposure profile for comparable swaps, the exposure profile of purchased options tends to be greater. In general, options do not have periodic payments, but are characterised by an upfront payment of the option premium and a final option pay-off. As such, the amortisation effect is limited to the time decay of the option price and is outweighed by the diffusion effect. In other words, the longer the time period, the greater is the scope for movements in the underlying variable, which can generate a large exposure on the option payoff.

In contrast to a swap, purchased options with the premium paid upfront initially create an immediate mark-to-market exposure equal to the option premium. If the option seller defaults immediately, the option buyer must pay another option premium to replace the option even if there has been no movement in the underlying variables.

Managing Credit Risk in Derivatives

Earlier, we examined the controls and measures that must be put in place in Treasury operations. These apply as well to managing credit risk in derivatives. As discussed, credit risk can be controlled and mitigated by having a well-designed and implemented oversight and management systems within and outside the treasury function, including internal controls, position and dealer limits, monitoring and control of the dealing operation, audit and compliance issues, management of conflicts of interest, and internalisation of the best-practice recommendations of *The Model*.

Treasury desks dealing in derivatives should make sure to carry out credit assessments of the counterparty, the underlying assets of the derivative, and the terms and conditions of the instrument. The prospectus or offer document for an issue provides investors with some information about the issuer, so that some credit analysis can be performed on the issuer before the instruments are placed on the market.

Banks typically employ specialists to carry out credit analysis. However, it is often too costly and time-consuming to assess every issuer in every market. Two other methods are commonly employed in managing credit risk of derivatives: name recognition and formal credit ratings.

Name recognition is when the investor relies on the good name and reputation of the issuer and accepts that the issuer is of such good financial standing, or sufficient financial standing, that a default on interest and principal payments is unlikely. However, the collapse of Barings Bank in 1995 and the bankruptcy of Lehman Brothers in 2008 suggest that it may not be wise to rely on name recognition alone in today's marketplace.

Name recognition needs to be augmented by other methods to reduce the risk of loss due to unforeseen events. One such method is credit ratings. The three largest credit rating agencies are Moody's, Standard & Poor's, and Fitch Ratings. These institutions undertake qualitative and quantitative analysis of borrowers and formally rate the borrower after their analysis. The issues considered in the analysis include:

- The financial position of the firm itself, for example, its balance sheet position and anticipated cash flows and revenues.
- Other firm-specific issues such as the quality of management and succession planning.
- An assessment of the firm's ability to meet scheduled interest and principal payments, both in its domestic and in foreign currencies.
- The outlook for the industry as a whole, and competition within it, together with general assessments of the domestic economy.

Figure 3.8 shows the credit ratings awarded by the three major agencies to long-term bonds, which are often the underlying assets of credit derivatives.

Note, however, that the reputation and credibility of the credit ratings agency have been somewhat tarnished in the wake of the Global Financial Crisis of 2007–08. They have been accused of assigning investment grades to collateralized debt obligations (CDOs) that had some U.S. sub-prime mortgages as underlying assets, along with triple-A credits. This situation underlines the need for banks to make sure their management of credit risk of derivatives is exhaustive and thorough, and not just dependent on one method such as credit ratings.

FIGURE 3.8   Credit ratings by major agencies, long-term bonds[11]

Fitch	Moody's	S&P	Summary description
Investmaent grade—High creditworthiness			
AAA	Aaa	AAA	Gilt-edged, prime, maximum safety, lowest risk
AA+	Aa1	AA+	
AA	Aa2	AA	High-grade, high credit quality
AA–	Aa3	AA–	
A+	A1	A+	
A	A2	A	Upper medium grade
A–	A3	A–	
BBB+	Baa1	BBB+	
BBB	Baa2	BBB	Lower medium grade
BBB–	Baa3	BBB–	
Speculative—Lower creditworthiness			
BB+	Ba1	BB+	
BB	Ba2	BB	Lower grade; speculative
BB–	Ba3	BB–	
B+	B+		
B	B	B	Highly speculative
B–	B–		
Predominantly speculative, substantial, risk or in default			
		CCC+	
CCC	Caa	CCC	Considerable risk, in poor standing
		CCC–	
CC	Ca	CC	May be in default, very speculative
C	C	C	Extremely speculative
		CI	Income bonds – no interest being paid
DDD			
DD			Default
D		D	

Summary

- Money markets exist in every market economy and comprise cash instruments and some derivative products such as forward rate agreements. The money market's main function is to transfer funds from lenders to borrowers through various financial instruments that have a tenor of a year or less.
- The Hong Kong dollar is one of the most traded currencies in the world. The HKMA is the regulator and its main priority is stability, which is kept through a link to the USD. The link is managed by the Exchange Fund.
- The money market is important to banks because of its ability to achieve a reasonable return on surplus funds and make trading profits. However, the first and foremost goal

---

[11] Choudhry, Moorad. "Bank Asset and Liability Management: Strategy, Trading, Analysis". Singapore: John Wiley & Sons (Asia) Pte Ltd, 2007. Pg. 752.

of the money market desk in using the money market is to make sure the bank's liquidity ratio and cash flow management meet, or even exceed, statutory requirements. In Hong Kong, the liquidity ratio requirement is 25% in each calendar month, although authorised institutions are encouraged to maintain a higher target ratio.

- The most common instrument in the money market is a loan/deposit transaction. The other popular on-balance sheet products include government (treasury) bills, certificates of deposit, banker's acceptance, commercial paper, and repurchase agreements.
- The tenor of money market instruments can range from overnight (O/N) to tomorrow next (T/N), to within one year, and up to 52 weeks for a treasury bill. Contracts follow business day convention. In certain markets and products, the year convention can be 365 days (ACT/365) instead of the usual 360 days (ACT/360). Traders should be cognisant of which conventions are in use to avoid losses.
- Quotation of a loan in the inter-dealer market is in terms of annualised interest rates and is given in the form of "offer-bid." The smaller number on the right hand side (the bid side) is the acceptance rate. The bigger number on the left hand side (the offer side) is the placement rate.
- Forward rate is the interest rate for a period of time that commences on a particular future time. For example, a one-month-against-four-months loan is a loan where the borrower will receive a three-month loan in one month's time, with the cost of that loan determined now.
- A treasury bill is a short-term debt obligation backed by a sovereign government such as that of the U.S. It has a maturity of less than one year (usually 13, 26, or 52 weeks). In Hong Kong, the analogous instrument is the Exchange Fund bill. In T-bills or any other discount instrument, the quotation is in terms of a discount rate.
- A forward rate agreement (FRA) is an over-the-counter short term interest rate derivative contract between two parties that agree on the interest rate to be paid at a future settlement date. The contract period is quoted as, for example, six against nine months (6 × 9), which means that the interest rate for a three-month period will commence in six months' time. The principal amounts are agreed, but never exchanged, and the contracts are settled in cash.

Key Terms

Banker's acceptance (BA)	Commercial paper (CP)
Basis conversion	Discount instrument
Business day convention	Discount rate
Buy/sell (B/S)	Eurodollar
Cash flow management	Euroyen
Central Moneymarkets Unit	Following business day convention
Certificate of deposit (CD)	Forward rate agreement (FRA)

Government (treasury) bill	Repurchase agreement (repo)
Hong Kong Monetary Authority (HKMA)	Rotation of the yield curve
Implied yield	Sell/buy (S/B)
Leap year	Short-date
Liquidity ratio	Spot rate
Loan/deposit transaction	Spot-next (S/N)
Market convention	Spot-one-month (S/1M)
Maturity date	Spot-one-week (S/W)
Money market	Stack hedge
Money/FX swap	Strip hedge
Notional sum	T-bill
Odd day loan	Tenor
Over the counter (OTC)	Term money
Overnight (O/N)	Tomorrow next (T/N or tom-next)
Parallel movement	Trade date
Preceding business day convention	True yield

Study Guide

1. Is it possible for the goals of liquidity ratio and cash flow management to achieve reasonable returns on surplus funds and serve as a key profit centre conflict with each other? Describe one situation when such a conflict may arise. What should the money market desk do in this case?

2. "The return of a financial instrument is affected by the market convention of the product." What are these market conventions? Enumerate and briefly describe each one. How may an ACT/360 convention affect the return on a deal compared with an ACT/365 convention?

3. A wealthy client wants to place USD1 million on three-month deposit with your bank, but he wants to get 6.5% on it. The market rate for a one-month deposit is currently 5.5%; 6% for a two-month deposit; and 6.5% for four months. You do not want to lose this client. What can you do to keep his goodwill without losing money for the bank?

4. The client plans to use the USD1 million in deposit to complete a purchase of a property in London in three months' time. How can he guard against a precipitous decline in the value of the USD against pound sterling when it comes time for him to pay for the property?

5. In stock trading, the mantra is "buy low, sell high." The opposite is true with treasury bills and other discount instruments, where the slogan is "buy high, sell low." Explain why this is the case.

Further Reading

Choudhry, Moorad. *Bank Asset and Liability Management: Strategy, Trading, Analysis.* Singapore: John Wiley & Sons (Asia) Pte Ltd, 2007. Print.

Flavell, Richard. *Swaps and Other Derivatives.* West Sussex: John Wiley & Sons, 2002. Print.

Hong Kong Government. "Liquidity Management." Banking Ordinance. Section 102. Web. 26 April 2010. <http://www.hklii.org/hk/legis/en/ord/155/s102.html>.

_____. "Liquidity Ratio." Banking Ordinance. Schedule 4. Web. 26 April 2010. < http://www.hklii.org/hk/legis/en/ord/155/sch4.html>.

Hong Kong Monetary Authority. "Liquidity Risk Management." *Supervisory Policy Manual.* Web. 26 April 2010. http://www.info.gov.hk/hkma/eng/bank/spma/attach/LM-1.pdf.

_____. "CMU Bond Price Bulletin." Web. 07 May 2010. https://www.cmu.org.hk/cmupbb_ws/eng/page/wmp0100/wmp010001.aspx.

Steiner, Robert. *Mastering Financial Calculations: A Step-By-Step Guide to the Mathematics of Financial Market Instruments.* FT Press, 2007. Print.

Bond Market

After studying this chapter, you should be able to:

1 Explain the basics of the debt security market and the types of debt securities that treasury desks use to manage the bank's trading liquidity book and generate trading profits.

2 Discuss the concepts around return on debt securities, including yield to maturity, credit spread, and Z-spread.

3 Describe the properties of various debt security products, such as fixed-rate bonds, zero coupon bonds, and floating rate notes.

4 Understand other issues around the debt market, including measurement of interest rate risk, portfolio duration and immunisation, and management of basis risk.

Introduction

The bank's treasury desk does not concern itself only with foreign exchange and money market instruments. It also needs to be aware of, and be familiar with, debt instruments, for example, when managing debt securities such as floating-rate notes as part of a liquidity book portfolio.

As we discussed briefly in the previous chapter, bonds are debt-capital market instruments that represent a cash flow payable during a specified time period heading into the future. This cash flow represents the interest payable on the loan and the loan redemption. So, essentially, a bond is a loan, but one that is tradable in the secondary market. This differentiates bond-market securities from commercial bank loans.

In this chapter, we discuss the general types of debt securities, their investment return, the various debt security products, and the management of interest rate risk.[1]

Basics of the Bond Market

A bank treasury may, at any time, need to consider long term bond issues on top of their traditional sources of funding such as bank deposits or short-term interbank funding. Long-term bonds provide banks with stable funding even in times of financial crisis or stress test conditions imposed by regulators. They can also supplement or become an alternative to equity financing to meet strategic investment objectives without diluting shareholders' control or reducing earnings per share—not to mention that interest expenses are tax deductible. At the same time, typical market conditions before the upturn of an interest rate cycle favor bond issuances.

A number of elements are typically considered during the planning of a bond issuance program including the target credit rating and risk profile of the issue, its size, maturity, currency, investor base, distribution, use of funds, pricing, use of derivatives in combination with the bonds, and the frequency of the issue. Market conditions will typically be key in determining the size and currency of the issue.

Most corporate bonds are straight bonds that are senior and unsecured with no derivative structure attached to them. A medium-term note (MTN) programme is a slight variation in terms of distribution and allows for some flexibility in terms of size, timing, currency, public or private placement, and disclosure/documentation. USD MTNs, for example, can be issued under Regulation S (not for sale to U.S. investors) or under 144A (only private placement to Qualified Institutional Buyers in the U.S.).

The offering circular, which is like a prospectus in an initial public offering, provides a wide range of information to investors including the size of the programme, its validity

---

[1] See Appendix B for a more lengthy discussion on how to measure the return on debt securities including yield to maturity, credit spread, Z-spread as well as a more detailed discussion of bond products and pricing.

and registration, rating, a summary of the programme and financial information, risks, terms and conditions, the use of the proceeds, information about the issuers, taxation, and various other relevant documents such as incorporation information. Under an MTN programme, the issuer has the choice of currency, maturity, size of each issuance tranche and the method of distribution (public or private placement). The form of pricing supplement is the standard document to be used in each tranche. The programme is usually updated annually when listed on the Stock Exchange of Hong Kong as debt securities with the understanding that the bonds are offered to professional investors.

Another approach is to use hybrid bonds to meet Basel III capital rules. Basel III requires buffer capital to cushion against adverse development in the banking book or trading book, which results in erosion of capital adequacy ratio below the statutory minimum level. The use of Contingent Convertible Capital Instruments (CoCos) has become increasingly popular and the bank treasury should be familiar with this kind of bond issuance.

The primary purpose of CoCos is to become a source of bank capital in times of crisis. CoCos need to automatically absorb losses prior to or at the point of insolvency. The activation of the loss absorption mechanism must be a function of the capitalization levels of the issuing bank. Their design has to be robust against to price manipulation and speculative attacks. CoCos can absorb losses either by converting into common equity or by suffering a principal write down. The trigger can be either mechanical (i.e., defined in terms of a capital ratio) or discretionary (i.e., subject to supervisory judgment). Discretionary triggers are also known as the point of non-viability (PONV).[2]

Types of Bonds

Bonds differ from each other in terms of issuer, tenor, coupon, rating, and other characteristics. We can categorise the different types of bonds in terms of these features. Note that a particular bond may share characteristics drawn from more than one category, for example, a zero coupon corporate bond or a sovereign junk bond (e.g., bonds issued by the Greek government).

By Issuer

Almost any organisation could issue a bond, although not all of them do because the underwriting and legal costs can be prohibitive, particularly for smaller companies. Regulations to issue bonds are also very strict. Bonds categorised by issuer include:

- **Supranational bonds.** These debt securities are issued by supranational agencies, such as the European Investment Bank and the Asian Development Bank.

---

[2]Stefan Avdjiev, Anastasia Kartasheva, Bilyana Bogdanova, "CoCos: a primer," BIS Quarterly Review, September 2013.

- **Government bonds.** These are issued by national governments and are denominated in the currency of the issuing country. Government bonds are usually considered risk-free bonds, because the government can raise taxes, reduce spending or simply print more money to redeem the bond at maturity.
- **Sovereign bonds.** These are also issued by governments, but in currencies other than their own, such as USD or yen. Investors in sovereign bonds run the risk that the issuer will be unable to obtain foreign currency to redeem the bonds.
- **Municipal bonds.** Also known as "munis" in the U.S., these are issued by provincial, state, municipal, and other sub-sovereign authorities.
- **Agency bonds.** These are issued by government-sponsored entities such as the Federal Home Loan Mortgage Corporation (Freddie Mac) and Federal National Mortgage Association (Fannie Mae) in the U.S., where they are also known as "agencies."
- **Corporate bonds** are issued by companies, which may be listed on an exchange or privately held.

By Tenor

Bonds are generally issued for a fixed term (the maturity) of longer than ten years. For example, the U.S Treasury issues bonds with a life of ten years or more. New debt between one year and ten years is referred to as a note, and new debt with a tenor of less than a year is a bill.

Some bonds have a term of up to 30 years; others have been issued with maturities of up to 100 hundred years, such as the Walt Disney bond due in 2093. The longest tenor so far in Hong Kong is 40 years.

Some bonds do not have a maturity date at all. These are called perpetual bonds or "perpetuities," which investors consider as equity capital. The most famous of them are the UK Consols, which are also known as Treasury Annuities or Undated Treasuries. Some were issued back in 1888 and still trade today. Some ultra long-term bonds (sometimes a bond can last centuries: West Shore Railroad issued a bond which matures in 2361 are sometimes viewed as perpetuities from a financial point of view, with the current value of principal near zero.

By Coupon

Coupon refers to the money (interest) that the issuer has promised to pay the bond holders. The types of bonds categorised by coupon include:

- **Fixed rate bonds**, which have a coupon that remains constant throughout the life of the bond.
- **Floating rate notes (FRNs)**, which have a coupon that is linked to a money market index, such as LIBOR or Euribor—for example three months USD LIBOR + 0.20%. The coupon is then reset periodically, normally every three months.

- **Zero coupon bonds** do not pay any interest. The issue price is at a discount to par; the difference between the price paid on issue and the redemption payment on maturity is the interest realised by the bondholder. Zero coupon bonds may be created from fixed rate bonds by "stripping off" the coupons. In other words, the coupons are separated from the final principal payment of the bond and traded independently.

By Rating

Credit rating agencies such as Standard & Poor's and Moody's assign credit ratings to bonds, ranging from triple-A (indicating almost no credit risk) down to D (indicating likely bankruptcy). In terms of rating, bonds can be categorised as:

- **Investment-grade bonds**, which are rated BBB- or higher (Standard & Poor's) or Baa3 or higher (Moody's). These are seen as prime debt securities that carry little credit risk and are therefore regarded as suitable investments for banks, insurance companies, and pension funds.
- **High yield bonds** are bonds that are rated below investment grade. Because they are relatively risky, investors expect higher coupons from them. These bonds are also called speculative grade bonds, junk bonds, and distracted bonds.

By Options Embedded

Some bonds include a provision in their offer particulars that gives the bondholder and/ or the issuer an option to enforce early redemption of the bond. Depending on the option embedded, these bonds are referred to as:

- **Callable bond.** A call provision grants the issuer the right to redeem all or part of the debt before the specified maturity date. The issuer's option to change the maturity date is considered harmful to the bondholder's interests; therefore, the market price of the bond at any time will reflect this risk.
  A Bermudan callable bond has several call dates, usually coinciding with coupon dates. A European callable bond has only one call date.
  An American callable bond can be called at any time until the maturity date.
- **Putable bond.** This bond allows the bondholder to change the maturity of the bond and sell the bond back to the issuer at par on specified dates. The advantage to the bondholder is that if interest rates rise after the issue date, thus depressing the bond's value, the investor can realise par value by putting the bond back to the issuer.
- **Convertible bond.** This is an issue that gives the bondholder the right to exchange the bond for a specified amount of shares (equity) in the issuing company. This feature allows the investor to take advantage of favourable movements in the price of the issuer's shares.
- **Exchangeable bond.** The investor has the right to exchange a bond for a number of shares of a corporation other than the issuer.

Other Bonds

Some bonds get their names from other specific features, although they share the common characteristics of bonds in general. We enumerate some of these bonds below:

- **Asset-backed security (ABS).** This is a bond whose interest and principal payments are backed by underlying cash flows from other assets. Examples include a mortgage-backed security (MBS) and a collateralised debt obligation (CDO). Some companies, including banks, create special purpose vehicles (SPVs), which are companies whose sole purpose is to contain assets against which mortgage-backed securities are issued.
- **Brady bonds.** These bonds are named after Nicholas Brady, who was U.S. Treasury secretary in the 1980s when he proposed converting bonds issued by mostly Latin American countries that were defaulting on their obligations into a variety of new bonds. The principal amount is usually but not always collateralised by specially issued U.S. Treasury 30-year zero coupon bonds purchased by the debtor country using a combination of International Monetary Fund, World Bank, and the country's own foreign currency reserves. Interest payments on Brady bonds, in some cases, are guaranteed by securities of at least double-A-rated credit quality held with the Federal Reserve Bank of New York.
- **Inflation linked bonds.** These bonds get their name from the fact that the principal amount is indexed to inflation, although their interest rate is lower than that on fixed-rate bonds with a comparable maturity. The UK was the first to issue inflation-linked Gilts in the 1980s. Treasury Inflation-Protected Securities (TIPS) and I-bonds are examples of inflation-linked bonds issued by the U.S. government.
- **Subordinated bonds.** These bonds carry a higher return to compensate for the fact that their holders get a lower priority in getting their money back in case the issuer is unable to service the bond or files for bankruptcy. The liquidator, government, and senior bond holders will be ahead of them. The main examples of subordinated bonds can be found in bonds issued by banks and in asset-backed securities, which are often issued in tranches. The senior tranches get paid back first, the subordinated tranches later.

Pricing Bonds

The market price of a bond is the sum of all discounted future coupon payments and the redemption value of the bond. The discount rate is yield to maturity (YTM) or the internal rate of return (IRR) of the bond. There are different ways to measure the yield of the bond. The most popular measures are yield to maturity, yield to call, or yield to put. The yield represents the market interest rate, credit spread for the issuer, and liquidity risk of the issue.

TABLE 4.1 Particulars of a 5% four-year bond

Year	Cash Flow	Discount Factor	Present Value
1	5	0.9524*	4.7619
2	5	0.9070	4.5351
3	5	0.8638	4.3192
4	105	0.8227	86.3838
Total			100

*0.9524 = 1/ (1 + 6%); 0.9070 = 1/(1 + 6%)²

Below is the general formula for pricing a fixed rate bond:

$$\text{Bond Price} = \sum_{i}^{n} CF_i \cdot DF_i$$

$$\text{Bond Price} = \sum_{i}^{n} \frac{(CF)_i}{(1+r_i)^i}$$

$$\text{Bond Price} = \frac{CF_1}{(1+r_1)} + \frac{CF_2}{(1+r_1)(1+f_2)} + \ldots + \frac{CF_n}{(1+r_1)(1+f_2)\ldots(1+f_n)}$$

Where
CF_i is the cash flow of the bond at time i
DF_i is the discount factor for the cash flow at time i
r_i is the spot rate from time 0 to time i
f_i is the forward rate between $i - 1$ to i

Table 4.1 shows the cash flow, discount factor, and present value of a 5% four-year bond that is trading at par (100) when its yield to maturity is 5%.

How do you know whether the current bond price presents good value or not? Keep the following relationships in mind to help you decide whether to buy, sell, or hold:

- When the YTM is the same as the coupon rate, the bond is trading at par on the coupon date.
- When the YTM is higher than the coupon rate of a bond, it is trading at discount.
- When the YTM is lower than the coupon rate of a bond, it is trading at premium.

Yield and Price Relationship

The yield and price relationship in a fixed rate bond (plain vanilla) is a convex-shaped curve, as shown in Figure 4.1. This means that the higher the interest rate (yield), the lower

FIGURE 4.1   Yield and price relationship of a fixed rate bond

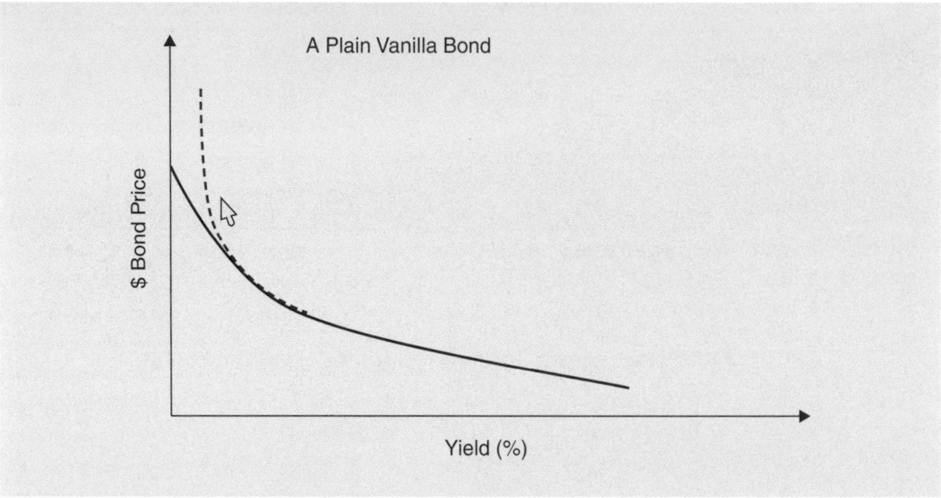

A Plain Vanilla Bond

$ Bond Price

Yield (%)

Source: HKIB

the price of the bond. In theory, when the market rate approaches zero, the bond price rises and equals the sum of all cash flows. The red broken line in the figure indicates a wrong relationship. The bond price is not a K/r function so that the bond price will not become infinite when the rate is zero.

This relationship changes when a bond has an embedded callable option (Figure 4.2). The bond price declines when the interest rate hits a certain point. The bond may be traded at a value above the call price over a narrow range of interest rates when the interest rate falls below some threshold level. Transaction costs and other

FIGURE 4.2   Yield and price relationship of a callable bond

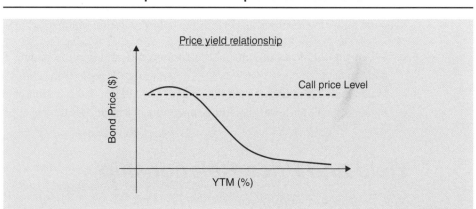

Price yield relationship

Bond Price ($)

Call price Level

YTM (%)

Source: HKIB

corporate finance considerations may allow the bond price to stay slightly above the call price.

Why? It is because at a certain interest rate point, the probability that the issue will be called by the issuer rises. Some bondholders (particularly the market traders) will sell their holdings before that event comes to pass to lock in their profits. This is the option risk or prepayment risk carried by callable bonds.

For example, borrowers aim to refinance their home mortgages at a lower rate and so the speed of mortgage prepayments increases when interest rates are low. The trigger point is somewhere around the transaction cost of switching from one loan to another loan. You will find that the price of callable bonds such as mortgage-backed securities behaves the same as a plain vanilla bond on the right hand side of Figure 4.2, but will see its value decline gradually on the left hand side of the diagram.

Discount Rates

The standard theoretical approach to the price of bonds is the discounting of cash flows, with discount rates as the interest rates. In practice, the calculations are more complex than in textbooks.

One formula (but not the only one) for the yield to maturity of bonds is the modified net present value formula, which is shown below:[3]

$$P + AI = \sum_{j=0}^{N} \frac{CF_{i+j}}{(1+y)^{\frac{n_2}{m}+j}}$$

$$AI = \frac{n_1}{m} \cdot C$$

where
  P = clean price of the bond
  AI = accrued coupon interest ($P + AI$ is dirty price or invoice price)
  CF = cash flows consist of coupon payments C and principal payment
  Y = yield to maturity as % p.a. in decimals
  n_1 = number of days from last coupon (incl) until (excl) settlement date
  n_2 = number of days from settlement (incl) until (excl) next coupon date[4]
  m = number of days in each coupon period
  N = number of remaining whole coupon periods
  CF_t = Cash flow in period t (t = 1, 2, 3,... N + 1)

---

[3] This approach, called the "Street Method," ignores the difference in number of days in future years. This is a mark-to-model approach that is subject to high modelling risk. No matter which model is used and what parameters are selected, the result will always be a theoretical value.
[4] Number of days depends on the day-year convention used, which sometimes excludes either the settlement day or the coupon day.

TABLE 4.2   A 5% four-year bond 0.25 year away from first coupon

Year	Cash Flow	Discount Factor	Present Value
0.25	5	0.9879	4.9394
1.25	5	0.9408	4.7042
2.25	5	0.8960	4.4802
3.25	105	0.8534	89.6033
Total			103.7270

For example, as Table 4.2 shows, a 5% four -year bond is 0.25 years away from the first coupon. The yield to maturity of the bond is 5%. What is the clean price of the bond?

Where

$$0.9879 = 1/(1+5\%)^{0.25}$$
$$0.9408 = 1/(1+5\%)^{1+0.25}$$
$$0.8960 = 1/(1+5\%)^{2+0.25}$$
$$0.8534 = 1/(1+5\%)^{3+0.25}$$

Present value of the cash flows is 103.7270 but this is not the clean price. We calculate the clean price below:

$$\text{Clean price} + \text{Accrual interest} \,(AI) = 103.7270$$
$$AI = 5\% \times D/Y = 5\% \times 0.75 = 3.75 \,(\text{simplified})$$
$$\text{Clean price} = 103.7270 - 3.75 = 99.977$$

Term Structure

The yield curve is the relationship between yield to maturity (or cost of borrowing) and the time to maturity of the debt for a given borrower in a given currency. This relationship allows the construction of various term structures for different issuers in different currencies.

For example, the current U.S. dollar interest rates paid on U.S. Treasury securities for various maturities are closely watched by many traders, and are commonly plotted on a graph such as the one shown in Figure 4.3. This is informally called the "yield curve." More formal mathematical descriptions of this relationship are often referred to as the term structure of interest rates.

Let us consider the zero coupon bond below.

$$\text{Value of zero coupon bond} = d(t) = 1/(1+Rt/2)^{2t}$$

Where Rt is the spot rate from now to time t and t is the number of years. Therefore:

$$0.9828125 = d(0.5) = 1/(1+R_{0.5}/2)^{1}$$

$$R_{0.5} = 0.034976 \text{ or } 3.4976\%$$

FIGURE 4.3   Normal yield curve

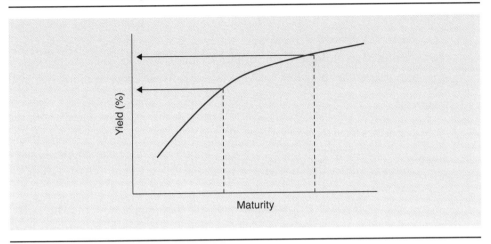

Source: HKIB

Maturity	Average Price or Discount factor	Spot Rate ($R_{0,t}$)
8/15/2014	98.28125	3.4976%
2/15/2015	96.20313	3.9085%
8/15/2015	94.01563	4.1565%
2/15/2016	91.59375	4.4389%
8/15/2016	89.28125	4.5870%

We are going to price a 2-year 15% coupon bond of the same credit rating:

Time (year)	R (%)	d(t)	Cash flow ($)	PV(CF) ($)
1	3.9085%	0.9620313	15	14.43047
2	4.4389%	0.9159375	115	105.3328
			Sum	119.7633

If the cash flows are discounted by the term structure, the theoretical value of the coupon bond is 119.7633. In reality, the actual value may diverge from this, because the term structure of government bonds might not be appropriate for a corporate issue, for example, or liquidity concerns might result in investors demanding a higher return.

Yield Curve

Figure 4.3 shows the comparative yields of securities in a particular class, such as Treasury securities, according to maturity. By depicting the market yield on the vertical axis and the maturity on the horizontal axis, yield comparisons between short-term instruments and long-term instruments are made more easily.

The yield curve for U.S. Treasury securities, which compares securities with maturities from three months to 30 years, is the benchmark for comparing yields of other fixed income investments. Corporate bonds, mortgage-backed bonds and asset-backed bonds are described as having a yield spread, measured in basis points, over Treasury securities.

Under ordinary conditions the yield curve slopes upward to the right, called a normal yield curve or positive yield curve, because long-term investments pay higher yields than short-term instruments, and borrowers are (supposedly) willing to pay a premium for long-term funds. When the yield curve is positive, no radical changes in rates are expected.

When short-term rates rise above long-term rates, an inverted yield curve or negative yield curve will appear, as shown in Figure 4.4. Inverted yield curves indicate unstable financial conditions. For example, the bursting of the subprime mortgage bubble in the U.S. in 2007 created a huge liquidity issue in the banking sector. The U.S. Fed had to do whatever it took to rescue the economy. [5]

FIGURE 4.4   Inverted yield curve

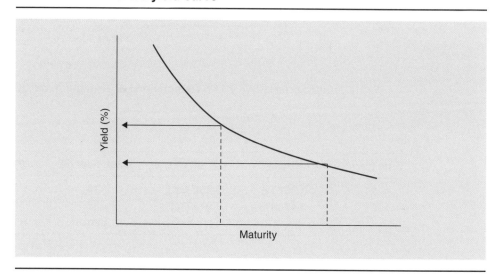

Source: HKIB

---

[5] This situation occurs in very short-term issues only. At one point, commercial banks could borrow short-term funds at 4–5%, but the one-year yield was less than 1%. This was a classic example of a liquidity trap during the progress of a financial crisis.

Investors expected the Fed to cut the interest rate from 5.25% to as low as 0% in the coming months. That is why the long end of the yield curve during the period dipped sharply lower. Meanwhile, financial institutions were unwilling to provide inter-bank credit, leaving many of them unable to finance loans. The situation of over-leveraged funds and so-called Special Investment Vehicles (SIVs) became extremely desperate. As a result, short end rates went up and exceeded the Fed fund target rate. The Fed had to inject additional liquidity into the market.

Theories of Term Structure

How do we explain the term structure of interest rates? There are many theories. We focus on three: the pure expectations theory, liquidity preference theory, and market segmentation theory.

Pure Expectations Theory

General interest rate theory explains that the anticipated yield on successive maturities of the same security is determined by investor expectations of future interest rates. An investor is said to be motivated by rational expectations when an investment decision is based on all available information.

The expectations theory seeks to explain the term structure of interest rates by saying that any combination of maturities produces roughly the same average yield. Investors willing to accept 6% on one-year certificates of deposit but who anticipate that next year's one-year rate will be 8% expect the current rate on two-year certificates of deposit will be 7%, the average of the two rates $((6\% + 8\%)/2 = 7\%)$. Investors anticipating rising short-term interest rates will buy more short maturity securities, which influence the slope of the yield curve.

The pure expectation theory implies that forward rates exclusively represent expected future spot rates. Under this view, a rising term structure must indicate that the market is expecting a higher interest rate in future, or vice versa. That is:

$$(1+R_{0,1})(1+F_{1,2})=(1+R_{0,2})^2$$

The theory also suggests that investors expect the return of any investment horizon to be the same regardless of the maturity strategy selected. For example, it makes no difference if a five-year or a 30-year bond is purchased, so long as they are held for the same period of time.

The pure expectations theory suggests as well that the return will be the same over a short-term investment horizon starting today, regardless of the maturities of the products that were bought. For example, if an investor has a six-month investment horizon, buying a one-year, five-year, or 10-year bond will produce the same six month return for that particular investor.

Liquidity Preference Theory

In Keynesian economics, investors are said to prefer having their money in liquid assets, such as checking accounts, rather than in non-liquid assets like stocks, bonds, and real estate). This preference is explained by:

- Transactional motivation, or the desire to keep money available for spending as needed.
- Precautionary motivation, characterised by the reluctance to keep money tied up in assets not readily convertible to cash.
- Speculative motivation, a belief that interest rates may be going up in the future.

According to the Keynesian theory, interest is the payment to investors to persuade them to give up their preference for liquidity. Longer-term investments, therefore, would command higher rates than shorter-term investments. This premium is known as the liquidity premium. As such, a higher long term rate does not imply that the market is expecting a higher spot rate in the future, a point on which the liquidity preference theory differs from the inference of the pure expectations theory.

The liquidity preference theory suggests there is a risk premium to compensate investors for holding a longer maturity of issue and implies that forward rates are not an unbiased estimate of the market expectations. Thus, an upward sloping yield curve may reflect expectations that future interest rates will either rise, will be unchanged, or even fall—but with a liquidity premium increasing fast enough with maturity so as to produce an upward-sloping yield curve. This reading is consistent with the empirical result that yield curves tend to be upward sloping more than they are downward sloping.

Market Segmentation Theory

This theory suggests that short-term and long-term markets act independently of each other and that investors have fixed maturity preferences. Proponents of this theory maintain that short-term and long-term rates are distinct markets, each with their own buyers and sellers, and are not easily substituted for each other.

This reading implies that there is no relationship between short-, medium-, and long-term interest rates. The shape of the yield curve is determined by supply and demand for securities within each maturity sector; demand and supply in each section of the curve determine the rates required by investors.

Reading the Yield Curve

The pattern of the yield curve and its relative change compared with others, such as the swap curve, is a useful tool for investors to interpret market conditions now and in the future.

FIGURE 4.5   UK Gilt and swap yield curves pre-recession

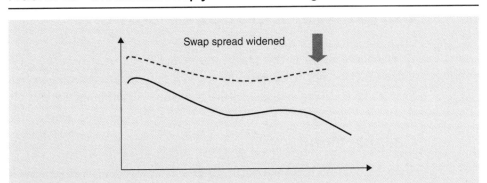

Source: HKIB

Consider the yield curves of Gilts and swaps in the UK before a recession there in 1990, as shown in Figure 4.5. The government bond yield curve was negative and so was the swap curve. The spread between the two curves was quite stable.

Things changed during the recession. Investors worried about the creditworthiness of corporate issues so they sold corporate bonds and bought government bonds. The "flight to quality" resulted in lower government bond yields (remember, yield falls when the bond price rises), but higher corporate bond yields. The spread widened sharply, as Figure 4.6 shows.

When the recession ended, the Gilt yield curve shifted down by another 4%, as Figure 4.7 shows, and then turned positive. The swap yield curve turned positive too, indicating that investors were regaining confidence in corporate issues and were willing to invest in them again to get higher returns. The spread between the two curves narrowed.

FIGURE 4.6   UK Gilt and swap yield curves during recession

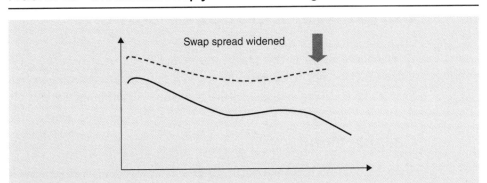

Source: HKIB

FIGURE 4.7   UK Gilt and swap yield curves after recession

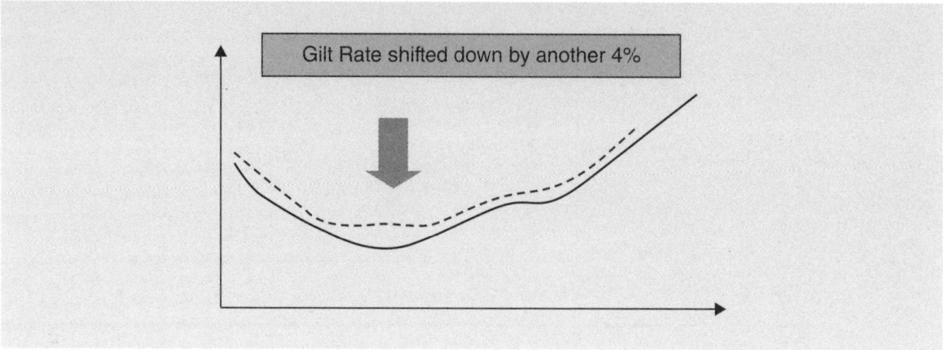

> Gilt Rate shifted down by another 4%

Source: HKIB

Does a negative yield curve foretell that the economy will fall into recession or is already in a recession? Not necessarily, because the expectations theory is not the only theory that explains a sharp yield curve. In fact, no one knows for sure what an inverted yield curve means. Before the outbreak of the recent global financial meltdown due to sub-prime mortgage problems, former U.S. Federal Reserve chairman Alan Greenspan described the phenomenon of a negative U.S. yield curve as a "conundrum."

In fact, after the outbreak of the aforesaid financial crisis, the signals derived from the yield curve correctly indicated that interest rates would go down and that the economy would slide into recession in the following years.

Other explanations have been proffered. The inverted U.S. Treasury yield curve may be due to the surprisingly strong demand for long-term bonds, for example. It may be that buying by the aging population in the U.S. and the rapid expansion of reserve money in the developing countries such as China and India are driving long-term yields lower, explaining the phenomenon in August 2007 of the overnight rate at 5.25% while the ten-year yield was at a lower 4.7%.

Bonds with Embedded Options

As mentioned earlier in this chapter, there are bonds that incorporate provisions giving the bondholder and/or the issuer the option to enforce early redemption of the bonds. We focus on two such instruments: callable bonds and putable bonds.

Callable Bond

A callable bond is a bond that can be redeemed by the issuer before maturity. There are certain call dates during which the issuer can exercise this option, which must be transacted at a call price. In other words, on the call dates, the issuer has the right, but not the obligation, to buy back the bonds from the bond holders at the call price. The bonds are not really bought and held by the issuer, but cancelled immediately.

The call price will usually exceed the par or issue price. In certain cases, mainly in the high-yield debt market (junk bonds), the call price will carry a substantial premium. To compensate the investor for the risk of early redemption, the issuer usually pays a higher coupon rate than a bond without an embedded call option.

Why would an issuer design a call option into its bond? It may expect that interest rates will fall, which will allow it to refinance the debt at a cheaper level at some point in the future. The issuer may also choose to offer a callable bond to get around the problem of long-term financing. For example, five-year loan capital is currently classified as long-term capital or Tier-1 capital. After one day, the term to maturity will become one day less than 5 years so that it will become a "short-term capital" or "Tier-2 capital." Issuing a five-year bond may therefore be inappropriate for the company's (or a particular bank's) capital structure.

However, ten-year loan capital is more expensive than a five-year one. The solution is a ten-year issue that is callable in five years. The capital raised will be a bit more expensive than a non-callable bond of the same tenor, but cheaper than a ten-year bond, and the company can classify the capital as long-term. It is almost certain to call the bond on the call date, which is why investors typically measure the yield-to-call or yield-to-first-call of a callable bond.

For his part, the investor enjoys the benefit of a higher return than he would have had with a bullet (that is, non-callable) bond. It is because the bondholder is holding a long bullet bond and has sold the call option to the bond issuer. The upfront premium of the call option will make the callable bond price lower than the bullet bond price. The risk is that if interest rates fall and the bond gets called, the investor will have to reinvest at the lower rates as new issues will be priced using the lower rates and existing bonds will be re-priced according to the same lower rates.

Putable Bond

A putable bond is the opposite of a callable bond—it can be redeemed by the investor, not the issuer, before the maturity date. Putable bonds are typically issued by companies that encounter difficulty in attracting bond investors, perhaps because they are in a risky industry, are seen as having uncertain financial prospects, or are unable to get an investment-grade credit rating.

A put is a very attractive feature for bond investors in the sense that investors have a right to get their money back from the issuers when they believe interest rates will go up or the issuer will not be able to repay the loan. The put option should be considered as an insurance against the default risk of the bond. Investors need to pay an upfront fee to purchase the bond so that the yield of the putable bond will be lower than the bullet bond from the same issuer. Should interest rates rise, bond holders can "put" the bond back to the issuer and reinvest the proceeds on other attractive yields. However, this places the issuer in a difficult financial position. It will likely have to borrow at even higher rates if too many investors put the bonds back to them over a short period of time.

Valuation

Suppose the holder of a callable bond entered into two separate transactions, such as a long non-callable bond (paid a price) and a short call option on the bond (received premium). The valuation formula is as follows:

$$\text{Long callable bond} = \text{Long non-callable bond} - \text{Call option}$$

If the owner of a putable bond entered into two separate transactions, such as a long non-putable bond (paid a price) and a long put option of the bond (paid premium), the valuation formula is:

$$\text{Long putable bond} = \text{Long non-putable bond} + \text{Put option}$$

Risks of Holding Bonds with Options

It should be clear that a key risk in a bond with embedded options is interest rate risk, particularly when the bond is not held to maturity (in which case liquidity risk also becomes prominent). But credit risk remains a major issue, as with all bond investments, particularly with putable bonds, whose issuers are almost always not investment-grade. These issuers may also pose a liquidity risk to bond-holders, in that an overwhelming volume of puts could cause an issuer to delay redemption payments while it sources funds to honour the options.

Interest Rate Risk

All our discussions in this chapter indicate that interest rate risk plays an important role after credit risk in bond investment. It is therefore important to measure this risk.

When the durations of a portfolio's assets and liabilities are the same, the portfolio is inherently protected against interest-rate changes. It is said to have immunisation. A duration-based strategy for portfolio management was introduced way back in the 1970s and remains in practice. In times of high volatility and interest rates increases, institutional investors have found duration and convexity as useful tools in immunising their portfolios.

The requirements for immunisation can be stated thus:

- The effective duration must be equal to the effective duration of the liability.
- The initial present value of the cash flow from the bond or bond portfolio must equal the present value of the future liability.[6]

---

[6] Fabozzi, Frank J.; Martellini, Lionel and Priaulet, Philippe. "Advanced Bond Portfolio Management". John Wiley & Sons: New Jersey, 2006. Pg. 358.

Let us examine the example of an insurance company that issued a $1m guaranteed investment contract with a guarantee of an annual effective yield of 8% for five years. The manager is faced with the problem of hedging the portfolio that is comprised, at the moment, of the following bonds:

- Bond 1: six-year par bonds with an 8% coupon
- Bond 2: five-year par bonds with an 8% coupon

The guaranteed investment contract will have cash outflow only five years later ($1,000,000 \times (1.08\%)^5 = \$1,469,328.08$) and thus can be treated as a zero coupon bond with duration of exactly the same as its life—five years. Par bond implies that the coupon rate is equal to yield-to-maturity (YTM).

Analysis:

Bond 1	YTM = 8%			
Terms	CF	d(t)	PV(CF)	tx PV(CF)
1	80	0.925925926	74.07407	74.07407
2	80	0.85733882	68.58711	137.1742
3	80	0.793832241	63.50658	190.5197
4	80	0.735029853	58.80239	235.2096
5	80	0.680583197	54.44666	272.2333
6	1080	0.630169627	680.5832	4083.499
		Bond 1's Price	1000	
		Duration =		4.99271

Bond 2	YTM = 8%			
Terms	CF	d(t)	PV(CF)	tx PV(CF)
1	80	0.925925926	74.07407	74.07407
2	80	0.85733882	68.58711	137.1742
3	80	0.793832241	63.50658	190.5197
4	80	0.735029853	58.80239	235.2096
5	1080	0.680583197	735.0299	3675.149
			1000	
		Bond 2's Price		
		Duration =		4.312127

Payoff of the Hedged Portfolio			
Portfolio	8%	7%	9%
Bond 1	1000	1047.665	955.1408
Bond 2	1000	1041.002	961.1035
Guarantee Fund (GF)	1000	1047.611	954.9624
Bond 1–GF	0	0.054	0.1784
Bond 2–GF	0	−6.609	6.1411

Guaranteed Fund		YTM = 8%		
Terms	CF	d(t)	PV(CF)	tx PV(CF)
1				
2				
3				
4				
5	1,469,328.08	0.680583197	1,000,000	5,000,000
		Sum Duration =	1,000,000	5

From the analysis, buying Bond 1 is a better fit to the Guaranteed Fund than buying Bond 2, even though Bond 2's maturity initially matched the Guaranteed Fund when yield-to-maturity was at 8%. This is because Bond 2's cash flow is different from that of the Guaranteed Fund. Matching the duration of the two assets is more important in hedging (portfolio immunisation) than matching the maturity without consideration of cash flows.

Duration is an important concept in asset and liability management because the assets (interest income) and liabilities (interest cost) of a bank can be considered as a portfolio with different durations.

While useful, duration has its shortcomings. One of them is its assumption of a parallel shift in the yield curve, which seldom happens in real life. Moreover, duration applies a flat rate for the whole life of the portfolio (YTM), which is also impractical. Nonetheless, many experts view the benefits of using duration to be far greater than the shortcomings.

Price Value of a Basis Point

Another way to measure the price volatility of a bond to interest rate risk is price value of a basis point (*PVBP*) or so-called dollar value of an 01 (*DV01*), which is the absolute value change in the price of a bond for a 1 basis point change in yield.

Terms	CF	DF(6%/2)			Yield		
					6%	6.01%	5.99%
1	3	0.970874	2.912621				
2	3	0.942596	2.827788	**Bond Price**	100	99.9574	100.0427
3	3	0.915142	2.745425	**PVBP(6.00%)**		−0.0426	+0.0427
4	3	0.888487	2.665461				
5	3	0.862609	2.587826				
6	3	0.837484	2.512453				
7	3	0.813092	2.439275				
8	3	0.789409	2.368228				
9	3	0.766417	2.29925				
10	103	0.744094	76.64167				
		Bond price	100				

Duration of Floaters

When the coupon is reset on the coupon date, its value will be worth par or 100% immediately. It follows that a floater is exactly the same as a bond with one coupon payment remaining and with maturity equal to the time until the next coupon reset. As a result, its Macaulay duration is the reset period of the floater. For example, if a three-year floater has a reset frequency of two times a year, its duration is six months or 0.5 year.[7]

Duration of Inverse Floater

As we learned above, the value of an inverse floater is equal to a long fixed rate bond and a short floater.

$$\text{Inverse floater} = \text{Fixed rate bond} - \text{Floater}$$

or

$$\text{Duration of fixed rate bond} = W_1(\text{Duration of floater}) + W_2(\text{Duration of inverse floater})$$

Given the duration of the 6% coupon bond is 2.81 and is worth 103.34,

---

[7] Tuckman, Bruce. "Fixed Income Securities: Tools for Today's Markets". New Jersey: John Wiley & Sons, 1992. Pg. 184.

Price of inverse floater = 103.34 − 50 = 53.34 . . . It is because the floater is about 100%.

And its duration is:

$$2.81 = (50/103.34)\,0.5 + (53.34/103.34)D_{\text{Inverse floater}}$$

Therefore, Duration of the inverse floater

$$= (2.81 - (50/103.34)*0.5)*103.34/53.34 = 4.98$$

Note that the duration of the inverse floater will exceed the duration of the fixed rate bond and its maturity.

Management of Basis Risk

To measure the basis risk of the yield curve, Thomas S.Y. Ho (1992) proposed the concept of "key-rate duration." This involves breaking down the assessment of interest rate risk into 11 key rates—at three months, one year, two years, three years, five years, seven years, ten years, 15 years, 20 years, 25 years, and 30 years. Thus, for a Treasury Bill with a coupon of 6% and maturity on 15 February 2026, the key-rate durations will be as shown below:

Type	Coupon	Maturity	3Mo	1Yr	2Yr	3Yr	5Yr	7Yr	10Yr	15Yr	20Yr	25Yr	30Yr	Eff. Dur
TB	6%	2/15/2026	0.02	0.06	0.12	0.26	0.47	0.73	1.33	1.69	1.57	1.45	4.6	12.3

Key-rate durations are defined as the sensitivity of the portfolio value to key rates at different points along the term structure. Note that the sum of key-rate durations is equal to the effective duration[8] or modified duration of the portfolio.

Mathematically, we can express key-rate durations thus:

$$\Delta P/P = -\sum KRD(i)*\Delta y(t_i)$$

where the yield curve is divided into m different key rates.

---

[8] The difference between effective duration and modified duration is that the former takes into account portfolio change when the movement of interest rates affects the portfolio cash flows. For vanilla bonds or portfolios, effective duration is the same as modified duration. However, if the portfolio has bonds with options embedded or linked with mortgage-backed securities (MBS), the effective duration of that portfolio may be significantly different from its modified duration.

Summary

- Bonds are debt-capital market instruments that represent a cash flow payable during a specified time period heading into the future. This cash flow represents the interest payable on the loan and the loan redemption. Essentially, a bond is a loan, but one that is tradable in the secondary market.
- Bonds are generally issued for a fixed term (the maturity) of longer than ten years. For example, the U.S. Treasury issues bonds with a life of ten years or more. New debt between one year and ten years is referred to as a note, and new debt with a tenor of less than a year is a bill.
- Bonds can be categorised in a variety of ways, with one instrument sometimes sharing characteristics from the various groups. In terms of issuer, we have supranational bonds, government bonds, sovereign bonds, municipal bonds, agency bonds, and corporate bonds.
- By coupon, we have fixed rate bonds, floating rate notes, and zero coupon bonds. By rating, there are investment-grade bonds and high-yield or junk bonds. By options embedded, there are callable bonds, putable bonds, convertible bonds, and exchangeable bonds. The other types of bonds include asset-backed bonds, Brady bonds, inflation linked bonds, and subordinated bonds.
- The yield on a debt security represents the return on the investor's investment. By yield, we mean the interest rate that can be earned on the bond, as currently quoted by the market or implied by the current market price. The yield is not the same as the coupon paid by the issuer, which is based on the coupon rate and the face value of a bond.
- When a bond's price goes up, its yield goes down. When its price falls, its yield goes up. There will be buyers for the bond in either direction because the various bond market players have different needs and purposes. Proprietary traders are primarily interested in price because their interest is to make money as soon as possible; long-term investors are mainly focused on yield because they have a long investing horizon.
- It is important to know how to measure the return on the various debt instruments in order to make the most appropriate investing decision. The measurements of return include yield to maturity (YTM), which is the most frequently used, credit spread, which is typically applied to corporate bonds, and Z-spread, used for zero coupon bonds.
- Interest rate risk is the key risk when investing in bonds. Duration, convexity, and price value of a basis point are some of the concepts that must be understood to measure interest rate risk.

Key Terms

Accrual interest

Agency bond

Asset-backed security

Bills

Bonds

Brady bond

Callable bond

Cash flow

Clean price

Contingent Convertible Capital
    Instruments (CoCos)

Convertible bond

Corporate bond

Coupon

Credit spread

Day count convention

Debt security

Discount rate

Duration

Exchangeable bond

Fixed rate bond

Floating rate note

Forward interest rate

Government bond

High yield bond (junk bond)

Immunisation

Inflation linked bond

Inverse floater

Inverted yield curve

Investment-grade bond

Liquidity preference theory

Market segmentation theory

Maturity

Medium-term note (MTN)

Municipal bond

Notes

Perpetual bond

Price value of a basis point (PVBP)

Principal

Pure expectation theory

Putable bond

Sovereign bond

Spot rate

Supranational bond

Tenor

Term structure

Yield curve

Yield to maturity (YTM)

Zero coupon bond

Z-spread

Study Guide

1. Taking into account the required liquidity ratio that banks in Hong Kong must maintain as well as the need for the bank to put excess cash to work, under what circumstances is the bank's trading desk justified in limiting its debt security positions only in U.S. Treasury bonds, bills, and notes?

2. Under what circumstances is it appropriate for the treasury desk to put some of the bank's money in zero coupon bonds and inverse floaters?

3. Under what circumstances is it appropriate for the bank to issue callable bonds rather than plain vanilla bonds to bolster its capital?

4. What do you think is the most appropriate strategy that a bank must follow in terms of the debt security market when the yield curve is inverted? Does it follow that an economic recession has started or will start?

5. When the price-yield relationship of a coupon bond is convex in shape, what is the difference in measurement between its duration and convexity? Explain why this is the case.

Further Reading

Choudhry, Moorad. *Bank Asset and Liability Management: Strategy, Trading, Analysis.* Singapore: John Wiley & Sons (Asia) Pte Ltd, 2007. Print.

Fabozzi, Frank J., Martellini, Lionel and Priaulet, Philippe, eds. *Advanced Bond Portfolio Management.* New Jersey: John Wiley & Sons, 2006. Print.

Fabozzi, Frank J., Pitts, Mark, and Dattatreya, Ravi E. "Price Volatility Characteristics of Fixed Income Securities" in *The Handbook of Fixed Income Securities.* McGraw Hill Professional, 2005. Print.

Gardner, Mona J., Mills, Dixie I. and Cooperman, Elizabeth S. *Managing Financial Institutions: An Asset/Liability Approach.* 4th Edition. South-Western College, 2004. Print.

SWX Swiss Exchange. "Accrued Interest & Yield Calculations and Determination of Holiday Calendars." Web. 05 May 2010. < http://www.six-swiss-exchange.com/download/trading/products/bonds/accrued_interest_en.pdf>.

Tuckman, Bruce. *Fixed Income Securities: Tools for Today's Markets.* New Jersey: John Wiley & Sons, 1992). Print.

U.S. Securities and Exchange Commission. "Zero Coupon Bonds." Web. 05 May 2010. < http://www.sec.gov/answers/zero.htm>.

Derivatives

Learning objectives

After studying this chapter, you should be able to:

1 Understand the use of derivatives for hedging interest rate and foreign exchange risks.

2 Describe the various credit derivative products of interest to bank treasury desks, including credit default swaps, total return swaps, and credit-linked notes.

3 Explain what collateralised debt obligations are, their role in arbitrage, and how they help in balance sheet management.

4 Understand how derivatives are priced and the various accounting principles that go into their valuation along with hedging techniques and risk considerations.

Introduction

Before the advent of credit derivatives, there was no instrument available that could be used to hedge credit risk in isolation. This changed during the 1990s. Credit derivatives, and structured credit products that incorporate credit derivatives in their construction, have transformed the way that credit risk can be managed and are a significant development in banking.

The importance of credit derivatives lies in the potential they generate for greater transparency and disintermediation for the market as a whole and transparency with regard to asset valuation, liquidity, and accessibility. The isolation of credit as an asset class, which has resulted in the creation of credit derivatives, is meant to create greater transparency in evaluating fair value, and increased opportunity to speculate and hedge in credit.

As with any complex financial instrument, however, credit derivatives can have a downside. The Global Financial Crisis of 2007–08 has been blamed, in part, on collateralised debt obligations (CDOs), which are credit derivatives backed by pools of financial assets such as bank loans, high-yield corporate bonds, emerging market securities and mortgage securities. Some CDOs were found to have been mixed with sub-prime mortgages in the U.S., even though those CDOs were still rated as investment grade because they were also backed by high-grade bonds and other assets.

Even so, it is unlikely that banks and other financial institutions will stop using credit derivatives because they are proving very useful in arbitrage and balance sheet management, including the monetisation of bank assets and transfer of risks. In this chapter, we will explore a few credit derivatives and their usefulness to hedging credit risk.

In its latest Triennial Survey of Central Banks in 2013, the BIS noted that trading activity rose in most categories of forex instruments. Through 2013, forex swaps were the most actively traded forex instruments, accounting for about 42% of all forex-related transactions. But it was the OTC derivatives market that grew the fastest in the three years covered in the survey, particularly forwards and options. Between 2010 and 2013, the rise in turnover of forex forwards and options accounted for about a quarter of the growth in global forex turnover.

Derivatives for Hedging

Credit derivatives are most useful for hedging interest rate. Credit risk, as we have explored earlier and in other books in this series, refers to the risk that a borrower will default on a debt or fail to make payments or meet obligations based on agreed terms. The risks include loss of principal and interest, disruption of cash flows, or higher collection costs and losses can be total or partial. For banks, credit risk is one of the most significant types of risk as the entire business of the bank is often based on lending. In broad strokes there are two types of credit risk: default risk and credit spread risk.

A strong regulatory environment and risk management practices have made Hong Kong into a relatively safe market. Even so, the amount of bad loans was on the rise in 2013, rising from 2.08% of total portfolios at the end of 2012 to 2.77% at the end of the first quarter of 2013, according to the HKMA. In Mainland China, the China Banking Regulatory Commission reported a ratio of bad loans for 2012 of 0.95%, although that number comes after years of efforts to clean up bad debt, and there are enormous fears that the number is not entirely accurate as banks may be carrying loans on their books that are actually non-performing.

To limit the exposure to credit risk, banks use a variety of hedging tools, engaging in swaps and the trade of derivative products that provide a balance for their loan business. The range of derivatives available for hedging has grown over the past few decades and is increasingly complex, allowing banks to hedge just about every aspect of their business, from their exposure to interest rate fluctuations to their exposure to movements in foreign currency and market performance.

Interest Rate Swaps

One well established way to hedge credit risk is to use interest rate swaps. Interest rate swaps are negotiated contracts between two parties that allow for the exchange of interest rate obligations. One party in a swap is almost always a bank. Because swaps are independent of debt or investments, they are useful hedging tools. The ultimate aim of a swap is to change the nature of an asset or a liability without any impact on the underlying exposure.

The aim of interest rate swaps is to exchange interest rate payments over a period of time, typically between one and ten years. By necessity, interest rate swaps are done in the same currency.

Swaps can be as complicated as the designer or the aims of those involved in it but in a typical swap, a party with a fixed interest rate payment would swap that with another with a floating interest rate payment. A swap allows, for example, to change a payment structure in anticipation of a shift in interest rates.

In a standard situation, a borrower with a weaker credit rating may have to pay a premium for a fixed rate on a loan or credit facility. In this situation, the organization may chose to borrow at a floating rate but then swap that rate with for a better fixed rate with another organization that may be looking for lower floating rates but has a long term commitment on its books.[1] The swap thus allows one party to predict its financing costs and avoid increased payments in the event of a hike in interest rates while the other party can benefit from lower interest payments than it would have otherwise had.

Interest rate swaps are hardly the only type of swap available. Other common swaps include asset swaps, basis swaps, zero-coupon swaps and forward interest rate swaps.

---

[1] Karen A. Horcher; "Essentials of Managing Treasury"; John Wiley & Sons; New Jersey; 2005; p 123.

Terminating a swap agreement early requires each party to determine the contractual obligations left to the end of the contract and netting the payments to determine what is owed to whom. A swap agreement may also be terminated and incorporated into a new agreement in what is known as a "blend and extend."[2] It is also possible to pass on the agreement to a third party, which then makes or receives payments until the end of the agreements.

Three risks are particularly important when considering a swap agreement[3]:

- **Basis risk** is caused by a mismatch between cash flows in the swap. This may happen when the interest on one borrowing is tied to one rate, such as HIBOR, while the other is tied to a different index. If the two rates do not move at lock-step, for example if HIBOR goes up by 0.3% and the other rate goes up by 0.5%, the swap may not work for one party or the other.
- **Counterparty risk** emerges if one party fails to meet its financial obligations, and the other party may face a liability. Usually, a bank or broker acts as intermediary between the two parties and can assume this risk for a fee.
- **Legal risk** can be caused by an error in a contract or if a signer does not have the right level of authorization to enter into the agreement.

A master agreement for a swap is available through the International Swaps and Derivatives Association[4] (ISDA), an organization that represents participants and maintains standard contracts.

ISDA Documentation

Before continuing with the discussion of derivatives, it is worth stopping briefly to discuss the dealing conventions and the documentation available through the ISDA. As the trade organization for traders of over-the-counter (OTC) derivatives, the ISDA has developed a standard contract. Based in New York, the ISDA is involved in a number of legal and policy activities and manages the Financial products Markup Langauage (FpML), an online message standard for the industry. The ISDA has more than 820 members in 57 countries, mostly derivatives dealers, providers, and end users. The ISDA is involved in the trading of credit derivatives and swaps, equity derivatives, interest rate derivatives, FX derivatives, energy and commodities and a structured products.

The ISDA was set up in 1985 as a swap dealers association before expanding to cover both swaps and derivatives. The group is best known for its ISDA Master Agreement,[5] which dealers and counterparties use when discussing a derivatives trade. There are various

---

[2] Steven M. Bragg; "Treasury Management: The Practitioner's Guide"; John Wiley & Sons; New Jersey; 2010; p 249.
[3] Ibid.
[4] www.isda.org.
[5] The ISDA Master Agreement is updated regularly and is available through the ISDA bookstore at http://www.isda.org/publications/pubguide.aspx.

forms of this Master Agreement covering either a single jurisdiction or currency or multiple jurisdictions and currencies. A schedule is usually attached to the agreement to set out the basic trading terms between the parties and is negotiated. The *Financial Times* has referred to the agreement as "fundamental . . . (for) the derivatives market".[6]

In Hong Kong, the HKMA and the SFC in July 2013, released the conclusion of a consultation on how to better regulate the OTC derivatives market with mandatory reporting and clearing of obligations on some interest rate swaps and non-deliverable forwards (NDFs). A Securities and Futures (Amendment) Bill would establish interim reporting arrangements for some OTC derivative transactions. Since 2010, the ISDA has made multiple submissions to the HKMA and other regulatory bodies in Hong Kong on how to best regulate the OTC derivatives trade.

Money/FX Swap

A money swap (FX swap) is a pair of FX transactions comprising a spot FX deal and an outright deal. Both parties of the swap transaction agree to enter into a spot deal now, at the same time agreeing to reverse the previous position at a particular contract rate in future. As with any other swap contract, an FX/MM swap contract effectively converts one cash flow into another. The tenor of the contract is relatively short at less than two years.[7]

$$FX/MM \text{ Swap deal} = Spot \text{ deal} + Outright \text{ deal}$$

Quotation of a Swap

It is quoted as a two-way price and is in the format of a number of pips of a currency pair. The bid (left-hand side) of the quotation is a buy/sell of the base currency. The offer (right-hand side) of the quotation is a sell/buy of the base currency. Figure 5.1 shows TT swap quotes. The right-hand side of the one-month swap is −84. This means the outright rate of USD/HKD is an 84 pips discount of the current spot rate.

For example, a one-month USD/HKD swap = $^{-87}/_{-84,}$ meaning that the market maker (i.e., a bank) is quoting at 87/84. Therefore:

- You (as a customer or market user) may execute a buy/sell (B/S[8]) swap of USD/HKD deal at −87 with the market maker. At the same time, the market maker has created a sell/buy (S/B) USD/HKD deal at −87. Suppose the spot rate is 7.7987? You buy spot USD/HKD at 7.7987 and, at the same time, sell one-month outright USD/HKD at 7.7900.

---

[6] Ishmael, Stacy-Marie; "Lehman, Metavante and the ISDA Master agreement"; FT Alphaville; 30 September 2009; at http://ftalphaville.ft.com/2009/09/30/74606/lehman-metavante-and-the-isda-master-agreement/.
[7] An FX/MM swap contracts are short term. However, other contracts such as interest rate swaps and commodity swaps usually have a longer maturity.
[8] "B/S" reads "buy-sell" and "S/B" reads "sell-buy".

FIGURE 5.1 TT swap quotes

	HKD	FWD
O/N	-3.2	-2.7
T/N	-7.5	-7.0
1WK	-21	-19
2WK	-39	-37
1MO	-87	-84
2MO	-666	-162
3MO	-258	-253
4MO	-333	-327
5MO	-417	-411
6MO	-502	-495
9MO	-707	-697
1YR	-905	-890
2YR	-1530	-1480
3YR	-2050	-1950
4YR	-2600	-2450
5YR	-3170	-2970

Source: HKIB

- You (as a customer or market user) may execute an S/B swap of a USD/HKD deal at −84 with the market maker. At the same time, the market maker has created a B/S USD/HKD deal at −84. You sell spot USD/HKD at 7.7987 and, at the same time, buy one-month outright USD/HKD at 7.7903.

Figure 5.2 is a graphic representation of the cash flow of the buy/sell USD/HKD transaction in the example above. You buy USD now and sell USD one month

FIGURE 5.2 Illustration of cash flow in a B/S USD/HKD deal

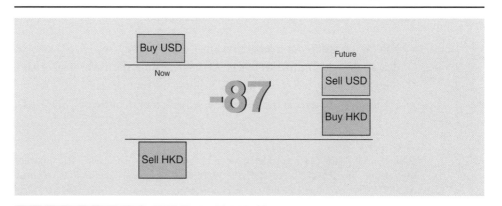

Source: HKIB

later. Meanwhile, the cash flow of HKD is always in the opposite direction of the USD leg.

The cash flow indicates that a B/S USD/HKD transaction reduces the cash of HKD (quote currency) on the spot day and the cash will be redeemed on maturity of the swap contract. On the other hand, a S/B USD/HKD transaction increases the cash of HKD on the spot day and the cash will be repaid on the maturity of the swap contract.

Swap Applications

How may a swap be used in the money market? The bank's money market desk can use swaps to fund another cash flow, fund an outright position, mitigate interest-rate risk and speculate on the interest rate movement.

A swap can be employed to fund the gap of cash flow of one currency with another currency. For example, in the coming two months, your clients are going to participate in a number of local initial public offerings. Since the oversubscription rate of these issues is expected to be over 100 times, the funding cost of HKD will be high.

One way to approach the problem is to borrow two-month HKD funds now. However, other would-be IPO buyers also have the same idea and the money lenders are swamped with borrowing requests. Your counterparties may not have sufficient credit facilities. So, instead of borrowing HKD directly, you may:

- **Borrow USD.** Since the supply of USD is abundant in the global money market, it is easier to borrow two-month USD than HKD.
- **Enter into a sell/buy USD/HKD deal** so that you swap your USD cash flow into HKD now.

Fund an Outright Position

The major risk of an outright position is the spot risk. Traders seldom employ back-to-back hedging against the outright transaction. They hedge the outright risk with spot deals because of the abundant liquidity of the spot market, which allows the trader to enjoy economies of scale. However, the mismatch of cash flows (the original outright deal and the spot hedge) exposes the trader to interest rate risk. To mitigate the risk or to close the mismatch of cash flows, money market traders employ swap transactions.

For example, a client has bought one-month forward USD/HKD 10mio from a trader. The trader has a short USD outright position and so is exposed to both foreign exchange and interest rate risk.

- If the trader does not cover the foreign exchange position, he will suffer a loss if the future spot rate goes higher.
- If the trader does not cover the gap of cash flows, he will also suffer a loss if the basis (the relationship between the spot rate and forward rate) changes.

- Normally, the trader will execute two transactions:
  - o The trader buys spot USD/HKD 10m to hedge the foreign exchange risk
  - o The trader enters into a sell/buy USD/HKD swap for USD10m (similar to previous argument) to cover the cash flows gap between now (actually the spot date) and future.

Mitigate Interest Rate Risk

Money market traders typically employ a swap contract to hedge against the interest rate exposure, because the swap market is more active and liquid than the traditional deposit market. Swap contracts also involve less credit risk (only replacement risk) before the settlement dates.

For example, a client has deposited HK$100m for one month. The trader executes a B/S USD/HKD for HK$100m for one month and then deposits the USD funds in the inter-dealer market to hedge the U.S. interest rate risk. The hedge works the other way too. Suppose another client borrowed HK$100m for one month from a trader. The trader may execute a S/B USD/HKD for HK$100m for one month to hedge against the interest rate risk.

The execution of a swap deal will achieve a return at the "implied yield." This yield is the return of the quote currency of a currency pair of the swap, which is measured from the swap point, and also the yield of the base currency. It means that there is an implied yield of HKD for a B/S USD/HKD deal and an implied cost of HKD for an S/B USD/HKD contract.

For example:

$$S \times \frac{1 + R_{HKD} \times \dfrac{D}{365}}{1 + R_{USD} \times \dfrac{D}{360}} = F$$

Where S = Spot USD/HKD, F = USD/HKD outright

$$R_{HKD} = \left[\left(\frac{F}{S} \right) \times \left(1 + R_{USD} \times \frac{D}{360} \right) - 1 \right] \times \frac{365}{D}$$

The R_{HKD} of the above formula is the implied yield of the swap. It means that if you execute a buy/sell USD/HKD for USD10m, you will have locked in the return at the implied interest rate of R_{HKD}, *provided you have done a hedge of the USD funds with the same tenor at the same time.*

What happens if you do not hedge the exposure of the U.S. dollar funds? If USD interest rates decline, you will get a lower amount of cash than the implied interest rate in HKD.

In practice, a trader likes to swap different foreign currency into USD. There are three reasons: the trader can save a lot of spread from the deals as compared to hedging individually; many tools are available for hedging USD interest rate risk, such as FRA, futures contract, and so on; and USD interest rates are less volatile than a minor currency.

For example, you may swap your long AUD position and short NZD position into USD. The first deal will give you a long USD position and the second will give you a short USD position. As a result, you may net the USD position from these two transactions and save at least the spread from the trades.

You may simply deposit your USD in an overnight loan to increase the liquidity of the firm despite the fact that the liability is, say, for three months. You can do this by buying or selling Eurodollar futures contracts to lock in the three-month interest rate.

Speculating on Interest Rate Movements

A trader may employ a set of swap contracts to speculate on the interest rate movement. The most popular approach is spread trading. The trader exposes himself to interest rate risk by a long (short) position of a long-dated swap contract and at the same time a short-dated position in the opposite direction.

Another form of speculation is to simply enter into a long-dated outright contract. For example, you may buy USD/HKD outright when the HK dollar interest rate is lower than the USD and is close to the undertaking rate of the government. Please note that USD/HKD is pegged with USD in a 7.75 – 7.85 trading range. Since the boundary is only 1.29%, if the interest differential is sufficiently large, the profit = is almost guaranteed.

For example, a trader believes that HKD interest rates are going to be set higher three months later. He has executed the following contracts:

- a S/B one-year USD/HKD swap for USD 1m at −810, and
- a B/S three-month USD/HKD swap for USD 1m at −210

Suppose the spot USD/HKD is 7.8. A trader does not have any outstanding position now; however, a gap is created between 3 months and one year. A summary of the cash flow is given in Figure 5.3.

Three months later:

- If the market rate for a nine-month swap is −200, the trader will execute a buy/sell nine-month USD/HKD swap for USD1m at −200 to cover the position.
- As a result, he loses HKD21,000, but makes a profit of HKD61,000 nine months later. He makes roughly (ignoring the time value) HKD40,000 or (USD1m * (0.0810–0.0210–0.0200)).

Forward Rate Agreement (FRA)

The money market also consists of a wide range of over-the-counter off-balance sheet derivative instruments. A forward rate agreement (FRA) is one these.

An FRA is an over-the-counter short-term interest rate derivative contract between two parties that agree on the interest rate to be paid at a future settlement date. The contract

FIGURE 5.3 Summary of cash flow in speculating on the interest rate movement

		Now	3-month	12-month
1Y swap	USD	(1,000,000.00)		1,000,000.00
	HKD	7,800,000.00		7,719,000.00
3m-swap	USD	1,000,000.00	(1,000,000.00)	
	HKD	(7,800,000.00)	7,779,000.00	
9m-swap	USD		1,000,000.00	(1,000,000.00)
	HKD		(7,800,000.00)	7,780,000.00
		0	(21,000.00)	61,000.00

P/L HKD

Assume TT = 7.8 for the first three month.

Now	1Y swap	−810
	3m swap	−210
3 months	9m swap	−200

Source: HKIB

period is quoted as, for example, six against nine months (6 × 9), which means that the interest rate for a three-month period will commence in six months' time.

The principal amounts are agreed, but never exchanged, and the contracts are settled in cash; exposure is limited to the difference in interest rates between the agreed and actual rates at settlement. One party pays a fixed interest rate, and receives a floating interest rate equal to a reference rate (the underlying rate). The reference rate is fixed one or two days before the termination date, depending on the market convention for the particular currency.

The payer of the fixed interest rate is also known as the borrower or the buyer, whilst the receiver of the fixed interest rate is the lender or the seller.

Put another way, an FRA is an agreement to borrow or lend a notional cash sum for a period of time lasting up to twelve months, starting at any point over the next twelve months, at an agreed rate of interest (the FRA rate). The "buyer" of an FRA is borrowing a notional sum of money while the "seller" is lending this cash sum.

Note how this differs from all other money market instruments. In the cash market, the party buying a CD or bill, or bidding for a stock in the repo market, is the lender of funds. In the FRA market, to "buy" is to "borrow." Of course, we use the term "notional" because, with an FRA, no borrowing or lending of cash actually takes place, as it is an off-balance sheet product. The notional sum is simply the amount on which interest payment is calculated.

For example:

$$3 \times 6 \text{ FRA} = 4\tfrac{1}{2} - 4\tfrac{1}{4}:$$

The buyer of an FRA hits 4 ½; the seller hits 4 ¼.

TABLE 5.1   Pros and cons of forward rate agreements

Advantages	Disadvantages
• Customised dates and amounts • Very liquid market, so small bid to offer spreads (relatively speaking) • No premiums or payments upfront • Can be reversed at any time at the then prevailing rate	• Only cover short-term interest rates • Less liquid than futures • Has counterparty risks • Involve credit limits

Source: HKIB

The terminology quoting FRAs refers to the borrowing time period and the time at which the FRA comes into effect or matures. The quote denoted as 3 × 6 or 3v6 (read 3 against 6 or simply "threes-sixes") refers to a three-month interest rate starting in three months' time.

- "ones-fours" – 1 × 4 FRA (three-month rate in one month time)
- "threes-nines" – 3 × 9 FRA (six-month rate in three months' time)

Like any other money market instrument, particularly an over-the-counter off balance sheet derivative, FRAs have their advantages and disadvantages. These are summarised in Table 5.1.

Terms of an FRA

The following are the terms you need to know in dealing with FRAs. They include:

- Notional sum
- Trade date
- Settlement date: the date when the two parties exchange the cash flow of the contract
- Fixing date: usually two business days before the settlement date
- Maturity date
- Contract period
- FRA rate: contract rate
- Reference rate: usually the LIBOR fixing rate
- Settlement sum

Settlement Value of an FRA Contract

The settlement value of an FRA contract is determined by the fixing of the reference rate, normally the LIBOR, on the fixing day. The settlement day is usually two business days after the fixing day. Both parties of the contract may also agree to settle the contract on any other day, such as the maturity day of the other underlying asset. In this case, the settlement value of the contract may differ from the original amount.

For example, suppose you would like to invest USD1m for three months, but the money will not be available until one month later. Currently, 1×4 FRA is 5.235/5.255. You sell an FRA contract for a notional amount USD1m at 5.235%.

If the three-month LIBOR is fixed at 4.235%, you will have the following cash flows:

- One month later, your investment (USD1mio) will get a smaller return of 4.235%, but
- You will get compensation from the FRA contract:
  o The loss on your investment $= 1,000,000 \times (4.235\% - 5.235\%) \times 92/360 =$ (USD2,555.56)
  o The gain on your FRA contract $= -1,000,000 \times (4.235\% - 5.235\%) \times 92/360 =$ USD2,555.56

Note that the amount of USD2,555.56 in the example is the future cash flow. The previous number is the interest receivable on the maturity of the three month deposit and the latter figure is the settlement cash flow supposed to happen for the FRA contract three months later.

On the settlement day of the FRA contract, the present value of the cash flow will be settled:

$$\text{Cash settlement} = 2,555.56 / (1 + 4.235\% * {}^{92}\!/_{360}) = \text{USD2,528.20}$$

Below is the generalised formula for the settlement value:

$$\text{Settlement value} = \text{Notional sum} \times \frac{(R_{ref} - R_{FRA}) \times \left(\dfrac{day}{year}\right)}{1 + R_{ref} \times \left(\dfrac{day}{year}\right)}$$

Year = 365 for GBP (money market convention)
Year = 360 for USD

Pricing an FRA

It is possible to construct a loan portfolio to replicate the cash flow of an FRA contract. For example, to replicate the bid of a 1×4 FRA, you place a four-month deposit and take a one-month loan. Figure 5.4 is a graphic representation of this operation.

One-month loan = 5.25%
Four-month deposit = 5.75%

$$(1 + 5.25\% \times 1/12)(1 + FRA \times 3/12) = (1 + 5.75\% \times 4/12)$$
$$FRA = 0.058909 \text{ or } 5.8909\%$$

It is important that an FRA contract is a financial derivative product and the loan portfolio is real money. The loan portfolio carries a higher spread to compensate for

FIGURE 5.4   Replicating bid of a 1 × 4 FRA

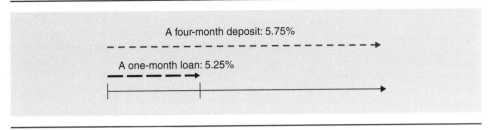

A four-month deposit: 5.75%

A one-month loan: 5.25%

Source: HKIB

counterparty risk. Therefore, the loan portfolio may not be good enough to explore the true value of an FRA contract. Another approach is to find the value by a portfolio of futures contracts, as discussed in the next section.

Hedging an FRA with Futures Contracts

Figure 5.5 illustrates a set of quotes for short term interest rate futures contracts and presents them graphically. The March contract is quoting at 93.80, meaning that the implied three-month USD LIBOR is 6.20%. The implied value of the underlying three-month loan commences on the settlement day of the March contract, which may be different from the fixing day of an FRA contract. Moreover, the value of the futures contract is settled on a daily basis, which is also different from an FRA contract.

$$6 \text{ Apr xx} - 15 \text{ Mar xx} = 22 \text{ days}$$

$$21 \text{ Jun xx} - 6 \text{ Apr xx} = 76 \text{ days}$$

The total number of contracts needed to hedge the FRA contract depends on the notional size of each futures contract. For example, if the Eurodollar futures contract is USD1m and the notional value of the FRA is USD10mio, you need 10 futures contracts to hedge the portfolio. If you take into consideration the daily settlement effect of the futures contract, however, the total number of contracts will be less than 10.

By interpolation, the theoretical value of the FRA contract is:

$$(76/98) \, 6.20\% + (22/98) \, 6.50\% = 6.2673\%$$

You therefore need 78% (76/98) or 7.8 March contracts and 22% (22/98) or 2.2 June contracts to hedge the FRA.

Some events can theoretically pose challenges to the above example of hedging an FRA with futures contracts. If the curve shifts upwards in parallel by 10 bps (parallel movement):

- The bank pays $10mio × 0.0010 × (91/360) = $2,527.78 for the FRA
- The bank receives (7.8 + 2.2) × 10 × 25 = $2,500 for the futures contracts

FIGURE 5.5   Short term interest rate futures contracts[9]

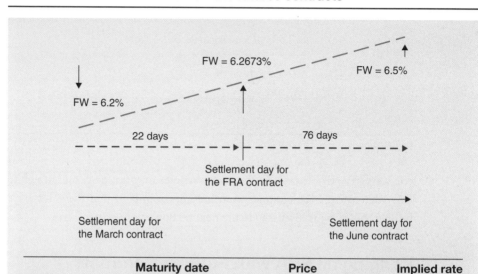

	Maturity date	Price	Implied rate
March	15 Mar 20xx	93.80	6.20
June	21 Jun 20xx	93.50	6.50

- The difference is due to the day count convention. This portfolio seems to be very good in hedging the market risk of interest rate.

  If the curve does not move in parallel (rotation of the yield curve) as shown by the numbers in Table 5.2:

- The March contract goes down by 6.8 bps, but the June contract rises 32.4 bps.
- The theoretical value of the FRA will be up 2 bps only.
- The value of your portfolio will result in a loss. This is the *basis risk* of the strategy.

  In addition to the non-parallel movement of the yield curve, the hedging strategy above is subject to various practical issues. For example, as the near month contracts expire, you will be able to hedge the exposure of the FRA contract only with far month contracts. *Liquidity* can be another problem because you must provide for additional margin as collateral to exchange when your contracts are losing money.

TABLE 5.2   Rotation of the yield curve

March	−6.8bps	7.8 × −6.8 × 25	−1326
June	+32.4bps	2.2 × 32.4 × 25	+1782
FRA	+2.0bps	10mio × 2 × 91/360	−505.56
Net			−49.56

Source: HKIB

---

[9] Adapted from Richard Flavell, *Swaps and Other Derivatives* (West Sussex: John Wiley & Sons, 2002), 18–20.

TABLE 5.3 Application of FRA contracts

Long FRA (hit the higher quote)	Expect higher interest rates	Cap the interest cost
Short FRA (hit the lower quote)	Expect lower interest rates	Protect the interest income

Source: HKIB

Application of FRA Contracts

The application of FRA contracts is summarised in Table 5.3. To hedge the rising interest rate cost of your loan, you should be holding a long position in FRA contracts. To hedge the falling interest rate return, you should be holding a short position in FRA contracts. FRA contracts are a short term interest rate derivative product. If you want to hedge a long term interest rate exposure, you will consider buying or selling a series of FRA contracts.

Non-Deliverable Forwards

In a typical forward contract, a party either acquires or delivers a foreign currency. Another type of forward is an agreement in which the exchange of currency does not happen. This is known as a non-deliverable forward (NDF) and it is often used to hedge currencies in emerging markets.

NDFs are like futures contracts. At a forward date, the current spot rate of a currency is compared to the rate at the contracted forward rate and a cash payment is made. There is no settlement of the foreign currency.

In the simplest case, two banks agree to a non-deliverable forward contract. For example, Bank A and Bank B agree to an NDF contract through which Bank A plans to acquire USD1 million three months forward at a rate of USD-RMB 6.17. Three months later, the two banks agree to settle at a rate of USD-RMB 6.27, which means that the dollar has appreciated in regards to the RMB. So Bank A will receive:

$$1,000,000\,(6.27 - 6.17) = \text{RMB}100,000.$$

Financial Futures

A futures contract is a legal agreement between a buyer (seller) and an established exchange or a clearing house, in which the buyer (seller) agrees to take (make) delivery of the underlying asset at a specified price at the end of a designated time period. When a party takes a position by buying (or selling) a futures contract, the individual is said to be in a long (short) futures position or to be long (short) futures.

What is the difference between a forward and futures contract? Table 5.4 compares the various features of these two derivative products. The differences include the fact that a forward contract is an OTC product while futures are traded on an organised exchange such as the Chicago Mercantile Exchange (CME) and Chicago Board of Trade (CBOT),

TABLE 5.4 Distinguishing forwards from futures

Forward contract	Futures contract
Non-standardised—traded in an over-the-counter market	Standardised—traded in organised exchanges such as CME and CBOT
The transacted parties are subject to counterparty risk	Clearinghouse stands between the transacted party and guarantees their performance
No need to mark-to-market	Mark-to-market on daily basis
Actual delivery of the underlying at settlement	Not obliged to settle by delivery (cash delivery is available)
Requires a credit facility from the market maker (the bank)	Requires a cash margin to start with

Source: HKIB

and that forwards require actual delivery of the underlying assets while futures are not so obliged (cash delivery is available).

There are usually at least four contract months for futures each year, namely March, June, September, and December. Most of the liquidity is concentrated in the near contract months; it is not easy to find a quote at the longer end. The Eurodollar futures contract is the most popular product. Other currencies are not as well accepted. For example, the liquidity of HKD interest rate futures contracts is poor. It is hardly possible to hedge HKD interest rate risk with this product.

The liquidity challenges with futures take different forms. The exchange where the product is traded may demand that the user adds more cash collateral to top up the margin account. It may amend the regulations, particularly on the margin requirement, from time to time or demand a particular account to increase the collateral.

The transparency of the market can also cause problems to small players. The exchange may not allow practitioners to have a net short position of the contracts. In this situation, the big players may force the small players to cover the short position with a power trade strategy. Thus, the implied yield of the futures may not only reflect the market risk of interest rates, but also the liquidity risk of the products themselves. Table 5.5 shows the advantages and disadvantages of futures.

Settlement of Contract

The Eurodollar futures contract is a cash settlement, meaning that the holder of the contract does not deliver the underlying asset. Instead, the holder deposits a sufficient amount of

TABLE 5.5 Pros and cons of futures

Advantages	Disadvantages
• High liquidity, and therefore small Bid/Offer spreads • Leverage due to margin trading ability	• Limited number of instruments covered • Limited number of maturities makes it impossible to hedge perfectly

Source: HKIB

TABLE 5.6   Application of interest rate futures

	Interest Rate Up	Interest Rate Down
Long Interest rate futures	Loss	Gain
Short Interest rate futures	Gain	Loss

Source: HKIB

cash in a collateral account as margin, in compliance with the regulations of the exchange. All the outstanding contracts are marked-to-market at the end of the day. The available margin will be adjusted according to the profit or loss on the contract on a daily basis.

The notional amount of each contract is USD1m. The minimum is a half tick or 0.005 or USD12.5 (one tick = USD25). Note that in using an interest rate futures contract to hedge against interest rate risk of an underlying asset, you will be taking a certain extension of basis risk.

Market players can take a long position or a short position on interest rate futures. Table 5.6 shows the correlation between the movement of interest rates and the position taken on the direction taken.

Below is an example of the use of interest rate futures:

- Three-month LIBOR at 5.1% is quoted as (100.00 – 5.1) 94.90;
- You buy a March contract at 94.50 (implied rate is 5.5%);
- The contract is settled at 95.50 (the implied three-month LIBOR rate is down to 4.5%);
- The contract generates a 100bps profit;
- The cash reward is 100×25 or USD2,500.

Implied Forward Interest Rate

In a perfect market (and the futures exchange is generally viewed as one), the pricing of the March contract at 94.50 in the example above indicates that the market expects the three-month LIBOR in March to be at 5.50%.

The quotation of a futures contract offers information of the implied interest rate of the cash market. For example, when a September contract is trading at 95.50, it implies that the three-month LIBOR rate in the third week of September will be at 4.50% (100 – 95.50).

Credit Derivatives

Credit derivatives are financial contracts designed to enable traders and investors to access specific credit-risky investments in synthetic (that is, non-cash) form. They can also be used to hedge credit risk exposure by providing insurance against losses suffered due to credit events.

Credit derivatives allow banks to manage the credit risk exposure of their portfolios or asset holdings, essentially by providing insurance against deterioration in credit quality of the borrowing entity. The simplest credit derivative works exactly like an insurance policy, with regular premiums paid by the protection-buyer to the protection-seller, and a payout in the event a specified credit event occurs.

The principle behind credit derivatives is straightforward. Investors desire exposure to debt that offers high returns. However, such exposure brings corresponding credit risk with it. This can be managed with credit derivatives. At the same time, the exposure itself can be taken on synthetically if, for instance, there are compelling reasons why a cash market position cannot be established. In addition, because credit derivatives are traded over-the-counter, they can be designed to meet specific user requirements.

What constitutes a credit event is defined specifically in the legal documents that describe the credit derivative contract. A number of events may be defined as credit events that fall short of full bankruptcy, administration, or liquidation of a company. For instance, credit derivatives contracts may be required to pay out under both technical as well as actual default.

We examine four basic structures of credit derivatives in this chapter: credit default swap (CDS), total return swap (TR swap), basket default swap, and credit linked note. In addition, we discuss collateralised debt obligations, or CDOs, in greater detail.

Credit Default Swaps (CDS)

A credit default swap is a contract in which one party (the protection-buyer) agrees to pay a lump sum periodically to another party (the protection-seller) over the life of the agreement in return for a contingency payment, in case a credit event specified in the contract occurs.

The credit default swap[10] illustrated in Figure 5.6 is a bilateral financial contract in which the protection-buyer pays a periodic fee, typically expressed in basis points on the notional amount, in return for a contingent payment by the protection-seller following a "Credit Event of a Reference Entity." The International Swap and Derivatives Association (ISDA) has completed a lengthy project to produce a standardised letter confirmation for credit swaps transacted under the umbrella of its ISDA Master Agreement.

Credit Events

The definition of what constitutes a credit event and the settlement mechanism used to determine the contingent payment are flexible and determined by negotiation between the counterparties at the start of the transaction. A credit event is usually defined as bankruptcy, insolvency, receivership, material adverse restructuring of debt, or failure to meet payment obligations when due.

---

[10] Extracted from "Credit Derivatives: A primer" issued by J.P. Morgan in February 1998.

FIGURE 5.6   Illustration of a credit default swap relationship

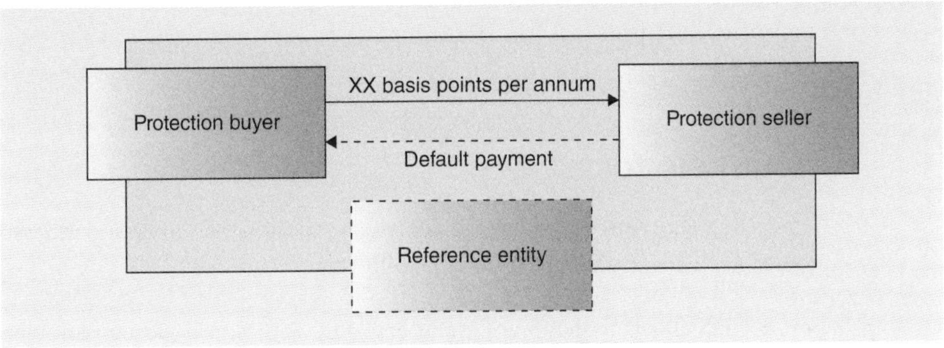

Source: HKIB

Where measurable, other elements are coupled with these credit events, such as a significant price deterioration (net of price changes due to interest rate movements) in a specified reference obligation issued or guaranteed by the reference entity. This latter requirement is known as a materiality clause.

Contingency Payment

A contingency payment is usually a cash settlement that compensates the creditors of the reference entity for losses incurred in a credit event. This payment is typically calculated as the fall in price of the reference obligation below par (or some other designated reference price or "strike") at some pre-designated point in time after the credit event.

As an alternative, the contingent payment may be fixed as a predetermined amount, called a "binary" settlement. Another option is for the protection-buyer to make physical delivery of a specified deliverable obligation in return for payment of its face amount. A default swap with its premium paid at inception is also called a default put.

A key distinction between physical delivery and cash settlement is that the protection-seller has recourse to the reference entity and gains the opportunity to participate in the workout process, as owner of a defaulted obligation following physical delivery of the obligation.

Value of a CDS

The value of a credit default swap depends on both the credit quality of the underlying reference entity and the writer of the CDS, also known as the counterparty. If the counterparty defaults, the buyer will not receive any payment even if a credit event occurs. Note also that the premium payments will end if the counterparty defaults. That is why the value of a default swap depends on the probability of counterparty default, the probability of entity default, and the correlation between them.

The valuation of a default swap is also affected by the recovery rate of a reference entity. In the case of a bond, the recovery rate can refer to the recovery rate of its principal only or to both principal and accrued interests. A recovery rate can also be deterministic or random.

Rationale for a CDS

There are many reasons why the bank's treasury desk, other investors, and issuer may want to deal with a CDS. These include the following:

- A CDS allows reduction of credit exposure without physically removing assets from the balance sheet.
- It is a confidential transaction in which the customer of the underlying does not need to be a party to the CDS or to even be aware of the transaction.
- It hedges the credit exposure of a position without triggering a sale for either tax or accounting purposes.
- A CDS can be completed even though the secondary market for the underlying loans and private placements is illiquid or does not exist at all.
- Low-rated entities that have high funding costs get the opportunity to take on credit exposure in off balance-sheet positions that usually do not need to be fully funded at inception.
- Highly rated entities with cheap funding costs can offset the risk of the underlying credit and still retain a net positive income stream.
- CDS users can sell the credit short, which is impossible with cash assets (i.e., you cannot short a bank loan).
- CDSs are off-balance-sheet instruments, which mean they are flexible and can be leveraged. Users gain exposure to certain credit risks while simultaneously avoiding the administrative costs of actually owning the assets and the cost of servicing those assets.

Total Return (TR) Swap

A total return swap is a contract that involves one party agreeing to swap the total return of a specific reference asset in return for fixed or floating payments from another party. This bilateral financial contract is designed to transfer credit risk between the parties. The protection-buyer (the TR payer) exchanges the total economic performance of a specified asset for another cash flow from another party (the TR receiver). Figure 5.7 illustrates the relationship between the two parties.

The term "total return" refers to the sum of interest, fees, and any change-in-value payments (positive or negative) with respect to the reference obligation. The change-in-value payment equals the appreciation (positive) or depreciation (negative) in the market value of the reference obligation, which is typically determined through a poll of reference dealers.

FIGURE 5.7   Illustration of a total return swap relationship

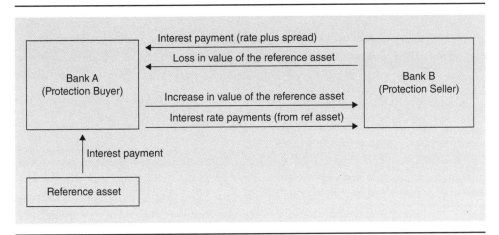

Source: HKIB

A net depreciation in value (negative total return) will result in a payment *to* the TR payer. Change-in-value payments may be made at maturity or on a periodic interim basis. Instead of cash settlement of the change-in-value payment, TR swaps may allow physical delivery at maturity of the reference obligation by the TR payer in return for the TR receiver paying the reference obligation's initial value.

How does a TR swap differ from a credit swap? The key difference is that TR swap payments are triggered by changes in the market valuation of a specified asset in the normal course of business. Payment on a credit swap, on the other hand, happens on a contingent or floating basis only if a specified credit event comes to pass.

Rationale for Using TR Swaps

The reasons for dealing in TR swaps include the following:

- A TR swap removes the TR payer's economic exposure to the underlying assets
- The transaction is done under the cloak of confidentiality and does not require a cash sale
- The TR payer retains servicing and voting rights to the underlying assets, although certain rights may occasionally be passed through to the TR receiver under the terms of the swap
- The TR receiver gains exposure to the underlying asset without having to make an initial outlay to purchase it
- Similar to credit swaps, a TR swap opens opportunities to both high funding cost and low funding cost entities.

Note that TR swaps involve issues of counterparty risk and the value of controlling rights over the reference obligation.

Basket Default Swap

In a basket default swap, the underlying is a basket of entities rather than one single entity. There are several types of basket default swaps, among which the most popular are:

- First-to-default;
- Nth-to-default;
- N-out-of-m-to-default;
- All-to-default swaps.

In a single entity credit default swap, the credit event is usually a default of the entity. With a first-to-default swap, a credit event occurs the first time any of the entities defaults. Such a swap will provide default protection against losses related to this first default. For a nth-to-default swap, the credit event occurs only when the nth default happens. The swap protects against losses that arise from that nth default only. An n-out-of-m-to-default swap protects the buyer against losses related to the first n defaults of the m-entity basket. An all-to-default swap protects against losses resulting from credit events of any of the entities in the basket.

Mechanism of Basket Default Swaps

In a first-to-default swap, whenever an entity in the reference basket defaults, the buyer stops paying the swap's premium and receives from the seller the difference between the principal amount of the entity in default and the recovered value. If the swap's counterparty defaults, premium payments will stop and both the buyer and the seller will walk away from the contract.

In an nth-to-default swap, whenever the nth default occurs in the reference basket, the buyer stops paying the premium and receives the difference between the principal amount of the latest (nth) entity in default and the recovered value. Note that the premium does not stop until the nth default as long as the counterparty does not default, even if there are already defaults in the basket.

In an n-out-of-m-to-default swap the seller pays the difference between the principal amount and the recovered value for each of the first n defaults. The buyer stops paying the premium after the nth default comes to pass.

In an all-to-default swap, the buyer continues paying the premium as long as there are un-defaulted entities in the basket and the counterparty does not default. The buyer receives from the seller any lost principal amount in the basket.

Credit-Linked Note (CLN)

A credit-linked note is a debt instrument that is bundled with an embedded credit derivative, typically a credit default swap. In exchange for a higher yield on the note, investors

FIGURE 5.8 How a credit-linked note works

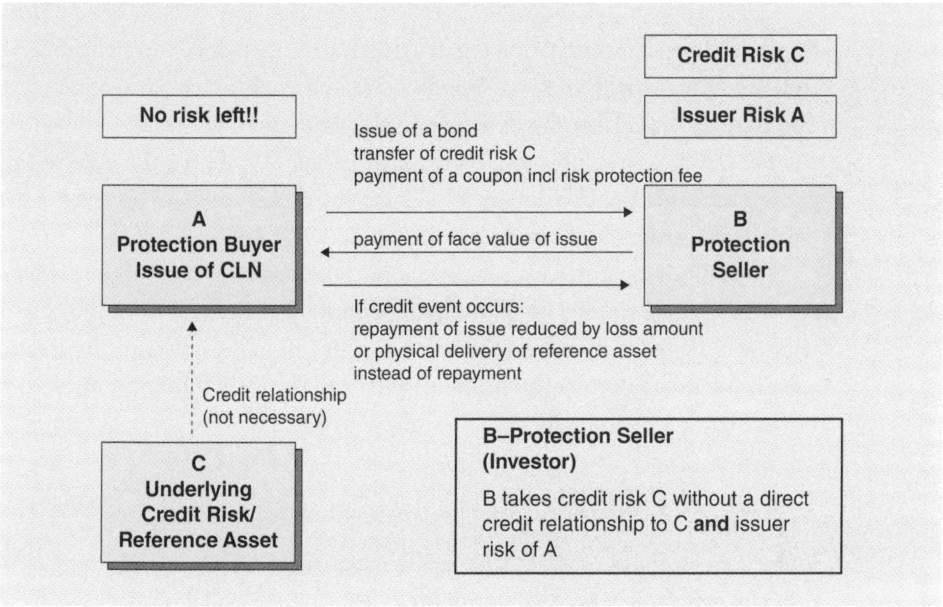

Source: HKIB

accept exposure to a specified credit event. For example, a note might provide for principal repayment to be reduced below par in the event that a reference asset defaults prior to the maturity of the note. Figure 5.8 shows how credit-linked notes work.

CLNs are issued by a protection-buyer (or hedger). The note is linked to the credit risk of a reference entity and is bought at par by an investor in exchange for a LIBOR spread. If none of the credit events specified in the contract occurs on the reference entity, the principal is returned to the investor and the transaction is complete. If a credit event comes to pass, however, the hedger pays the investor at par minus the amount due under the credit default swap.

In some ways, credit-linked notes can be considered as a funded version of a credit default swap. Such a security that is bundled with a credit default swap allows the issuer to transfer a specific credit risk to investors.

Created through a trust or Special Purpose Company (SPC), CLNs are backed by triple-A-rated securities. In effect, investors buy securities from a trust or SPC that pays a fixed or floating coupon during the life of the note. At maturity of the CLN, the investors receive par.

However, if the referenced credit defaults or declares bankruptcy, investors will receive an amount equal to the recovery rate. The trust or SPC enters into a credit default swap with a deal arranger. In case of default, the trust or SPC pays the dealer par minus the recovery rate in exchange for an annual fee that is passed on to the investors in the form of a higher yield on the notes.

Collateralised Debt Obligation (CDO)

A collateralised debt obligation is a structured security that is backed by diversified pools of bank loans, high yield corporate bonds, emerging market securities, or mortgage securities. The CDO can issue floating or fixed rate obligations in tranches according to seniority and payment, such as a senior note consisting of triple-A credit, a "B" note of single-A credit, and a mezzanine tranche note of BB credit. The obligations can be revolving, may include delay draw features, and may be guaranteed by a third party.

CDOs issue notes from a special purpose vehicle (SPV) to investors. These SPVs, which are set up so they are bankruptcy-remote and isolated from the originator's credit risk, are designed to transfer risk from the originator to the investor. The creation of an SPV usually involves a nominal amount of equity and the main funding comes from the issue of notes. Figure 5.9 shows the cash flow of a generic CDO.

Types of CDOs

There are two types of CDOs, namely balance sheet CDO and arbitrage CDO. The main differences between these two structures are the type of collateral backing the newly created

FIGURE 5.9   Generic cash flow of a CDO[11]

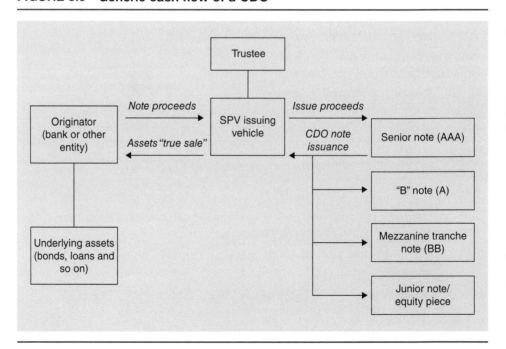

Source: HKIB

---

[11] Moorad Choudhry, *Bank Asset and Liability Management: Strategy, Trading, Analysis* (Singapore: John Wiley & Sons (Asia) Pte Ltd, 2007), 1025.

FIGURE 5.10   Balance sheet and arbitrage CDOs[12]

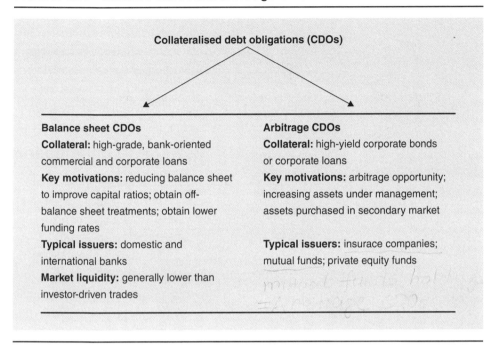

Collateralised debt obligations (CDOs)

Balance sheet CDOs
Collateral: high-grade, bank-oriented commercial and corporate loans
Key motivations: reducing balance sheet to improve capital ratios; obtain off-balance sheet treatments; obtain lower funding rates
Typical issuers: domestic and international banks
Market liquidity: generally lower than investor-driven trades

Arbitrage CDOs
Collateral: high-yield corporate bonds or corporate loans
Key motivations: arbitrage opportunity; increasing assets under management; assets purchased in secondary market
Typical issuers: insurace companies; mutual funds; private equity funds

securities in the CDO structure, and the motivations behind the transaction. Figure 5.10 shows a summary of the characteristics of these two types of CDOs.

Balance sheet transactions are initiated by holders of securities assets, such as commercial banks, which desire to sell assets or transfer the risk of assets. The motivation may be to shrink the balance sheet and/or reduce required regulatory capital or economic capital.

Arbitrage transactions seek to capture excess spread from securitising diversified pools of high yielding below investment grade loans or securities, and financing them largely through issuing relatively low cost investment grade debt. An arbitrage CDO's assets are purchased from a variety of sources in the open market, over a period that may stretch for months, from a warehousing period before the CDO closes to a ramp-up period after the CDO closes.

Tranches

A CDO typically issues several classes of equity and debt, classified into tranches according to seniority in bankruptcy and timing of repayment, as shown in Figure 5.11. The equity tranches, called junior subordinated notes, preferred stock, or income notes, are at the

[12] Moorad Choudhry, *Bank Asset and Liability Management: Strategy, Trading, Analysis* (Singapore: John Wiley & Sons (Asia) Pte Ltd, 2007), 1029.

FIGURE 5.11   Typical tranching of CDOs

Typical CDO Tranching

TRANCHES		RATINGS
A-1 Floating Rate Revolving Facility	**A-2** Fixed Rate Tranche	Triple-A or Double-A
B-1 Floating Rate Tranche	**B-2** Fixed Rate Tranche	Single-A
C Fixed or Floating Rate Tranche		Triple-B
D Fixed or Floating Rate Tranche		Double-B
Equity (Most Subordinate Tranche)		Not Rated

Source: HKIB

bottom of the CDO's capital structure. They bear the brunt of the risk of payment delays and credit losses first in order to make the debt tranches less risky in credit terms.

Subordinated CDO debt tranches protect more senior debt tranches against credit losses but they are assigned a higher coupon for taking on greater credit risk. Coupon payments on subordinated tranches might be deferrable if the CDO does not have sufficient cash flow or if it fails certain tests.

Credit Structures

A CDO can have either a market value or a cash flow credit structure, depending on the way it protects its debt tranches from credit losses.

In a market value structure, the asset manager makes sure the haircut value of the underlying assets is higher than the obligation of the CDO. The market value of the CDO assets is periodically calculated and then multiplied by a factor (called the advance rate) to arrive at haircut asset values. The sum of each asset's market value, times each asset's advance rate, must be greater than or equal to the debt tranche par and accrued. If the haircut value of assets falls below debt tranche par, underlying assets must be sold and debt tranches repaid until the haircut asset value once again exceeds debt tranche par.

There is no market value test in a CDO with a cash flow structure. The ability of the CDO to withstand portfolio default losses and still pay its debt tranches determines the credit quality of cash flow debt tranches. This credit quality, in turn, is based on the assessment of default probability, default correlation, and loss in the event of default. A common cash flow structuring technique is to divert cash flow from subordinated tranches to senior tranches if the quality of CDO assets diminishes by some objective measure.

Ways to Gain Exposure

There are two ways for a CDO to gain exposure to underlying assets. One is to purchase the assets outright using cash, a process described as a "true sale of assets." The other method is to use other credit derivatives to gain exposure to assets synthetically, rather than by a true sale. The credit risk of the underlying assets is transferred to the SPV through credit default swaps and/or total return swaps.

As shown in Figure 5.12, the originator sells assets to the SPV, resulting in the reduction of the balance of the originator. The transaction is financed by the investors of the CDO in different tranches. This results in the "true sale" of the assets to the SPV. The SPV gains an asset-and-liability profile that must be managed during the life of the CDO.

The ownership of the assets is transferred to the SPV. This asset transfer, if performed and structured properly, removes assets from the balance sheet of the originator. As a result, the securitised assets would not be included in the calculation of capital ratios, thus providing regulatory capital relief if the originator is a bank, for example.

In a synthetic CDO, the transfer of credit risk is achieved "synthetically" via a credit derivative, rather than by a "true sale" to an SPV, as Figure 5.13 shows. The most common contracts used are credit default swaps, with a portion of the credit risk sold in the form of credit-linked notes. Typically, a large majority of the credit risk is transferred via a supersenior CDS, which is dealt with a swap counterparty, but usually sold to monoline

FIGURE 5.12   Structure of a cash CDO

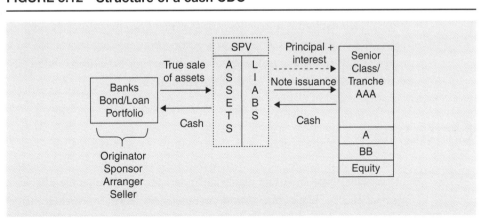

Source: HKIB

FIGURE 5.13   Structure of a synthetic CDO

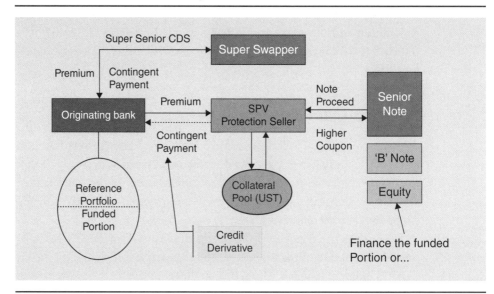

Source: HKIB

insurance companies at a significantly lower spread over LIBOR compared with the senior AAA-rated tranche of cash-flow CDOs.

In a synthetic CDO, unlike a cash CDO, the credit risk of the underlying loans or bonds are not legally transferred to the SPV; these assets remain on the originator's balance sheet. A bank originator can still obtain some regulatory capital relief because reference assets that are protected by credit derivative contracts attract a lower regulatory charge under Basel rules, though not to the same extent as the relief obtained via a cash CDO. And of course the bank will not raise much in the way of new funds, since it is not monetising the assets, but merely using them as a reference portfolio for the credit derivatives.

Most synthetic CDO deals are structured with mezzanine notes sold to a wider set of investors, the proceeds of which are invested in risk-free collateral such as U.S. Treasury bonds. The most junior note, known as the "first-loss" piece, may be retained by the originator. If a credit event comes to pass among the reference assets, the originating bank receives funds remaining from the collateral after they have been used to pay the principal on the issued notes, less the value of the junior note.

Options

Interest-rate swaps and other plain vanilla derivatives can meet the interest-rate risk management needs of banks, but in some circumstances, it is more efficient and cost effective to use option products to hedge risks. The banking professional therefore needs to be familiar with the use and application of options.

As a risk management tool, option contracts allow banks not only to hedge market risk exposure, but also to gain from upside moves in the market. Because they confer the right to conduct a certain transaction, but not an obligation, options function more like an insurance policy rather than a pure hedging instrument. The buyer of an option for hedging purposes needs only exercise it if required. The price of the option is in effect the insurance premium that has been paid for peace of mind.

Options are also used for purposes other than hedging, as part of speculative and arbitrage trading. Many banks also act as option market-makers and generate returns from profitably managing the risk on their option books.

An option is a contract in which one party (the **option holder**) has the right, but not the obligation, to buy or sell an underlying asset at a predetermined price during a specified period of time. The seller of the option, known as the **option writer,** grants this right to the buyer in return for receiving the price of the option, known as the **premium**.

An option that grants the right to buy an asset is a call option, while the corresponding right to sell an asset is a put option. The option buyer has a long position in the option and the option seller has a short position in the option.

Option contracts trade on exchanges or over-the-counter (OTC). They are linked to a variety of underlying assets (the underlying). Most exchange-traded options have stocks or futures as the underlying assets. OTC options have a greater variety of the underlying, including bonds, currencies, physical commodities, swaps, or baskets of assets.

Options are popular financial instruments among banks and other financial institutions and investors because they have the following advantages:

- **Unlimited gain but limited loss:** A well-designed option gives the holder potentially unlimited upside, while putting a floor on losses, which are limited to the loss of the premium paid in the worst case.
- **Work around regulations:** Some regulatory regimes are not as flexible as banks would like in terms of making possible effective management of interest-rate, market, and other risks, as well as maximising trading profits. Through such strategies as taking a synthetic short selling position in an underlying asset, an option holder is able to work around exchange and country rules without violating them.
- **Leverage effect:** Options allow speculation involving huge notional amounts of an underlying asset without the need to lay out an equally large sum of money for the premium.
- **Complex structure:** Options make possible the construction of complex portfolios that express, and benefit from, a particular view of the market, allowing traders to potentially make money regardless of the direction of the market (both upturn and downturn).

However, options can also be difficult to understand and manage, particularly for smaller banks and less sophisticated retail investors. The disadvantages of options include:

- **Expensive:** Percentage-wise, the cost of trading options is significantly higher than trading the underlying asset, and can significantly reduce profits.

- **Difficult to manage:** Options can be very complex and require a great deal of monitoring and professional skill.
- **Time-decay:** Holders of options run the risk of time decay, which erodes the value of option contracts over time.
- **Prone to misunderstanding:** Contracts, particularly for uncovered options, may be interpreted differently by the option writer and the option holder, given their open-ended nature and complexity.
- **Illiquid:** When revising a position, it is sometimes difficult to find a counterparty without incurring significant cost.

Types of Options

Plain vanilla options are the most well-known and used, but there is a wide variety of exotic options that are custom-designed to meet exceptional and unique needs and circumstances.

Plain Vanilla Options

As the term indicates, plain vanillas are straightforward structures, involving a bet that the option will reach a certain price level on a pre-agreed date. There are two plain vanilla options:

- **Call options** provide the holder the right, but does not oblige him, to purchase the underlying at a specified price.
- **Put options** provide the holder the right, but does not oblige him, to sell the underlying at a specified price.

Exotic Options

While following the basic template of an option, which is to grant the right but not the obligation, exotic options embed twists and conditions not found in their plain-vanilla counterparts. There is a long list of exotic derivatives, even as new ones continue to be created. They include:

- **Binary/Digital options** pay a fixed amount or nothing at all, depending on the price of the underlying instrument at maturity.
- **Barrier options** include a mechanism where, once the underlying crosses a price, the option starts to exist or ceases to exist at that particular time
- **Average/Asian options** determine the payoff not by the underlying price at maturity, but by the average strike price or average reference price over a pre-set period of time.
- **Chooser options** give the purchaser a fixed period of time to decide whether the derivative will be a vanilla call or put.

- **Compound options** are options on another option. They present the holder with two separate exercise dates and decisions. If the first exercise date arrives and the "inner" option's market price is below the agreed strike, the first option will be exercised but the holder still has a further option at final maturity.
- **Rainbow options** are usually calls or puts on the best or the worst of the underlying assets in a basket. For example, a "maximum option" is a bundle of vanilla options with different features—different strike prices and underlying assets, some may be puts, others calls—but generally with the same expiration date. Whichever is most favourable to the holder is the one exercised at expiration. A "minimum option" is the same as a maximum option, except that the option exercised at expiration is the one most favourable to the issuer.
- **Quanto options** are cash-settled derivatives that have an underlying asset denominated in one currency (foreign currency), with settlement in another currency (domestic currency) at a fixed rate. This is why a quanto (for "quantity adjusting option") is also known as a cross-currency derivative. Both the strike price and underlying asset are denominated in the foreign currency, which is also used to calculate the option's intrinsic value in the foreign currency at expiration. The resulting number is then converted to the domestic currency at the fixed exchange rate.
- **Lookback options** grant the option owner the right to buy (sell) the underlying instrument at its lowest (highest) price over some preceding period.

Terminology

Like the other financial instruments we have studied, options have their own terminologies that are unique to them. It is important for the banking professional to understand and use these option terms to avoid misunderstandings and mistakes that can result in losses.

- **Strike price:** The strike price of a call (put) option is the contractual price at which the underlying asset will be purchased (sold) if the option holder decides to exercise the option.
- **Expiration date:** The expiration date is the last day on which an option can be exercised.
- **American exercise:** The holder of an option has the right to exercise at any time up to the expiration date. This is usually the exercise mode of stock option trading on the Hong Kong stock exchange.
- **European exercise:** The holder of an option has the right to exercise only on the expiration date. OTC currency options are usually European exercise.
- **Bermudan exercise:** The buyer has the right to exercise the option on a set number of discretely spaced times. For example a Bermudan swaption (swap option) may confer the right to enter into an interest rate swap. The option holder may decide to enter into the swap at the first exercise date (and so will enter into, say, a ten-year swap) or defer

that opportunity and do so in six months' time (and so will enter a nine-year and six-month swap). Most exotic interest rate options are Bermudan exercise.

Moneyness States

There are three basic moneyness states in options trading: in-the-money (ITM), at-the-money (ATM), and out-of-the-money (OTM), which are summarised in Table 5.7.

- **In-the-money** is a situation where an option's strike price is below the current market price of the underlying asset (for a call option) or above the current market price of the underlying asset (for a put option). An option in this moneyness state has intrinsic value (see Table 5.7).
- **At-the-money** is a situation where the strike price of an option is or is nearly equal to the market price of the underlying security (for both a call option and a put option).
- **Out-of-the-money** is a situation where the strike price of a call option is higher than the market price of the underlying asset, or the strike price of a put option is lower than the market price of the underlying asset.

As applied to actual option contracts, these three basic moneyness states can have variations that are important for the options trader to know:

- **Deep out-of-the-money** refers to an option which is so far out-of-the-money that it is unlikely to go in-the-money prior to expiry.
- **Deep in-the-money** refers to an option in a situation where the market price of the underlying asset is far away from the strike price of the option. For a call option, the market price is much higher than the strike price. For a put option, the market price is much lower than the strike price.
- The trading of deep ITM options is a sensitive issue. There is typically no real reason for anyone to buy a deep ITM option, since an option has little time value. Writing a deep ITM option may be considered a way to borrow money from the market. The trading of deep ITM options is highly suspicious from the point of view of risk management. This was the case in the 2002 fraud at Allied Irish Banks (AIB), where a rogue trader was found to have written many deep ITM options to cover up his losses.

TABLE 5.7 Summary of moneyness states

Suppose:

S = An underlying asset

X = The strike price of the option

	S > X	S = X	S < X
Call option	In-the-money	At-the-money	Out-of-the-money
Put option	Out-of-the-money	At-the-money	In-the-money

Source: HKIB

- **At-the-money-forward option** (also known as ATMF) refers to an option that involves traders quoting a strike price that is the prevailing outright foreign exchange rate.

Value of an Option

The total value of an option is its intrinsic value and its time value. By expiration, the value of an option consists only of its intrinsic value.

The intrinsic value of an in-the-money option is the difference between the actual price of the underlying asset and the strike price of the option. The intrinsic value reflects the effective financial advantage that would result from the immediate exercise of that option.

For example, if a call option has a strike price of $45 and the underlying asset, say a stock, is trading at $55 a share, that call option will have an intrinsic value of $10 per share. If the stock price is lower than the strike price, the call option will have no intrinsic value.

Let us take another example, this time of a put option. If a put option has a strike price of $70 and the underlying asset, again let us say is a stock, is trading at $40 a share, the put option will have an intrinsic value of $30 per share. If the stock price is greater than the strike price, the put option will have no intrinsic value. Table 5.8 shows examples of call and put options and their intrinsic values.

Mathematically, where S = the price of the underlying asset and X = the price of the option:

$$\text{Intrinsic value of a call option} = \max{(S - X, 0)}$$
$$\text{Intrinsic value of a put option} = \max{(X - S, 0)}$$

Also known as the time premium, time value is the amount that an option's premium exceeds its intrinsic value (see Table 5.8). Time value is determined by the remaining lifespan of the option, its volatility, and the cost of refinancing the underlying asset in interest rate terms.

TABLE 5.8 Examples of intrinsic and time values

Option	Strike	Option Price	Stock Price	Intrinsic Value	Time Value
Call	$28	$3	$29	$1	$2
Put	$54	$4	$52	$2	$2
Call	$25	$2	$25	$0	$2
Put	$100	$3	$100	$0	$3
Call	$17	$1.50	$16	$0	$1.50
Put	$50	$0.50	$55	$0	$0.50

Source: HKIB

Mathematically:

$$\text{Time value} = \text{option price} - \text{intrinsic value}$$

In Table 5.8, there are four options that have zero intrinsic value, but positive time values. This is the case because the options may still regain intrinsic value given that there is still time left before the expiry. By the time of expiry, however, the time value would have disappeared and the option's premium will consist only of intrinsic value.

Variables in Value of a Stock Option

Table 5.9 shows the variables that can affect the value of a stock option and what the direction of that effect will be if a particular variable is changed while all others remain constant. We summarise the variables and the effect on the value of the option below:

- **Stock price:** If the price of the underlying asset rises above the strike price, the value of a call option goes up as well, but the value of a put option falls. This is because the call option goes further in-the-money, but a put option moves further out-of-money.
- **Strike price:** Setting a higher strike price makes a call option less in-the-money and thus lowers its value. However, it makes a put option more in-the-money and increases its value.
- **Time to expiration:** In general, the value of a call/put option is higher the further it is from maturity. However, a special situation may arise in a European option. If a dividend is distributed for an underlying asset before the maturity of the option, the event may cut the value of its call option and boost the value of its put option. This is because the price of the underlying typically declines after the stock goes ex-dividend. As a result, there is no certain relationship between option value and the expiration date for European call/put options.
- **Volatility:** The more volatile the price changes of the underlying asset, the higher the value of a call or put option tends to be.
- **Risk-free rate:** When interest rates rise, the price of a call option typically rises, while the price of a put option falls. Since investors pay only the premium on a call option, the finance cost of investing in the underlying asset becomes cheaper for them in light of higher interest rates. At the same time, investors get higher interest income from selling the underlying asset immediately, rather than holding on to a put option. But if the rise in interest rates results in a fall in the stock price, which may be the knee-jerk reaction of the stock market in general soon after the central bank raises interest rates, this relationship falls apart, at least in the short term.
- **Dividend:** When the underlying asset declares a higher dividend, the value of a call option falls while the value of a put option rises. This is because the holder of a call option is not entitled to dividends and the price of the underlying asset usually falls when it goes ex-dividend. The holder of a put option is not entitled to dividends either, but if the stock price falls, the value of the put option will increase.

TABLE 5.9   Effect on price, increasing one variable while all others are fixed[13]

Variable	European Call	European Put	American Call	American Put
Stock price	+	−	+	−
Strike price	−	+	−	+
Time to expiration	?	?	+	+
Volatility	+	+	+	+
Risk-free rate	+	−	+	−
Dividends	−	+	−	+

Currency Options

The terminology discussed above applies mainly to stock options, although the principles are similar to currency options. In this section, we will discuss the terminology that applies to currency options, primarily to at-the-money-forward (ATMF) options we referenced earlier.

- **Exercise conventions.** Interbank players trade mainly European type options that allow the buyer to exercise the contract on the expiry date with a 24-hour window. The most popular expiration cut-off times in foreign-exchange options are the New York Cut (NY time 10 am) and Tokyo Cut (Tokyo time 3 pm).
- **Settlement.** Once the buyer has committed to a transaction, he has to pay the premium to the option seller in two business days, like a spot FX transaction. The exercise of the option leaves the option buyer with an open position. If the option holder (or seller) does not want to keep that position, he will square the position in the spot market.
- **Quotation.** Traders quote in terms of volatility. For example, a one-month ATMF USD put/JPY call is 20.25/20.35. This means the volatility (vol) is at 20.25% and 20.35% in terms of the bid and offer, respectively. Given the vol data, the trader can work out the dollar premium of the option using the Black-Scholes model, such as $230,827, $231,966.
- **Strike.** A trader may ask for a specific strike, say 125 for a USD call/JPY put. Another practice is to quote according to the level of delta, a concept we will discuss later. For ATMF options (most quotations in the market refer to ATMF options), the delta, or rate of change in the price, is roughly 50%. This means that a quotation of 25-delta indicates an out-of-money option; a 15-delta option is further out-of-money.
- **Hedged position.** Sometimes, a dealer buys or sells an option only when it accompanies a hedge that equals the delta of the face value of the contract. For example, a buyer buys a 50-delta USD call/JPY put option for USD10m. At the same time, the buyer sells USD5mio USD/JPY to the seller of the option. This is called delta-neutral basis.

---

[13] John C. Hull, Options, *Futures, & Other Derivatives*, Fourth Edition (Prentice Hall, 2000), 169.

Properties of Options

Amongst the most important properties of options are upper bound and lower bound, put-call parity, early exercise, and negative time value. These properties often differ depending on whether the instrument is a call or a put, and whether the exercise mode is American or European.

Upper Bound

At any particular point in time, the value of a call option or a put option cannot exceed a particular price. The upper bound is the maximum possible price for a call option or a put option. However, call options and put options have different upper bounds.

In the case of an American or a European call option, an options contract cannot be worth more than the underlying asset under any circumstances. Therefore, the value of a call option should be lower or equal to the underlying asset price. If there is a violation of this rule, an arbitrageur will quickly enter the market to make a riskless profit by buying the underlying asset and selling the call option.

Mathematically, this rule can be represented as:

$$c \leq S_t \quad \text{and} \quad C \leq S_t$$

In the case of an American or European put, the upper bound is the strike price. Under any circumstances, the value of a put will be lower than or at most equal to the strike price of the option. If this condition is violated, then an investor will make use of the arbitration opportunity by writing the option and investing the proceeds at the risk-free rate of interest.

Mathematically, this rule can be presented as:

$$p \leq X \quad \text{and} \quad P \leq X$$

A European option cannot be exercised before the expiration day. It is necessary to consider the present value of X when its value (the put) is being measured. Mathematically:

$$p \leq Xe^{-r(T-t)}$$

Lower Bound for European Calls on Non-Dividend-Paying Assets

The lower bound for a European call option can be mathematically presented as:

$$S_t - Xe^{-r(T-t)}$$

The value of a European call option must be worth more than its intrinsic value in $(S_t - X)$, as $S_t - Xe^{-rt}$ is always higher than $(S_t - X)$.

FIGURE 5.14 Slope of a European call option at expiry

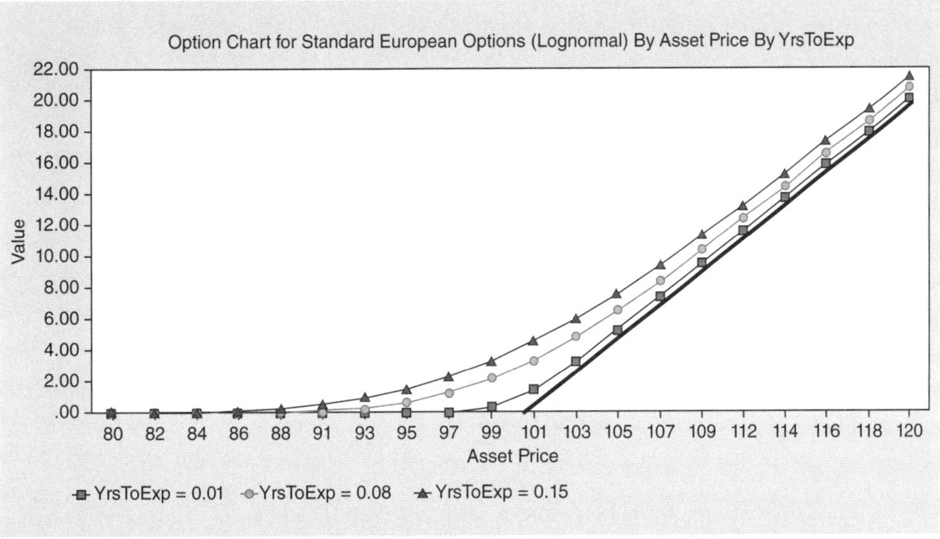

Option Chart for Standard European Options (Lognormal) By Asset Price By YrsToExp

— YrsToExp = 0.01   — YrsToExp = 0.08   — YrsToExp = 0.15

Source: HKIB

The slope in Figure 5.14 is the intrinsic value of the call option at expiry. As the option draws closer to expiration, its value also comes closer to the intrinsic value. Non-zero is another lower bound of the call option.

For example, suppose $S_t = \$20$, $X = \$18$, $r = 10\%$ p.a., and $T - t = 1$ year. The lower bound of the European call is:

$$S_t - Xe^{-r(T-t)} = 20 - 18e^{-0.1^*1} = 3.71$$

Then consider the situation where the European call is at $3 (instead of $3.71), indicating that it has been oversold. An arbitrageur can buy the call and short the stock. The portfolio generates a cash inflow of $17 (sell short the stock and buy the option at $20 − $3). If the proceeds are invested for one year at 10% per annum, the portfolio will become $17e^{0.1^*1} = \$18.79$.

At the end of the year, the stock price might be:

Greater than the strike price ($18). The arbitrageur exercises the call option at $18 to cover the short position in the stock. The net cash flow will be $18.79 − $18 = $0.79.

Lower than the strike price ($18). The arbitrageur does not exercise the call option but buys the stock at the current market price (say, $17) to cover the stock position. The net cash flow of the portfolio will be $18.79 − $17 = $1.79 (the risk-free profit is greater).

Mathematically, the lower bound of a European call option is:

$$c \geq S_t - Xe^{-r(T-t)} \text{ and } c \geq 0$$

Therefore, $c \geq \max\left(S_t - Xe^{-r(T-t)}, 0\right)$.

Consider a European call option (no dividend) where the stock price is $51, the exercise price is $50, the time to maturity is six months, and the risk-free rate of interest rate is 12% per annum. In this case, the lower bound of the option price is:

$$c \geq S_t - Xe^{-r(T-t)} = 51 - 50e^{-0.12*0.5} = \$3.91$$

Any fall in the price of the call option to below $3.91 will open up an arbitrage opportunity.

Lower Bound for European Puts on Non-Dividend-Paying Assets

Mathematically, the lower bound of a European put option is presented thus:

$$Xe^{-r(T-t)} - S_t$$

As Figure 5.15 shows, the value of the European put option is always lower than its intrinsic value $(X - S_t)$. In addition, non-zero is another lower bound of the put option.

Suppose $S_t = \$37$, $X = \$40$, $r = 5\%$ pa, and $T - t = 0.5$ year. The lower bound of the European put is:

$$Xe^{-r(T-t)} - S_t = 40e^{-0.05*0.5} - 37 = 2.01$$

FIGURE 5.15   Slope of a European put option at expiry

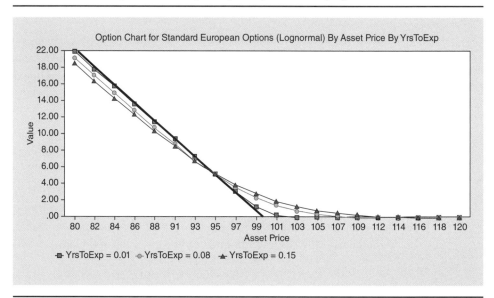

Source: HKIB

The theoretical value of the European put is $2.01. Any put price below this value will create arbitrage opportunity.

Consider another situation where the European put price is $1 (instead of $2.01). An arbitrageur can borrow $38 for six months to buy one stock (at, say, $37) and one put ($1).

Six months later, the total payout for the loan will be $38e^{0.05*0.5} = \$38.96$.

If the stock price is below the strike of $40, the arbitrageur will exercise the put option and sell the stock at $40. Then, the net cash flow will be $40 - \$38.96 = \$1.04$.

If the stock price is above the strike of $40, the arbitrageur will not exercise the put option but will liquidate the stock on hand at market price, say at $42. Then, the net cash flow will be $42 - 38.96 = \$3.04$.

Mathematically, the lower bound of a European put option is:

$$p \geq Xe^{-r(T-t)} - S_t \text{ and } p \geq 0$$

Therefore $p \geq \max\left(Xe^{-r(T-t)} - S_t, 0\right)$.

Let's look at a third example. Consider a European put option (no dividend) where the stock price is $38, the exercise price is $40, the time to maturity is three months, and the risk-free rate of interest rate is 10% per annum. In this case, the lower bound of the option price is:

$$p \geq Xe^{-r(T-t)} - S_0 = 40e^{-0.1*0.25} - 38 = \$1.01$$

Any fall in the price of the call option below $1.01 will create an arbitrage opportunity.

Put-Call Parity

One important property of option pricing is that at a particular point in time (t), the value of a European call option with a particular exercise date and exercise price can be obtained from the value of a put with the same exercise date and strike price. This is known as put-call parity, a relationship that is strictly only the case with European options.

Mathematically, put-call parity can be presented thus:

$$c + Xe^{-r(T-t)} = p + S_t$$

The concept of put-call parity is better understood with an example. Consider the situation where the stock price is currently $31, the exercise price is $30 and the risk-free rate is 10% per annum. The price of a three-month European call option is $3, and the price of a three-month put is $2.25. Then:

You sell the stock short, write the put, and buy the call. The cash flow is equal to -3 (call) $+2.25$ (put) $+31$ (short stock) $= \$30.25$.

You deposit the proceeds for three months $= 30.25e^{0.1*0.25} = \$31.02$

Three months later:

- If $S_T > \$30$, you allow the put option to expire and exercise the call option at $30 to cover your short position in the stock. The net cash follow will be $31.02 − $30 = $1.02.
- If $S_T < \$30$, you allow the call option to expire and exercise the put option to put the stock at $30. The net cash flow will also be $31.02 − $30 = $1.02.

Early Exercise: American Calls on a Non-Dividend-Paying Asset

It is never optimal to exercise an American call option on a non-dividend-paying stock before the expiration date. This is because the underlying asset does not generate income (assumption) and the early exercise of the American call option will also incur a financial cost. However, the above statement does not mean the holder of an in-the-money (ITM) call option should not do anything. In fact, the option holder should sell the call option to lock in the profit.

Mathematically:

Intrinsic value of American call option is max $(S_t - X)$
American call $C \geq$ European call c

This is because an American option offers the holder the right of early exercise so that it should be worth more than a European option, everything else being equal.

$$c \geq S_t - Xe^{-r(T-t)}, \text{ therefore}$$

$$C \geq S_t - Xe^{-r(T-t)}$$

If an investor exercises an American call option when it is in-the-money, he will get $S_t - X$ only. However, $C \geq S_t - Xe^{-r(T-t)} \geq S_t - X$, because $Xe^{-r(T-t)} \leq X$ given $r > 0$. The equation implies that the time value of the American option is not zero. If you exercise the call, the holder will give up the time value of the option. The optimal strategy is thus to sell the ITM call option directly.

Early Exercise: American Puts on a Non-Dividend-Paying Stock

It is optimal to exercise an American put option on a non-dividend-paying stock early. If a stock is traded at $0 (zero) and the strike price of a put option is $10 (very deep-in-the-money), the holder of the put option should exercise the put since it is obvious that the stock price cannot drop below $0. When the American put option is deep in-the-money, the holder should exercise the right immediately. This is because the proceeds received from the put option will at least earn a positive interest income.

Mathematically:

$$p \geq Xe^{-r(T-t)} - S_t$$
$$P \geq X - S_t$$

Value of the American put = Intrinsic value + Time value

When the American put option is deep in-the-money, $X - S_0$ is always bigger than $Xe^{-r(T-t)} - S_t$.

Negative Time Value for a European put

When the American put is deep in-the-money, it is desirable to exercise the option early and capture its intrinsic value. However, the same advice does not always apply to European put options, which are sometimes worth less than their intrinsic value $\left((X - S_t) \geq Xe^{-r(T-t)} - S_t \right)$.

Recall the formula:

Option = Intrinsic value + Time value

If the European put is deep in-the-money, its intrinsic value will be positive, but may be smaller than $X - S_t$. Since European puts cannot be exercised before the expiry date, the time value of even a deep ITM European put option will carry a negative value. This is not the case with an American put option in the same situation, since an American put option can be exercised any time before expiration.

Relationship between American put and Call Prices

As we have learned, put-call parity holds only for European options. However, it is possible to derive a relationship for the American pair. Mathematically, this is presented as:

$$S_t - X \leq C - P \leq S_t - Xe^{-r(T-t)}$$

Volatility

As discussed earlier in this chapter, volatility is a key variable that influences the value of an option; the more volatile the price is, the higher the value of the option is.

The volatility of an asset measures the variability of its price returns. It is defined as the annualised standard deviation of returns, where variability refers to the variability of the returns that generate the asset's prices, rather than the prices directly. The standard deviation of returns is given by the formula below:

$$\sigma = \sqrt{\sum_{i=1}^{N} \frac{(x_i - \mu)^2}{N-1}}$$

where x_i is the i'th price relative, μ the arithmetic mean of the observations, and N is the total number of observations.

The value is converted to an annualised figure by multiplying it by the square root of the number of days in a year, usually taken to be 250 working days. Using this formula from market observations it is possible to calculate the historical volatility of an asset.

However, what is required is a figure for future volatility, since this is relevant for pricing an option, which expires in the future. Future volatility cannot be measured directly, by definition. Market-makers get around this by using an option-pricing model "backwards." An option-pricing model calculates the option price from volatility and other parameters. Used in reverse, the model can calculate the volatility implied by the option price. Volatility measured in this way is called implied volatility.

Historical Volatility

Historical volatility is approximated by the standard deviation (the square root of the variance) of the return of an underlying asset for a reference period. Each asset has a unique historical volatility.

Note that it is the asset price returns on which the standard deviation is calculated, and the not the actual prices themselves. This is because using prices would produce inconsistent results, as the actual standard deviation itself would change as price levels increased.

Implied Volatility

The implied volatility of the underlying asset is based on the backward calculation of the market value of an option, as explained earlier. It reflects market sentiment and supply and demand of the option at a particular moment. The value of implied volatility for an underlying asset varies from time to time and from model to model.

From the perspective of market practitioners, implied volatility is superior to historical volatility in that implied volatility utilises current market information to calculate a volatility estimate. However, the calculation process is cumbersome and typically requires the use of a computer, not just a calculator.

Several assumptions regarding the underlying distribution of prices remain open to debate among the various mathematical models in use. There are several option-pricing models, among them the Black-Scholes Model, Hull-White Model, Black-Derman-Toy Model and Cox-Ross-Rubenstein Model. We will discuss some option-pricing models later in this chapter.

Volatility Smile

In calculating the implied volatilities of options, a pattern resembling a "smile" has been observed when plotting the implied volatility against the moneyness of the option. This phenomenon is not well understood theoretically and different markets displays different characteristics. In particular, American equity options did not show a volatility smile before the Crash of 1987, but began showing one afterwards.

A closely related concept to volatility smiles is that of term structure of volatility, which refers to how implied volatility differs for related options with different maturities. An implied volatility surface is a 3-D plot that combines volatility smile and term structure of volatility into a consolidated view of all options for an underlying asset.

Option Pricing Models

Most option-pricing models are based on one of two methodologies, although both types employ essentially identical assumptions. The first method is based on the resolution of the partial differentiation equation of the asset–price model, corresponding to the expected payoff of the option security. This is the foundation of the Black-Scholes model.

The second type of model uses the martingale method, and was first introduced by Harrison and Kreps (1979) and Harrison and Pliska (1981), where the price of an asset at time 0 is given by its discounted expected future payoffs, under the appropriate probability measure, known as the risk-neutral probability. There is a third type that assumes lognormal distribution of asset returns but follows the two-step binomial process.

The most popular models for the beginner include the binomial model developed by Cox, Ross, and Rubinstein and the Black-Scholes model.

Binomial Model

The binomial model is relatively simple, but it is required to work in accordance with a simulation technique such as Monte Carlo modelling. The binomial model breaks down the time to expiry into potentially a very large number of time intervals, or steps. A tree of stock prices is initially produced working forward from the present to expiry. At each step it is assumed that the stock price will move up or down by an amount calculated using volatility and time to expiry.

This produces a binomial distribution, or recombining tree, of underlying stock prices. The tree represents all the possible paths that the stock price could take during the life of the option. At the end of the tree—that is, at expiry of the option—all the terminal option prices for each of the final possible stock prices are known, as they simply equal their intrinsic values.

Next, the option prices at each step of the tree are calculated working back from expiry to the present. The option prices at each step are used to derive the option prices at the next step of the tree using risk neutral valuation based on the probabilities of the stock prices moving up or down, the risk free rate, and the time interval of each step.

Let us look at the one-step model and the two-steps binomial model to gain a clearer understanding of this concept.

One-Step Model

Suppose a European call option has the following characteristics:

- S0 = $20
- K = $21
- r = 12%
- S1u = $22
- S1d = $18
- t = 0.25 year

Using the above data, we can produce a binomial distribution (recombining tree), as shown below:

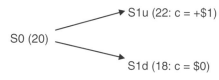

$$S0 = \$20, K = \$21, r = 10\%, S1u = \$22, S1d = \$18$$

Now suppose the change from state 0 to 1u is p, and then 0 to 1d is $(1-p)$. Under a risk-neutral condition, the expected present value of S1u and S1d must be identical to S0.

$$S0 = \$20 = (p*22 + (1-p)*18) e - 0.12*0.25$$

Therefore:

$$p = (20*e0.12*0.25 - 18)/4 = 0.6523$$

Since, $c0 = (p*(+1) + (1-p)*(0)) * e - 0.12*0.25 = 0.505*e - 0.12*0.25 = 0.633$

To calculate the delta of the call (remember, delta is defined as $\partial c/\partial S$):

$$\text{Delta} = (1-0)/(22-18) = \tfrac{1}{4} = 0.25$$

If $22 = 20 * u$, and $18 = 20 * d$,

$$S0\, e^{rt} = pS0u + (1-p)\, S0d$$
$$\rho = (e^{rt} - d)/(u-d)$$
$$\Delta = (cu - cd)/(S0u - S0d)$$

Two-Steps Binomial Model

Let us consider the same call in the previous example. Suppose:

- S0 = $20
- K = $21

- $r = 12\%$
- $S1u = \$22$
- $S1d = \$18$
- $S2uu = \$24.2$
- $S2ud = \$19.8$
- $S2dd = \$16.2$
- $t = 0.5$ year (two steps of 0.25y)

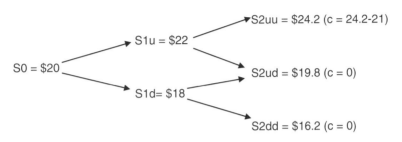

Consider the node between S2uu and S2ud,
Like the one-step model,

$$S1u = \$22 = (p*(S2uu) + (1-p)*(S2ud))*e - 0.12*0.25$$
$$p = 0.6523, \text{then}$$
$$c1u = (p*3.2 + (1-p)*0)*e - 0.12*0.25 = 2.0257$$

Consider the node between S2ud and S2dd,
Like the one-step model,

$$S1d = \$18 = (p*(S2du) + (1-p)*(S2dd))*e - 0.12*0.25$$
$$p = 0.6523, \text{then}$$
$$c1d = (p*0 + (1-p)*0)*e - 0.12*0.25 = 0$$

Consider the node between S1u and S1d,
Like the one-step model,

$$S0 = \$20 = (p*(S1u) + (1-p)*(S1d))*e - 0.12*0.25$$
$$p = 0.6523, \text{then}$$
$$c0 = (p*2.0257 + (1-p)*0)*e - 0.12*0.25 = 1.2823$$

Delta of the previous tree:

$$D1 = (2.0257 - 0)/(22 - 18) = 0.5064$$
$$D2u = (3.2 - 0)/(24.2 - 19.8) = 0.7273$$
$$D2d = (0 - 0)/(19.8 - 16) = 0$$

Black-Scholes Model

The Black-Scholes (B-S) model is more complicated than the binomial model. It is used to price many European-type options. To understand the B-S model, one should know the meaning of Wiener processes or Brownian motion, as shown below:

$$\Delta x = a\Delta t + b \in \sqrt{\Delta t}$$

Δx is the change of the underlying asset.
$a\Delta t$ is the constant growth of the asset.
$b \in \sqrt{\Delta t}$ is the noise of the asset.

Remember that investors expect to reap a return from an asset that is higher than the risk-free rate. The constant "a" is actually the risk-free rate of the market while "b" represents the volatility of the assets and $\in$ is a random number of the distribution. The variable t is number of year. Mathematically:

$$\text{Mean of the distribution } \Delta x = a\Delta t$$
$$\text{Standard deviation of } \Delta x = b\sqrt{\Delta t}$$

In terms of stock price:

$$\Delta S/S = \mu \, \Delta t + \sigma \in \sqrt{\Delta t},$$

The B-S model assumes that the return of the underlying asset follows a log normal distribution and assumes further that the natural logarithm of the distribution has a mean and standard deviation equal to 0 and 1, respectively, as shown in Figure 5.16.

We can now render the B-S model as follows:

$$C = SN(d1) - Ke^{-rT}N(d2)$$

Where:
C = Theoretical call premium
S = Current stock price
T = (T − t) or time to maturity in number of years
K = Strike price of the option
r = Risk-free interest rate
N () = Cumulative standard normal distribution
e = Exponential term (2.71828.....)
σ = Annualised standard deviation of stock returns
In = Natural logarithm
$d1 = [\text{In}(S/K) + (r + \sigma^2/2)T]/(\sigma\sqrt{T})$
$d2 = d1 - \sigma\sqrt{T}$

From the formula and keeping everything unchanged, when the share price S increases by one dollar, the call value rises one dollar times N (d1).

FIGURE 5.16   Log normal distribution

$\mu = 0 \quad \sigma = 1$

LOG NORMAL DISTRIBUTION: f(X)

VALUE STOCHASTIC VARIABLE

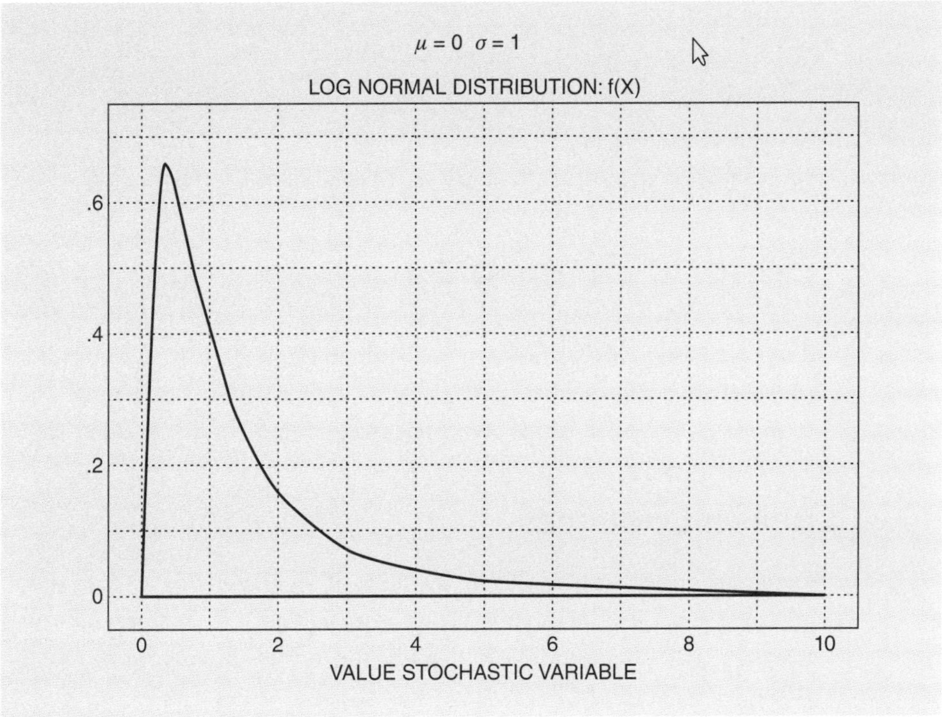

Source: HKIB

In other words, we have N (d1) as the option delta, representing the changing rate of the option price as a result of the stock price change. Moreover, N (d2) actually is the probability the option will be exercised. Since d1 is always larger than d2, it follows that the cumulative probability function N (d1), the option delta, should always be larger than N (d2), the probability to exercise.

Furthermore, because the difference between d1 and d2 is ó √T, such a difference will be more significant for long dated options (large T) on highly volatile (larger ó) equity stocks, hence the difference between the option delta and probability to exercise.

Trading Strategies

There are two broad types of trading strategies, and position trading.[14] Volatility trading is used by traders who feel that the volatility of the underlying asset is about to go higher or lower. All the various volatility trading strategies can achieve results so long as they are in delta-neutral position.

---

[14] Cormac Butler, *Mastering Value at Risk: A Step-by-Step Guide to Understanding and Applying VAR* (Financial Times/Prentice Hall, 1999), 142.

Traders engage in position trading because they believe the underlying asset is set to go in one direction. Bull call or put spreads may be used whenever traders feel the underlying asset will rise in price. Similarly, bear call or put spreads are used to speculate a downward movement of the underlying.

We will first look at generic trading strategies and then focus on volatility trading strategies, including bullish and bearish on volatility, straddle, strangle, and butterfly, and on spread strategies (position trading), such as bull spread, bear spread, and calendar spread.

Generic Strategies

There are three generic strategies: bullish strategies, where the asset prices are expected to rise; bearish strategies, where asset prices are expected to fall; and neutral or non-directional strategies, which assume that asset prices will not move much in either direction.

Bullish Strategies

When the options trader expects the price of the underlying asset to shoot upwards, he considers the use of bullish option strategies. However, it is important to assess how high the asset price can go and the time frame for the rally in order to choose the best trading strategy.

The most bullish options trading strategy is the simple call buying strategy employed by most freshman options traders.

In most cases, however, an asset seldom goes up by leaps and bounds. Moderately bullish options traders usually set a target price for the expected bull run and utilise bull spreads to reduce cost. While these strategies cap maximum profit, they are usually not expensive to employ. The bull call spread and the bull put spread are common examples of moderately bullish strategies.

Mildly bullish trading strategies make money as long as the underlying asset price does not go down on the expiration date of the option. These strategies usually provide a small downside protection as well. Writing out-of-the-money covered calls is a good example of a mildly bullish trading strategy.

Bearish Strategies

Bearish strategies are the mirror opposite of bullish strategies. Bearish options strategies are employed when the options trader believes that the price of the underlying asset will move downwards. The trader must assess how low the asset price can go and the time frame during which the deterioration will happen in order to select the most appropriate trading strategy.

The most bearish of option trading strategies is the simple put buying strategy utilised by most new options traders.

But asset prices rarely slide down precipitously. Moderately bearish traders usually set a target price for the expected decline and utilise bear spreads to reduce cost. The maximum profit is capped, but these strategies are usually cheap to employ. The bear call spread and the bear put spread are common examples of moderately bearish strategies.

Mildly bearish trading strategies make money as long as the underlying asset price does not go up on the option's expiration date. These strategies usually provide a small upside protection. Writing out-of-the-money puts is an example of such a strategy.

Neutral or Non-Directional Strategies

When a trader is not sure whether the price of the underlying asset will rise or fall, he will resort to neutral strategies. Also known as non-directional strategies, they get their name from that fact that the opportunity to make money does not depend on whether the price of the underlying will rise or fall. Instead, the opportunity to turn a profit depends on the volatility of the underlying asset price.

Figure 5.17 summarises the various trading strategies that are at the options trader's disposal depending on his views of the market's direction or non-direction.

FIGURE 5.17   Summary of strategies in options trading

		Option Trading Strategies		
	Bullish	**Bearish**		**Neutral**
Most bullish/ bearish	Buy call	Buy put	**Bullish on volatility**	Long straddle, long strangle, and short condor or short butterfly
Moderately bullish/ bearish	Buy bull call spread/bull put spread	Buy bear call spread/put spread		
Mildly bullish/ bearish	Sell covered OTM call	Sell covered OTM put	**Bearish on volatility**	Short straddle, short strangle, ratio spreads, long condor and long butterfly

Source: HKIB

Volatility Trading

As its name indicates, volatility trading is used by traders who feel that the volatility of the underlying asset is about to go higher or lower. The volatility trading strategies are those **bullish on volatility**, exemplified by the long straddle, long strangle, and short condor or short butterfly, and **bearish on volatility**, among them the short straddle, short strangle, and long butterfly. Appendix 6.1 shows a graphical representation of these strategies as well as their delta, gamma and theta.

Long Straddle

When the options trader believes that the price of the underlying asset will become significantly volatile in the near term, he may construct a long straddle to make money on the volatility. This non-directional options strategy involves purchasing a long put and a long call at the same strike price. Mathematically:

$$\text{Long Straddle} = +C_{k1} + P_{k1}$$

Table 5.10 summarises the characteristics of a long straddle. It is an unlimited profit, limited risk strategy. When the positions expire, the investor will make profits if the asset price has moved strongly enough in either direction. As the market moves strongly in one direction, the gain made on one leg exceeds the losses incurred on the other, and the straddle increases in value.

Profits can be taken early in the life of the straddle, but only if the expected movement occurs quickly. Since the structure consists of two options, time decay works strongly against the bought straddle. The longer the straddle is left in place, the greater the loss due to time decay. Only rarely will this strategy be held to expiry. Once the

TABLE 5.10   Characteristics of a long straddle

Long straddle	
Construction	long call X, long put X
Point of entry	market near strike price X
Break-even points (at expiry)	strike price plus net premium paid strike price less net premium paid
Maximum profit (at expiry)	unlimited
Maximum loss (at expiry)	limited to premium paid
Time decay	hurts the long straddle

Source: HKIB

FIGURE 5.18   Impact of "smile" on a long straddle

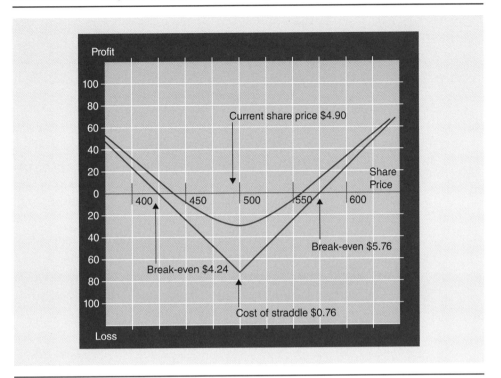

Source: HKIB

investor's market view proves correct, the straddle should be unwound to lock in the profits. The position must be closely monitored and may need to be closed out well before expiry.

Traders should be aware of the impact of a "smile" on the straddle strategy, as shown in Figure 5.18. Because both the long call and long put options are at-the-money, both have a minimum volatility. Once the price of the underlying moves away from ATM, however, the smile indicates that both options will experience greater volatility, as one now becomes out-of-the-money while the other will become in-the-money.

As an example, let us look at a hypothetical gold mining company called XYZ Corp. It had been involved in an extensive exploration program over the last few months. The results are due to be made public in a month. You do not know whether it will find gold deposits or not, but you expect the current share price of $4.9 to move sharply in either direction depending on the news. You therefore construct a long straddle:

- BUY 1 three-month Call @$0.38
- BUY 1 three-month Put @$0.38

Short Straddle

What about the investor who believes the price of the underlying asset will stagnate for some time? Constructing a short straddle may be an appropriate way to turn a profit in such a situation. Mathematically:

$$\text{Short Straddle} = -C_{k1} - P_{k1}$$

Table 5.11 summarises the characteristics of a short straddle. It is a high-risk strategy—the maximum loss at expiry is unlimited, while the maximum profit is limited to the premium. The investor faces the possibility of getting hit with damaging losses if the asset price moves sharply in either direction. The net premium received for selling the straddle provides some protection, but beyond that, unlimited losses can be incurred. The stronger the move, the greater this loss will be.

Since the short straddle consists of two short positions, time decay assists the combination. In order to get the greatest benefit from time decay, however, it may be best to trade options with near-month expiries, when time decay is starting to accelerate.

Unless the asset price is exactly at the strike price of the two options sold, one of the legs will be in-the-money. Therefore, there is always a risk of early exercise on one leg or the other. The trader who is unhappy about being exposed to possibly unlimited losses may consider taking a put and a call option with out-of-the-money strike prices. In the event of an adverse market movement, he may decide to close one or both legs of the straddle.

An increase in volatility will be damaging to the short straddle. The two written options may rise in value, making them more expensive to buy back. The higher volatility also signals that the market may be about to move strongly. The options trader must monitor volatility closely and be prepared to take action should it increase unexpectedly.

Long Strangle

In a market that has been consistently stagnant and where implied volatilities are low, buying a long strangle may prove to be an appropriate strategy. The taker of this spread believes

TABLE 5.11   Characteristics of a short straddle

Short strangle	
Construction	short call X, short put X
Point of entry	market near strike price X
Break-even points (at expiry)	strike price plus net premium received strike price less net premium received
Maximum profit (at expiry)	limited to premium
Maximum loss (at expiry)	unlimited
Time decay	helps the short strangle

Source: HKIB

TABLE 5.12   Characteristics of a long strangle

Long strangle	
Construction	long call Y, long put X
Point of entry	market between the two strike prices
Break-even points (at expiry)	higher strike price plus net premium paid
	lower strike price less net premium paid
Maximum profit (at expiry)	unlimited
Maximum loss (at expiry)	limited to premium paid

Source: HKIB

the long period of stagnation is due for an explosive move in either direction. The long strangle is a cheaper strategy than the long straddle; however, a larger move in the share price will be required for it to be profitable. Mathematically:

$$\text{Long strangle} = +C_{k1} + P_{k2}; \quad \text{where both } C \text{ and } P \text{ are OTM}$$

Table 5.12 summarises the characteristics of a long strangle. It is constructed as a long slightly out-of-the-money put and a long slightly out-of-the-money call. The long strangle has unlimited maximum profit, and limited maximum loss, which equals just the premium paid.

A long strangle will pay off if there is a sharp move in the asset price or a dramatic increase in volatility. Profits can be made when the asset price has gone beyond the strike price of either option to cover the premium paid. Long straddle profits can be taken early in the life of the strategy if there has been a big enough move in the asset price.

The long strangle should not be held too close to the expiration date. If the expected move in the asset price has taken place, the position can usually be unwound at a profit well before expiry. If the asset's direction becomes clear, it will be appropriate to close out the leg that is losing its value and hold the profitable leg.

If the expected increase in volatility has not taken place, it may be advisable to close the position out before time decay starts to seriously damage the strategy. As with the long straddle, the long strangle is exposed to time decay.

Since the long strangle comprises out-of-the-money options, its cost is lower than that of a straddle. However, the asset price must move further for a long strangle to turn a profit. You must consider constructing a long strangle only if you believe a really significant move is in the making. If the increase in volatility or change in asset price does not come to pass, both the long call and long put will end up as worthless.

As an example, let us look again at XYZ Corp. The results of the exploration were not conclusive and so the company has extended the exploration exercise period for three more months. The stock price fell after the announcement but has since stayed steady at around $4. You:

- BUY 1 three-month $4.5 Call @$0.19 and
- BUY 1 three-month $3.5 Put @$0.1

Short Strangle

When the trader regards current option premiums as overpriced and also believes that the underlying assets will stay within a fairly narrow price range, he may consider constructing a short strangle. This strategy can result in a lower profit than does the short straddle. However, it offers greater protection to the writer since the asset price must move further to result in a loss.

Table 5.13 summarises the characteristics of the short strangle. The strategy is constructed by selling an out-of-the-money call and another out-of-the-money put, both expiring on the same date. The maximum profit that can be earned from the short strangle is the premium received from the sale of the options. The strangle yields a smaller potential profit than the straddle because writing out-of-the-money options command lower premiums.

A profit is made if the asset price finishes between the two strike prices at expiry. As the asset price moves beyond the strike price of either option, the profits decrease. A loss will result if the move is large enough to erode the premium received at the time of writing the options. If the asset price becomes unexpectedly volatile, the strangle writer faces potentially unlimited losses.

Like the short straddle, the short strangle gains from time decay. When constructing the strangle, it is usually best to utilise contracts with near-month expiries so as to gain most from time decay.

Because the strangle is constructed with out-of-the-money options, there is a lower risk of early exercise compared with a straddle. However, a dramatic change in the asset price can bring one of the options in-the-money, thus introducing the risk of exercise.

The impact of "smile" on a short strangle is different from the effect on a straddle because the short strangle strategy involves two out-of-money options. The volatility of these two options would have been already high and reflected in being discounted in the premium. Once the underlying moves to the strike of either the put or the call, that option will lose its volatility. The volatility of the other option will increase, but only slightly because the initial level of volatility was already high. In general, the trader may lose value from the volatility smile.

TABLE 5.13   Characteristics of a short strangle

Short strangle	
Construction	short call Y, short put X
Point of entry	market between the two strike prices
Break-even points (at expiry)	higher strike price plus net premium received lower strike rate less net premium received
Maximum profit (at expiry)	limited to premium
Maximum loss (at expiry)	unlimited
Time decay	helps the short strangle

Source: HKIB

Long Butterfly

A long butterfly is the combination of a long strangle and a short straddle. It can be utilised to yield extra income for the investor who expects the market to stagnate, but is nevertheless wary of an unexpected rise or fall in prices.

Mathematically:

$$\text{Long butterfly} = +P_{k1} + C_{k3} - P_{k2} - C_{k2},$$
$$\text{Long butterfly} = +C_{k1} - 2 \times C_{k2} + C_{k3},$$
$$\text{Long butterfly} = +P_{k1} - 2 \times P_{k2} + P_{k3},$$
$$\text{Long butterfly} = +P_{k1} - P_{k2} - C_{k2} + C_{k3}, \text{ where } k3 > k2 > k1$$

Table 5.14 summarises the characteristics of the long butterfly. It is constructed as long two call options with different strikes and short two calls with a strike that lies between the two other strikes. The long butterfly will earn the maximum profit if the market finishes at the middle strike price when the options expire.

If this happens, the lower strike price call will be the only one to finish in-the-money. The trader will profit on the difference between the middle and lower strike prices, minus the cost of the spread. Most of this profit will develop in the last month as time decay accelerates. The maximum loss for the trader is the cost of the spread, which will happen if the market ends past either of the long butterfly's "wings."

The presence of short options in the strategy means that an increase in the market price above the central strike price introduces the risk of exercise. Thus, if the asset price moves sharply up, the trader may consider liquidating the position in order to avoid exercise. If the asset price moves sharply down, the trader may close out in order to salvage some time value from the taken legs of the strategy. If the asset price remains steady, the position may be left until close to expiry since the profit develops almost entirely in the last month.

One problem with the use of straddles and strangles is that both may result in unlimited losses (short straddle or strangle). However, the butterfly strategy in general

TABLE 5.14   Characteristics of a short strangle

The long butterfly	
Construction	long call X, short 2 calls Y, long call Z
Point of entry	market around central strike price
Break-even points (at expiry)	lower strike plus cost of spread upper strike less cost of spread
Maximum profit (at expiry)	central strike less lower strike less cost of spread
Maximum loss (at expiry)	cost of spread
Time decay	market around upper or lower strike: hurts market around central strike: helps

Source: HKIB

does allow traders to trade only the volatility without too much exposure to excessive market risk.

For example, you believe that asset prices are likely to remain steady for some time but you will still derive some income during this period. You consider selling a straddle, but you are concerned that an unexpected break either way in the market could be very damaging. You therefore buy a butterfly:

- BUY 1 three-month $2.75 Call @ $0.45
- SELL 2 three-month $3.00 Call @ $0.27
- BUY 1 three-month $3.25 Call @ $0.14

Spread Strategies

Unlike volatility trading, where the trader makes money from the volatility of price movements in any direction, spread strategies earn profit by betting that the market will move in one direction. Spread strategies include bull and bear spreads, ratio call spread, calendar spread, and collar. Appendix 6.1 shows a graphical representation of these strategies as well as their delta, gamma, and theta.

Bull Spread

Also called a call spread, a bull spread consists of a long call at one strike price and a short call at a higher strike price. Both options are for the same expiration. Mathematically, a bull spread is rendered thus:

$$\text{Bull Spread} = +C_{k1} - C_{k2}; \quad \text{where } k2 > k1$$

If the investor is not bullish enough to buy a call outright, but expects the underlying asset price to rise moderately, the bull spread is a lower cost way to gain exposure to such a market movement. The strategy has limited upside potential, but the income from selling the high-strike call offsets the cost of purchasing the low-strike call.

Table 5.15 summarises the characteristics of the bull spread strategy. While the short call in the bull spread reduces the cost inherent in taking an outright call, it also limits the profit to be made. The maximum profit obtainable is the difference between the strike prices of the two options, less the cost of the spread. Maximum profit will occur if, at expiry, the asset price is at or above the strike price of the sold option.

If the asset price rises quickly to this level, the spread will often be unwound early in order to avoid the risk of early exercise on the short leg. The higher delta of the long call means that the spread will increase in value as the asset price rises (delta of C_{k1} is higher than C_{k2} because C_{k1} is always more in-the-money than C_{k2}). The maximum loss possible is the cost of the spread, and will be incurred when the asset price is at or below the strike price of the bought option at expiry.

TABLE 5.15   Characteristics of the bull spread strategy

Bull spread	
Construction	long call X, short call Y
Point of entry	market around the lower strike
Break-even point (at expiry)	lower strike plus cost of spread
Maximum profit (at expiry)	difference between strike prices less cost of spread
Maximum loss (at expiry)	net premium paid
Time decay	market around lower strike: hurts market around higher strike: helps

Source: HKIB

The bull spread strategy can be replicated with puts instead of calls. In this approach, the investor buys the lower strike option (P_{k1}) and sells the higher strike option (P_{k2}). Called a bull put spread, this strategy can be rendered mathematically as:

$$\text{Bull put spread} = +P_{k1} - P_{k2}; \quad \text{where } k2 > k1$$

Figure 5.19 shows a graphical representation of the construction of a bull put spread on the stock price of hypothetical gold mining company, XYZ Corp. The stock has been rising strongly for a long time and is currently trading at $3.70. You think the price will rise

FIGURE 5.19   Example of a bull put spread, XYZ Corp

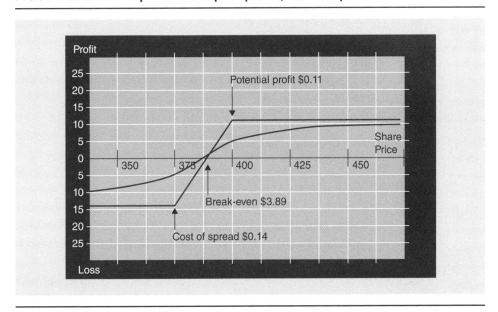

Source: HKIB

further to around $4.00 over the next three months. But buying the ATM call option is expensive, so you decide to buy the spread for $0.14 using a bull put spread:

- BUY 1 three-month $3.75 Call @$0.43
- SELL 1 three-month $4.00 Call @$0.29

Bear Spread

Also known as a put spread, a bear spread is constructed by putting together a long put at a higher strike and a short put at a lower strike. It is utilised when the investor expects a moderate fall in the market, but is not prepared to pay to purchase a put outright. Mathematically:

$$\text{Bear spread} = -P_{k1} + P_{k2}, \quad \text{where } k2 > k1$$

Table 5.16 summarises the characteristics of a bear spread. Like the bull spread, the written leg of this strategy serves to reduce the cost of entering the position. However, it also caps the profits that can be earned.

The maximum profit to be earned is the difference between the strike prices of the two options, less the cost of the spread. If, at expiry, the asset price has fallen to the strike price of the sold option, the maximum profit will be earned.

But if the asset declines to these levels, the trader may well choose to unwind the spread early, in order to avoid the possibility of exercising on the short leg. The maximum potential loss is the cost of the spread. This will occur at expiry, when the asset price is above the exercise price of the bought option.

If the price of the underlying asset unexpectedly falls sharply, it may be advisable to exit the bear spread strategy once the lower strike price is reached. Time decay will benefit the spread around the lower strike price; however, the trader will usually be more concerned with avoiding the exercise of the short leg.

If the asset price rises suddenly, the spread may be unwound before the put loses too much time value.

TABLE 5.16   Characteristics of a bear spread

Bear spread	
Construction	short put X, long put Y
Point of entry	market around upper strike
Break-even point (at expiry)	upper strike less cost of spread
Maximum profit (at expiry)	difference in strike prices less cost of spread
Maximum loss (at expiry)	net premium paid
Time decay	market around lower strike: helps market around upper strike: hurts

Source: HKIB

FIGURE 5.20 Example of a bear spread, XYZ Corp

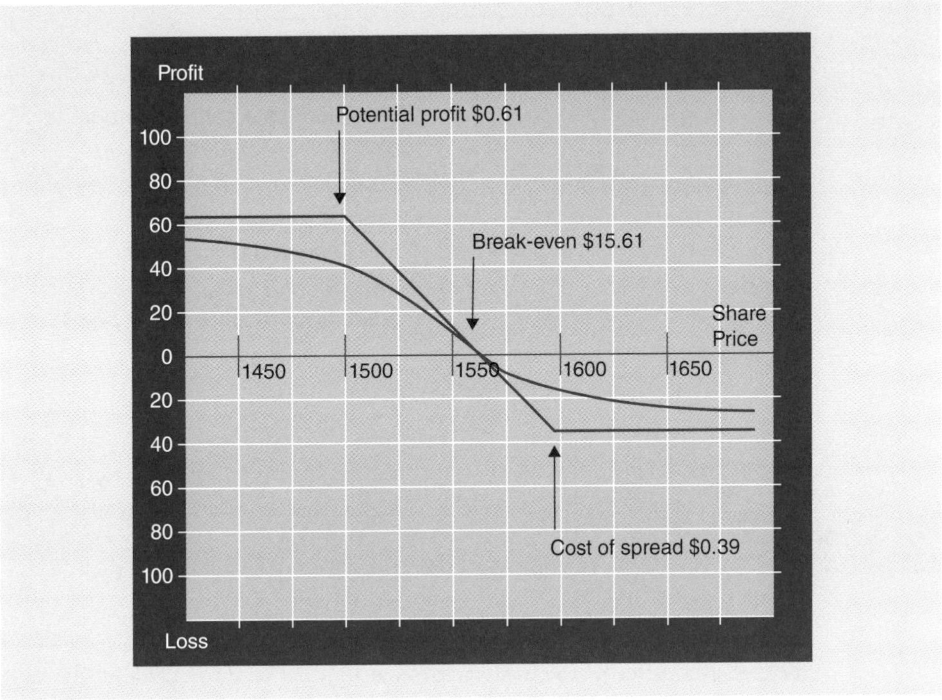

Source: HKIB

As an example, let us take a look again at XYZ Corp. Figure 5.20 shows a graphical representation of a bear spread on XYZ's stock price. After a series of price rises, you feel that a minor correction is about to take place on XYZ's share price. It is currently trading at $16.1, but you expect it to pull back to $15 over the next three months. You construct a bear spread on XYZ:

- BUY 1 three-month Put ($16.0 strike) @$0.61
- SELL 1 three-month Put ($15.0 strike) @$0.22

Ratio Call Spread

Also referred to as a "call ratio vertical spread," a ratio call spread has low and high strike calls that are not bought and sold in equal proportions. It is often used when traders have views both on the volatility and direction of the market. The ratio call spread can be an appropriate strategy for the investor who is expecting the market to rise slightly, but also sees the possibility of a sell-off.

Table 5.17 summarises the characteristics of the ratio call spread strategy. It is actually the same as a short straddle, except that the loss for the downward (left-hand side of

TABLE 5.17   Characteristics of a ratio call spread

Ratio call spread	
Construction	long call X, short calls Y
Point of entry	market around X
Break-even points (at expiry)	lower strike plus cost of the spread upper strike plus maximum profit of spread
Maximum profit (at expiry)	difference between strike prices less cost of spread
Maximum loss (at expiry)	unlimited if shares rise cost of spread if shares fall
Time decay	market around lower strike: hurts market around upper strike: helps

Source: HKIB

the movement) is limited. A ratio spread may be constituted by a long call with a strike at k_1 and short two calls at k_2, where k_2 is higher than k_1. Mathematically:

$$\text{Ratio spread} = +C_{k1} - 2 * C_{k2}; \text{ where } k2 > k1$$

The strategy involves uncovered written positions that carry the risk of exercise. If, at expiry, the price of the underlying is at the higher strike price of the ratio call spread, the trader will receive the maximum profit, which is the difference of the strikes minus the cost of the spread. The size of the profit depends in part on how many calls have been sold against each call taken. Generally the ratio is at 1:2. It rarely goes higher than 1:3 because this increases the risk if the price of the underlying rises strongly.

If, at expiry, the price of the underlying asset falls, the trader will lose no more than the cost of the spread. This protection is greater than in a bull call spread because of the higher number of written positions in place. However, the trader can face unlimited losses if there is an unexpected strong upward movement. The bigger the number of unprotected calls, the larger the losses.

The main downside in a ratio call spread is that the rise in price of the underlying is greater than anticipated market strength. If this happens, the trader may consider closing out the spread or else closing out the sold options to reduce the risk. If the market falls dramatically, the trader may have to sell back the long call before it loses too much time value. The danger in closing out the long position is that a reversal in the market direction exposes the trader to risk on the short legs.

To illustrate the use of a ratio call spread, suppose the market has been rising over the last couple of weeks and you believe a further increase is still possible. However, given the recent high, you fear the possibility of a downward correction. You buy a ratio call spread:

BUY 1 one-month $5 call @$0.38 and
SELL 2 one-month $5.50 calls @$0.13

Calendar Spread

A calendar spread has two calls or two puts. Both options are at the same strike, but each has a different maturity. Calendar spreads are useful in purchasing assets below the current market price. If the trader believes the underlying will rise in price but not within the next month, buying a calendar spread in effect gives him a call option once the near-month expiry has passed—at a lower cost than taking a call outright. Mathematically:

$$\text{Long calendar spread} = -C_{k1t1} + C_{k1t2}; \text{ where } t2 > t1$$

Table 5.18 summarises the characteristics of the calendar spread strategy. One of the options is a short call near expiry and the other is a long call far from expiry. Because the time decay of the near-month option is faster than that of the far-month call, the trader can capture the relative change of the rate to make money.

When the market is stagnant, the calendar spread allows the trader to turn a profit purely from time decay, and without the risk of having an uncovered sold position. However, because the calendar spread involves two expiry months, it is not possible to construct an accurate payoff diagram for the strategy at expiry of the sold position. The value of the long position can be estimated only by using pricing models.

The trader will make the maximum profit, which is undetermined but is limited, if the price of the underlying is at the strike price of the options at the near-month expiry. The sold call will then become worthless, while the long call will contain the most possible time-value remaining.

The maximum loss is limited to the cost of the spread. Maximum loss will be sustained if the long call has very little time value left at expiry, that is, if the price of the underlying has dramatically risen or fallen at maturity.

Both legs will be in-the-money if the price of the underlying goes up, but the trader will face the possibility of early exercise on the short leg. The long leg acts as a hedge, but the cost and inconvenience of exercising it must be considered. A calendar spread may be damaged by an increase in short term volatility, since this works against the desired fall in value of the sold call option.

TABLE 5.18   Characteristics of a calendar spread

Calendar spread	
Construction	short call X, near expiry long call X, far expiry
Point of entry	market around strike price
Break-even points	undetermined in advance
Maximum profit (at expiry)	undetermined but limited
Maximum loss (at expiry)	limited to cost of spread
Time decay	helps the calendar spread

Source: HKIB

TABLE 5.19 Summary of outcomes of a calendar spread

At maturity of near-month option	Outcome
It is below the strike	The near call expires as worthless and the far option will have a reduced time value
It equals the strike	Maximum profits are achieved. The near option has zero intrinsic value and so expires as worthless. The far month option is at-the-money and so has a high time value
It is above the strike	Both options are in-the-money, but they are set off with each other. The time value of the far option is also low, which may create a loss to the trader

Source: HKIB

If the market remains steady, the trader may do nothing and let time decay take its course. This means the short call will become worthless. The long call can then be closed out or the trader may choose to hold on to it if the expectations going forward are bullish. By retaining the call, the trader in effect converts the calendar spread into a simple taken option position.

What if the price of the underlying falls precipitately? The investor may decide to close the spread before the long call loses all time value. Alternatively, the position could be left alone in case the market recovers and the value of the long call goes up.

If the market rises, the investor must decide whether to close out the spread to avoid exercise or maintain it in the hope that the market retreats and time decay can take effect. Table 5.19 summarises all these possible outcomes.

Collar

A collar, which is also referred to as a fence, is a spread consisting of a long (short) call and a short (long) put, with both options out-of-the-money and sharing the same expiration month. The spread can be designed in such a way that the premium received for writing the call offsets the cost of the put. The spread then becomes a **costless collar**.

Mathematically, a collar can be rendered thus:

$$\text{Collar} = +C_{k2} - P_{k1}, \text{ where } K2 > k1$$

The main objective of buying a collar is to protect the gains already made in the underlying asset. An investor using this spread strategy usually has hefty profits that he does not yet want to realise because he anticipates further rises or has other reasons, while at the same time recognising that it can all fall apart. A collar will protect his gains in case the underlying asset's price deteriorates. If the underlying continues to climb and hits the call strike, he will be able to sell the shares at that higher price.

If the price of the underlying is between the strikes of the call and put at the collar's maturity, the two options will be worthless at expiration. The trader will neither lose nor gain if the spread is a costless collar. If the premium received is higher than the cost of the put, which is possible, the trader will end up with a small profit. Whatever the outcome, the goal of protecting the unrealised gains on the underlying would have been achieved.

To illustrate the use of a collar, let us look at a listed Internet company during the dotcom frenzy in the late 1990s. Before the bubble burst, the owners of a high technology company knew very well that their shares were overpriced. It made sense for them to sell the shares, but they felt the bull market still had some time to run. They could buy a put option to protect their gains in case the bubble bursts, but such a contract was very expensive—counterparties knew what was going on, too.

The solution was to design a collar. The owners decided to buy a put option and sell a call option at two different strikes at a relatively cheap net cost because both were out-of-the-money and the premium received from writing the call offset in part the premium paid for buying the put. In the end, the dotcom bubble burst while the owners still owned the shares, but the put protected their gains.

Hedging with Interest Rate Futures

We discuss two strategies that traders typically use to hedge exposures using interest rate futures: strip hedge and stack hedge.

Strip Hedge

Figure 5.21 shows a strip hedge strategy. A trader takes a series of futures positions in successively longer expirations to hedge a series of exposures. In this strategy, short

FIGURE 5.21 Strip hedge strategy

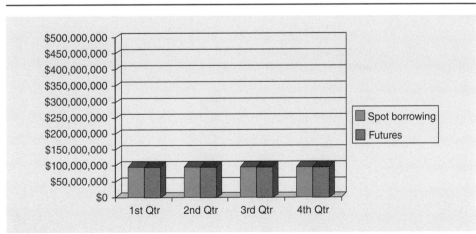

Source: HKIB

date futures are purchased to hedge against the interest rate risk of a portfolio. When the contracts mature, new futures contracts are purchased to replace them, and profits and losses are invested in cash. This process is continued until the horizon date is reached.

Stack Hedge

Figure 5.22 shows a stack hedge strategy, in which a trader enters the futures market and takes a number of positions that can be stacked in the front month and then rolled forward.

For example, a market maker in the FRA market sells a EUR 100 million 3×6 FRA, that is, an agreement to make a notional deposit (without exchange of principal) for three months in three months' time, at a rate of 7.52%. He is exposed to the risk that interest rates may have risen by the time the FRA is settled in three months' time.

- Date: 14 Dec
- 3×6 FRA: 7.52%
- March futures price: 92.50
- Current spot rate: 6.85%

We can calculate the nominal value of a basis point move in LIBOR (basis point value or BPV) on the FRA settlement payment thus:

- $BPV = FRA \times 0.01\% \times N_{3,6} / 360$
- $BPV = USD100mio \times 0.01\% \times 90/360 = 2,500$

FIGURE 5.22 Stack hedge strategy

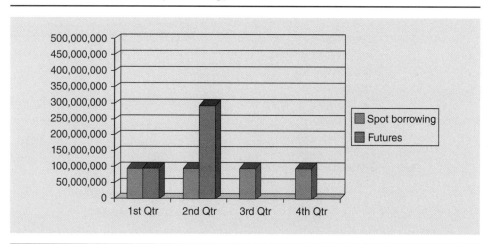

Source: HKIB

FIGURE 5.23 Hedging interest rate risk

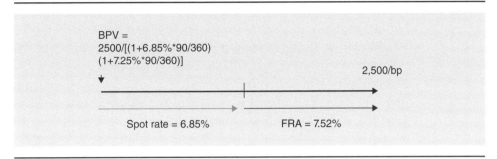

BPV =
2500/[(1+6.85%*90/360)
(1+7.25%*90/360)]

2,500/bp

Spot rate = 6.85%   FRA = 7.52%

Source: HKIB

We can also find present value (PV) by discounting back to the transaction date using the FRA and spot rates, and determine the correct hedge ratio accordingly:

- $PV = BPV/[(1 + SP \times N_{0,3}/360)(1 + FRA \times N_{3,6}/360)]$
- $PV = 2500/[(1 + 6.85\% \times 90/360)(1 + 7.52\% \times 90/360)] = 2,412$
- Hedge ratio $= USD2,412/25 = 96.48$

To hedge the risk of an increase in interest rates, the trader sells 96 EUR three months' futures contracts at 92.50 (see Figure 5.23).

Practical Issues

In sum, there are a number of issues that traders and users need to consider when dealing with interest rate futures. To recapitulate:

- **No counterparty risk.** A margin system is in place so that all traders must place sufficient collaterals with the exchange. Basically, the trader is trading against the exchange, not any individual. If the authority of an exchange knows a trader is taking a huge position or is suspected of having liquidity problems, they will increase the margin requirement of the trader.
- **Imperfect hedge.** Since the contract is standardised, it is impossible to hedge your underlying asset perfectly with a futures contract. As a result, they are all cross-hedges or economic hedges, and the trader is subject to basis risk.
- **Profit and loss.** The futures contract is supposed to result in a cash flow that offsets the underlying asset. However, the profit and loss of the contracts are settled on a daily basis, so it is also impossible to match the underlying asset. For example, the interest on daily profit and loss will make it difficult to determine exactly how much you have hedged.
- **Anonymity.** Some traders are not willing to disclose their identities so they can trade behind the exchange and guard against being examined by others.

- **Cost of margin account.** Since traders must deposit money into the margin account, the cost of maintaining the margin money is part of the transaction cost that must not be forgotten.
- **Tailing effect.** The actual number of contracts a trader needs may be fewer than what the numbers on the surface indicate. Suppose you need to hedge a $500 risk in the future. At first glance, you need 20 contracts to do the hedge. However, the futures you buy will generate a profit or loss as of today. You actually need to hedge less than $500, and as a result, you need fewer contracts to do it.

Summary

- Credit derivatives are financial contracts designed to enable traders and investors to access specific credit-risky investments in synthetic (that is, non-cash) form. They can also be used to hedge credit risk exposure by providing insurance against losses suffered due to credit events.
- Credit risk can be defined as the potential that a bank borrower or counterparty will fail to meet its obligations in accordance with agreed terms. There are two main types of credit risk that a portfolio of assets, or a position in a single asset, is exposed to. These are credit default risk and credit spread risk.
- Interest rate swaps are used to hedge credit risk. They are independent of debt or investments. The aim of an interest rate swap is to exchange interest rate payments over a period of time. By necessity, interest rate swaps are done in the same currency.
- The International Swaps and Derivatives Association (ISDA) is the body that represents participants in the over-the-counter (OTC) derivatives market. One of the most useful services that the ISDA provides is the Master Agreement, widely used around the world as a contract for OTC derivatives trades.
- A money swap, also known as an FX swap, is a pair of foreign currency transactions involving a spot FX deal and an outright deal. The parties agree to a spot deal now and to reverse to the previous position at a future date.
- A forward rate agreement (FRA) is an OTC off-balance sheet derivative, short-term interest rate derivative contract between two parties. Both agree on the interest rate to be paid at a future settlement date.
- A non-deliverable forward is a forward agreement in which an exchange of currency does not actually occur.
- A futures contract is an agreement between a buyer or seller and an exchange clearinghouse to take or make delivery of an underlying asset at a specified price after a time period. A forward is an OTC product whereas a futures contract is traded on an exchange.
- Credit derivatives are financial contracts that allow traders and investors to access specific credit-risky investments in synthetic or non-cash forms. They allow banks to manage credit risk exposure in their portfolios.

- A credit default swap is a contract in which one party (the protection-buyer) agrees to pay a lump sum periodically to another party (the protection-seller) over the life of the agreement, in return for a contingency payment in case a credit event specified in the contract occurs. A total return swap is a contract that involves one party agreeing to swap the total return of a specific reference asset in return for fixed or floating payments from another party. The term "total return" refers to the sum of interest, fees, and any change-in-value payments (positive or negative) with respect to the reference obligation.

- A credit-linked note is a debt instrument that is bundled with an embedded credit derivative, typically a credit default swap. In exchange for a higher yield on the note, investors accept exposure to a specified credit event.

- A collateralised debt obligation is a structured security that is backed by diversified pools of bank loans, high yield corporate bonds, emerging market securities, or mortgage securities. A CDO typically issues several classes of equity and debt, classified into tranches according to seniority in bankruptcy and timing of repayment.

- Regulators require banks to measure the credit exposure of their holdings in credit derivatives through the current exposure method, which entails adding together total replacement costs of all contracts with positive value and an amount for potential future credit exposure. To determine credit exposure for interest rate and foreign exchange related contracts, banks may be allowed to use the original exposure method.

- Banks dealing in derivatives should carry out credit assessments of the counterparties, the underlying assets of the derivatives, and the terms and conditions of the instrument. The prospectus or offer document allows some credit analysis before the instruments are placed on the market. Name recognition and ratings by credit-rating agencies are also used.

- An options contract is a contract in which one party (the option holder) has the right, but not the obligation, to buy or sell an underlying asset at a predetermined price during a specified period of time. The seller of the option, known as the option writer, grants this right to the buyer in return for receiving the price of the option, known as the premium.

- Plain vanilla options are the most well-known and used, but there is a wide variety of exotic options that are custom-designed to meet exceptional and unique needs and circumstances. Vanilla options include call options and put options. Exotic options include binary/digital options, barrier options, and average/Asian options.

- In terms of exercise mode, options can be classified as American, where the holder of the option has the right to exercise it at any time up to the expiration date, European, where the holder has the right to exercise only on the expiration date, and Bermudan, where the buyer has the right to exercise the option on a set number of discretely spaced times.

- Options can have three basic money states: in-the-money, where the strike price is below the market price (call) or above it (put); at-the-money, where the strike price is equal or nearly equal to the market price; and out-of-the-money, where the strike price is higher than the market price (call) or lower (put).

- There are two broad types of trading strategies. Volatility trading is used by traders who expect the volatility of the underlying asset to go higher or lower. Position trading is used when the underlying asset is expected to move in one direction.
- Generic trading strategies include bullish strategies, bearish strategies, and neutral or non-directional strategies. Volatility trading strategies include the long straddle, short straddle, and long butterfly. Spread trading strategies include the bull spread, bear spread, ratio call spread, calendar spread, and collar.
- There are a number of approaches to using interest rate futures as a hedge including the strip hedge and stack hedge.

Key Terms

Add-on	Expected exposure
All to default	First-to-default
Arbitrage CDO	Hedging
Balance sheet CDO	International Swaps and Derivatives
Basket default swap	Association (ISDA)
Cash CDO	Market value structure
Cash flow structure	Master Agreement
Collateralised debt obligation (CDO)	Maximum exposure
Contingency payment	Name recognition
Credit default risk	N-out-of-m-to-default
Credit default swap (CDS)	Nth-to-default
Credit derivative	Original exposure method
Credit exposure	Over-the-counter (OTC)
Credit ratings	Physical delivery
Credit risk	Replacement cost
Credit spread risk	Strike
Credit-linked not (CLN)	Synthetic CDO
Current exposure method	Total return swat (TR swap)

Study Guide

1. Explain why CDOs have been blamed for worsening the 2007–08 Global Financial Crisis. How may the structure, use, and other issues around CDOs be improved to mitigate the risk that they can make the next crisis worse?

2. Under what circumstances is it appropriate for the treasury desk to use credit default swaps instead of total return swaps? What are the differences between these two types of credit derivatives?

3. Under what circumstances is it better for a bank to issue and trade in a credit-linked note rather than a credit default swap? When is a credit-linked note a better option than a total return swap?

4. Distinguish between the use of a CDO for arbitrage and for balance sheet management. Is it possible for the same transactions to serve both the purpose of arbitrage and reducing regulatory and economic capital requirements?

Further Reading

Butler, Cormac. Mastering Value at Risk: A Step-by-Step Guide to Understanding and Applying *VAR*. Financial Times/Prentice Hall, 1999. Print.

Choudhry, Moorad. *Bank Asset and Liability Management: Strategy, Trading, Analysis*. Singapore: John Wiley & Sons (Asia) Pte Ltd, 2007. Print.

Rajendra, Rajiv. *The Handbook of Global Corporate Treasury*. Singapore: John Wiley & Sons (Asia), 2013. Print

Horcher, Karen A. *Essentials of Managing Treasury*. New Jersey: John Wiley & Sons, 2005. Print.

International Swap and Derivatives Association. Home page. Web. 2 May 2013. http://www.isda.org/.

PART 2

TREASURY OPERATIONS

6

Treasury Operations

After studying this chapter, you should be able to:

1 Understand and analyze the roles of the front office, including such activities as proprietary trading and corporate treasury.

2 Describe the importance of the middle office, particularly as it relates to operational risk management and the internal audit function.

3 Explain the role of the back office and its importance, including interbank transfers.

4 Discuss the revaluation of bank assets and liabilities, including those meant for the trading book.

5 Discuss the issues associated with accounting and revaluation of securities.

Introduction

Financial institutions typically have a treasury function with a front office, a middle office and a back office. These are mainly involved in the bank's proprietary and customer-driven trading and the management of risks that emanate from such activities.

But hedging risk is only one part of the operations of the treasury. The front office, for example, has to deal with other banks as much as it has to deals with clients. The middle office, often independent, has a key role to play in operational risk management. The back office, in turn, is integral to the smooth and safe functioning of the bank by managing cash and access.

Front Office

The front office performs the most public and visible operations of any bank or financial institution as it focuses on areas like planning, dealing and trading, investments, risk management, interactions with clients and other banks, and handling accounts.[1]

In broad strokes, the front office is responsible for:

- Initiating and executing transactions;
- Funding operations;
- Investments;

In planning and deciding on cost-effective funding, the front office has to consider market conditions such as the interest rate outlook, yield curve changes, competition, central bank policies, and market demand for credit, as well as internal factors like the ratio between wholesale and retail funding, target credit rating and bank product mix.

The investment and trading process of the front office is managed to maximize returns with minimum cash balances that meet the cash flow needs of clients and at the same time smooth short term liquidity surplus and shortfalls. Investing longer term assets requires consideration of the size and mix of high quality liquid assets to earn a reasonable return and at the same time enabling client trades in the bank's role as market maker, meet contingent funding needs and satisfy the new OTC derivative collateral margining requirement.

Bank Trading Activities

The front office acts as the interface between the bank and the market, including both clients and other banks. One of the most visible roles of the front office is to put in place

---

[1] Rajendra, Rajiv. "The Handbook of Global Corporate Treasury". John Wiley & Sons: Singapore, 2013. Pg. 48.

and execute trades and transfers between banks, whether in fulfillment of client activities or to meet the needs of the bank's own proprietary trading and dealing. As with all other bank activities in Hong Kong, it is the HKMA that regulates interbank trades and transfers.

The front office is often staffed by traders who execute transactions for the bank, as part of its proprietary trading, to optimise cash flows and earn profits, and by dealers who trade based on the needs of the clients. The traders and dealers typically specialise in the following financial instruments:

- Foreign exchange, such as spot, outright contracts, and non-deliverable forward (NDF), although in some banks the swap desks are responsible for outright contracts/NDF;
- Money market products, including loans and deposits, money swaps, forward rate agreements, interest rate swaps, and interest rate futures;
- Debt security instruments, including all kinds of debt securities issued by government or corporate, plain vanilla, and option embedded;
- Financial derivatives/structured products, such as plain vanilla and exotic options of various underlying assets, credit derivative products.

The decisions on the size and the direction of the trade and the resulting exposure and risk for the banks have to be well managed. The prime cautionary tale is Barings, the venerable British bank that collapsed in 1995 because of the activities of Nick Leeson, who was general manager of Barings Securities (Singapore). Leeson was not supposed to trade himself, but he managed to get a license to do so on the Singapore International Monetary Exchange. He became the chief trader and also de facto head of the back office, whose staff he hired and therefore felt some loyalty to him.

On paper, Leeson reported huge profits (and thus was rewarded with lucrative bonuses), but in reality, he was racking up losses that he managed to hide because of his control of the back office. When his deception was discovered, Leeson had open futures and options positions that ultimately cost Barings almost USD1.4 billion, which far exceeded the bank's trading capital. In the end, Barings was sold for a symbolic £1 to Dutch bank ING in return for assuming its liabilities. There are now industry best practices including *The Model Code* and the TMA *Code of Conduct and Practices*, which bank treasury operations are expected to follow.

For the front office, *The Model Code* stipulates that the official recognition of individual dealers' roles and authority must be set out in writing by management so that there is no ambiguity as to the transactions, instruments, markets or trading platform in which the dealer is empowered to trade. Such mandates may include persons authorized to deal, limits on open positions, mismatch positions, counterparties, stop-loss limits etc. Dealers must take a minimum of two consecutive weeks of holiday each year. *The Model Code* also includes do and don't for the front office. For example, when setting the rates for an FX swap to extend the maturity, the spot rate should be fixed immediately within the current spread, to reflect current rates at the time the transaction was done. There should be safeguards in rate setting to ensure there is no manipulation of the rates. Deals at non-market rates should be avoided, as such practices may result in concealment of a profit or loss, in the perpetration of a fraud, tax evasion, or the giving of an unauthorized extension of credit.

Corporate Treasury

Treasury operations in banks involve managing cash, collections, payments, managing investments, and investment concentrations, and trading in instruments like bonds, currencies, derivatives and various issues associated with risk management.

Although the actual structure of the treasury may differ from bank to bank, treasuries are often made up of a fixed income or money markets desk, a foreign exchange desk, a capital markets or equities desk, a proprietary trading desk, an asset liability management desk, and a transfer pricing or pooling function.

The role of the corporate treasury within a bank is not totally dissimilar from that of a treasury department in other major corporations, although banks often have to deal with greater regulatory oversight and the corporate treasury is a key interface in the relationship between regulators and the bank or financial institution. Overall, the corporate treasury, which is part of the front office of a bank's larger treasury function, has to deal with any or all of the following external parties:

- **Regulators:** The heavily regulated nature of the business of banking requires that the treasury department interface with various regulators. In Hong Kong, this includes a number of bodies with the HKMA at the top of the list. The corporate treasury is directly responsible for the movement of money and market participation due to its management of investments, risk, foreign currency, trade flows, collections, and payments.
- **Exchanges:** Most banks are listed on exchanges, so not only do treasuries have to deal with exchanges as a result of trading activities—both on behalf of clients and of a proprietary nature—but also due to the fact that the shares of the bank or financial institution may be publicly traded.
- **Banks:** The corporate treasury is also a point of contact for other banks and companies that the bank may have to deal with. The treasury implements a number of operational aspects of the bank, which includes dealing with geographical, operational, funding, trade, hedging, markets, and operational factors.
- **Rating agencies:** The corporate treasury is also responsible for the credit rating of the firm and of the various products that the firm may issue, such as bonds or derivatives.
- **Other institutions:** It is up to the treasury to deal with a variety of other institutions, such as banks or groups, that play a role in financing products or providing services to customers.

- **Technology firms:** The modern bank relies heavily on technology. From account management to trading and the settlement of trades on electronic exchanges, technology is central to the smooth functioning of a bank. The treasury often deals with technology firms that provide services ranging from risk engines to forecasting technologies and reporting tools.
- **Service providers:** As some of the treasury's operations can be outsourced, the corporate treasury also has to deal with a number of outside service providers.

Middle Office

Banks developed the concept of the middle office, which works closely with the front and back office but reports independently and provides a check to the operations of the other two.[2] The focus of the middle office is control, valuation, and reconciliation of the operations of the front and back office. The middle office evaluates performance, validates models, generates risk reports, and monitors limits. In this regard, the middle office has oversight over both the front and back office operations thanks to its reporting and control responsibilities, which are typically independent.

To ensure its independence, the middle office typically reports directly to the treasurer, the chief financial officer, or the head of risk. The middle office is typically responsible for:

- Controls;
- Valuations;
- Reconciliation of trades;
- Performance evaluations;
- Model validation;
- Monitoring risk;
- Monitoring limits.

The Model Code provides middle office best practices on risk control procedures such as trade surveillance and internal review, as well as how to deal with crisis situation, reconciliations, and mark-to-market best practices. On the role of investment banks as prime-brokers for hedge funds, *The Model Code* has guidance on reputational risks, operational risks, credit risks, post-trade event risks, and how to handle disputes and confidentiality. The middle office is something of an anomaly that exists predominantly in banks. Corporate treasury, risk management, and strategic management all might be part of middle office operations, for example.

---

[2] Rajiv Rajendra; "The Handbook of Global Corporate Treasury"; Singapore; John Wiley & Sons, 2013.

Treasury Accounting

One of the more important roles of the middle office of the treasury function in banks and financial institutions is the application of treasury accounting in the valuation and revaluation of financial assets and liabilities, based on applicable accounting standards. In Hong Kong, accounting and financial reporting is done on the basis of the Hong Kong Financial Reporting Standards (HKFRSs), which includes both standards and interpretations developed by the Financial Accounting Standards Committee of the Hong Kong Institute of Certified Public Accountants (HKICPA).[3]

In general, HKFRS is identical to the international equivalents known as the International Financial Reporting Standards (IFRS), developed by the IFRS Foundation and the International Accounting Standards Board (IASB), a linked organization.

One of the more relevant standards for the treasury operations is HKAS 39 on "Financial Instruments: Recognition and Measurement." The standard took effect on January 1, 2005. HKAS 39 "establishes principles for recognizing and measuring financial assets and financial liabilities and provides additional guidance on selected matters such as derecognition, when financial assets and financial liabilities may be measured at fair value, how to assess impairment, how to determine fair value and some aspects of hedge accounting."[4]

HKAS 39 will be replaced by HKFRS 9 "Financial Instruments" but no earlier than 2017. The key changes related to bank treasury are the elimination of the "Available for Sale" category to classify financial assets, more principle-based applications of hedge accounting and permitting the use of "macro hedging" in management of aggregated risks.

Risk Management

The Nick Leeson affair[5] at Barings Bank underlined the importance of segregation of duties. A good checks and balances system must be put in place. Without unduly holding back the activities of the front office, other treasury units must effectively monitor all trading and hedging positions, processes, and other control areas, to ensure full compliance with the bank's policies and regulatory requirements.

The middle office is staffed by operations managers, risk managers, product specialists, and compliance officers. Among its responsibilities are:

- Risk management, including modelling of risks associated with the derivatives positions the front office is taking, and tracking its compliance with approved trading, counter-parties, financial instruments, and other limits.

---

[3] Hong Kong Institute of Certified Public Accountants.
[4] HKAS 39, Par IN3, p. 6.
[5] Nick Leeson carried out a series of unauthorized and fraudulent trades that resulted in losses of GBP827 million for Barings Bank. The losses led to the downfall of the bank, the oldest in the UK.

- Analytical support, such as industry and company-specific research, technical analysis of market trends, and creating, testing, and modifying new financial products for front-office trading.
- Management and regulatory reporting, including analysing income from and costs of each trading desk financial instrument traded, and reporting financial information to the bank unit responsible for submitting reports to external regulators.

These days, the functions of the middle office also include the following:

- Ensuring compliance with trading limits, including the position, stop loss, or value at risk limit of the traders, department, or any risk-taking business units.
- Monitoring compliance with trading procedures, including the operational procedure of trading, sale of products to clients, and anything related to the procedures of the dealing room.
- Determining the appropriate models, data, and anything related to mark-to-market or mark-to-model revaluation of the financial products.

Regulatory Compliance

Ensuring regulatory compliance is a key function of the middle office. Considering that banking is a heavily regulated industry, this role takes particular significance. Regulations cover just about every aspect of the business, from the opening of individual accounts by customers to trading and the amount of capital banks must hold in reserve. Regulatory breaches can generate significant risks for a bank and expose it to financial loses, reputational loses, fines, and other risks. Contracts may be invalidated. Customers may walk away or regulators decide to exercise even greater oversight over day-to-day operations. By ensuring regulatory compliance, the middle office is key to limiting these operational risks.

Different functions within the bank have to deal with different regulatory requirements but it is often important to ensure compliance with all of them. One useful tool, explored in greater depth in *Operational Risk Management*, another volume in this series, is the use of a heat map. A heat map provides a detailed outlook of the different operations within the bank and covers a number of variables such as performance, maturity of process and units, interconnectedness of the different units, the strength of processes in place, and the governance and compliance requirements of each unit. The focus on operational risk management, and on regulatory compliance as part of this effort, is unique to the middle office.

There are quite a number of regulatory issues that the middle office has to be aware of and track. Following the Global Financial Crisis, regulations have become even more stringent and regulators less lenient with oversight, whether as a result of weak processes, human error, or negligence.

In the United States, for example, a number of new regulations were introduced throughout the first decade of the century, which drastically impact operations.

Perhaps the most famous example is the Sarbanes-Oxley Act of 2002, officially known as the Public Company Accounting and Investor Protection Act of 2002. This piece of legislation affects all listed companies, not just banks, but banks have to be particularly aware of any potential breaches due to the wide-ranging nature of its operations. At times, new laws and regulations have impact across borders. The U.S. Bank Secrecy Act, the Patriot Act, and anti-money laundering regulations all can generate risks for banks that operational risk managers should monitor carefully, to avoid significant penalties and fines.

In Hong Kong, the HKMA is the regulator and the overarching piece of legislation is the Banking Ordinance. Increasingly, bank regulation internationally and in Hong Kong, is concerned with operational risk, which includes legal risk. The HKMA defines operational risk as "the risk of loss resulting from inadequate or failed internal processes, people and systems or from external events."[6] A key function of the middle office is operational risk management, and regulatory compliance falls clearly within its scope.

The Banking Ordinance[7] also requires banks and other AIs to operate with "integrity, prudence, competence and in a manner which is not detrimental to the interests of depositors or potential investors." This is a wide-ranging mandate that requires those in charge of regulatory compliance to be at the top of their game. Failures to comply can emerge, for example, for poor legal documentation. Given that banks generate enormous amount of paperwork and documentation, ensuring that all of it complies with existing regulations is a significant task. The HKMA provides some guidance regarding what banks should do when reviewing their documentation, including making sure it complies with all regulatory and legal requirements, that it uses standard and non-standard terms, that the communication is done through multiple channels, and ensuring confirmation of acceptance of terms from customers.

Changes to the legal system or code of a country can also prove expensive for the bank and result in failures in regulatory compliance.[8] The advent of a slew of new regulations to deal with the perceived failures of the financial industry in the past two decades (particularly since 2008) have led to a series of such risks.

---

[6] Hong Kong Monetary Authority, *Supervisory Policy Manual: Operational Risk Management*; 28 November 2005. Pg. 3.

[7] The entire text of the Banking Ordinance is available through the Hong Kong government website here: http://www.legislation.gov.hk/blis_pdf.nsf/6799165D2FEE3FA94825755E0033E532/5A827AA51F4 96D08482575EE004568 BC/$FILE/CAP_155_e_b5.pdfhttp://www.legislation.gov.hk/blis_pdf.nsf/ 6799165D2FEE3FA94825755E0033E532/5A827AA51F496D08482575EE004568 BC/$FILE/ CAP_155_e_b5.pdf.

[8] Anna S. Chernobai, Svetlozar T. Rachev, Frank J. Fabozzi, *Operational Risk: A Guide to Basel II Capital Requirements, Models, and Analysis* (New Jersey: John Wiley & Sons, Inc., 2007).

To facilitate this process of compliance, the HKMA has issued a *Supervisory Policy Manual*, which is regularly updated.[9] The manual includes the supervisory policies and practices along with minimum standards that banks and AIs are expected to attain and maintain, to meet the requirements of the Banking Ordinance and best practices. The manual is not, however, the letter of the law. Rather, it is a reference document that helps AIs, auditors, advisors, and supervisory staff. What's more, the Banking Ordinance is much more wide ranging in scope. To ensure regulatory compliance, says the HKMA, "(t)here is no substitute for AIs continuing to consult the relevant laws of Hong Kong and taking appropriate legal advice to ensure compliance with the standards expected of them."[10]

Even though it is not law, the Supervisory Policy Manual is a useful guideline for banks and financial institutions. One section of the manual relevant to the issue of compliance considers the link between treasury accounting and fair value considerations. The HKMA reviews fair value disclosures and the policies of financial institutions that ensure that those disclosures are both adequate and fair. The HKMA requires that these policies be consistent with the institution's approach to risk management. It also expects a balance between qualitative and quantitative information so that the overall risk profile is balanced.[11]

Internal Audit

Another important role of the middle office, one that is particularly significant to banks, is to carry out internal audits. Internal audits are important to control operations and limit risk while ensuring that the bank's operations conform with any operational risk framework in place.[12]

The HKMA's *Supervisory Manual* devotes a section to the internal audit function of banks or financial institutions.[13] The Banking Ordinance requires AIs to maintain adequate control systems and an internal audit function is key to this end, as it provides both the

---

[9] The Supervisory Policy Manual is available online at http://www.hkma.gov.hk/eng/key-functions/banking-stability/supervisory-policy-manual.shtml.

[10] HKMA. "Supervisory Policy Manual: Introduction". 19 January 2001. Online. Accessed in May 2013 at http://www.hkma.gov.hk/media/eng/doc/key-functions/banking-stability/supervisory-policy-manual/IN.pdf.

[11] HKMA. "Supervisory Policy Manual: Fair Value Practices". CA-S-10. 10 December 2013.

[12] For more information on operational risk frameworks see "Operational Risk Management", another volume in this series.

[13] HKMA. "Supervisory Policy Manual: Internal Audit Function". 14 July 2009. Online at http://www.hkma.gov.hk/media/eng/doc/key-functions/banking-stability/supervisory-policy-manual/IC-2.pdf.

board of directors and senior management with an independent and objective evaluation of the state of affairs within the bank or institution on a regular basis. Ideally, internal audits are carried out by an independent internal audit function (IAF). This function is typically part of the middle office, which is uniquely positioned to carry out effective supervision of both front and back office functions.

The responsibilities of this function include assessing:

- Compliance with internal policies, risk management controls, laws, regulations, and supervisory guidelines;
- The reliability and timeliness of financial and management information;
- The continuity and reliability of management and financial information systems;
- The accuracy of accounting records and financial reports;
- The efficiency of operations; and
- The effectiveness of systems and processes for risk management and control.

The ideal internal audit function meets a number of criteria that the HKMA's Supervisory Manual outlines.

The first is independence from day-to-day operations and functional units. The IAF should report directly to the Board, independent of the bank management through its Audit Committee. However, the workings of the IAF should be subject to independent review, mostly likely by an outside party.

The second is authority and standing. The IAF can hardly be expected to do its job if it does not have the recognition of the board and senior management. Banks and other financial institutions should have an audit charter that enhances the authority of the IAF and sets out its objectives and scope, position within the organization, powers, responsibilities, relations to other control functions, accountability, and terms and conditions under which it operates. The IAF should be able to communicate directly with the board as it sees fit.

The third set of criteria includes objectivity and impartiality. The IAF must avoid conflicts of interest at all costs, although it may provide consulting services to other functions from time to time.

Fourth, the IAF should have both the resources and professional competence to do its job. Enough planning and budget should be allocated for professional development and staff within the IAF; staff should have the right qualifications and technical proficiency, skills, and knowledge of the business to do their jobs.

Finally, the IAF should have continuity. The IAF should be a permanent function of banks and other AIs in Hong Kong and adequate documentation is necessary, to ensure the function continues to operate unimpeded should staff leave. There should be a written track record of all work and the HKMA should be informed of who the head of the IAF is and if that person changes.

The process of internal auditing is clearly outlined in the Supervisory Manual. Its ultimate goal is two-fold: accountability and transparency. Both of these are ensured through structured and well-defined processes with clear stages of work.

Back Office

The treasury operation of a bank is usually referred to as the back office and it has a range of responsibilities including processing, settling, and confirming transactions, and ensuring operations are reconciled and recorded. Ideally, the back office should provide independent reports.

The operations of the back office include[14]:

- Processing transactions;
- Confirmation of transactions;
- Settlement of transactions;
- Reconciliation;
- Accounting entries.

The back office is the least visible of the three offices. In general, the back office includes departments such as information technology (IT) operations and accounting—functions that are often associated with support or processing. This does not mean that the way the back office operates is in any way less important than the front or middle office. Hong Kong's Treasury Markets Association (TMA) points out in its Code of Conduct, a voluntary code, that the "independent checking and confirmation of transactions by back office is a powerful defense against erroneous and even fraudulent trades." In fact, the TMA dedicates an entire section to the back office, covering both the types of transactions it does and how it should do them. In the Code of Conduct, the TMA also includes confirmation procedures for transactions and deal amendments and cancellations as key operations of the back office.

Cash Management

One important function of the back office is cash management, which includes liquidity risk management. This includes, on the one hand, the forecasting, control, and oversight of the financial assets and liabilities of an organization. On the other, cash management also includes the protections of financial assets against fraud, error, or loss.[15] Although it is often easy for outsiders to overlook or underestimate the role of the back office, this particular responsibility makes the back office a key component of the treasury management of a bank or financial institution.

Effective cash management includes accurately forecasting the timing and amount of cash flows and making provisions (often under regulatory pressure) to pre-empt liquidity risk, controlling disbursements and ensuring collections are speedy, limiting losses due

---

[14] Rajendra, Rajiv. "The Handbook of Global Corporate Treasury". Singapore; John Wiley & Sons, 2013.
[15] Horcher, Karen. "Essentials of Managing Treasury". New Jersey. John Wiley & Sons. 2006. Print. P 15.

to fraud or error, ensuring enough funds are in hand to avoid short-falls of liquidity, and investing excess cash to minimize risk and maximize returns while ensuring liquidity.

The HKMA has issued statutory guidelines on liquidity risk management that take into account international standards and practices. On the one hand, banks are required to meet capital adequacy standards set by the BCBS. The current set of standards, known as Basel III, are being implemented in Hong Kong in stages.[16]

In most businesses, cash flow management is a relatively internal matter—although the very survival of the business may depend on how effectively it is done. Banks, on the other hand, often deal with deposit money from the general public. Any whisper of a failure to adequately manage cash flows could lead to a dangerous bank run. As a result, the HKMA supervises both cash flow management approaches and the management of liquidity risk.

Banks and other financial institutions in Hong Kong are required to submit management reports that cover cash-flow analysis in normal business conditions, and cash-flow analysis and stressed liquidity reports "for individual currencies in which an AI has significant positions."[17]

Managing cash flow can be challenging in most corporations but banks have to deal with added variables including non-performing loans, bad debt charges, changes in interest rates, the credit ratings of both the institution and clients, and more. As the HKMA points out, many bank failures have been caused by a combination of credit and liquidity issues.

There are multiple approaches to forecasting cash flow. The more common ones include:

- **Scheduling:** In simple terms, maintaining a schedule of expected cash inflows and outflows.
- **Distribution:** More frequently used for items like cheque clearings, distribution forecasts a number of different cash flow items when put together. Although the individual value of each item is hard to forecast, their combined value may be more range-bound.
- **Statistical analysis:** There are a number of approaches to using statistical analysis to forecast cash flows. Simple regression, for example, can be used to create a formula that makes links between a particular event and the resultant cash flows. Multiple regression analysis is also likely to be useful as it can be used to consider several events and the impact on cash flow.

Payment and Settlement Processing

With the advent of electronic and straight-through trading and processing, the inputting part is now often done at the front office, with the trader inputting orders that the

---

[16] For more on Basel III see "Operational Risk Management."

[17] HKMA. Supervisory Policy Manual: Liquidity Risk Management. 1 April 2011. Par 6.5.3. Online.

trading platform automatically captures, checks for technical correctness, and confirms in real time.

These days, the functions of the back office include the following:

- Completing transactions, including examining the transactions that have been inputted into the system to check what else needs to be done to complete them. Some trades may require settlement instructions such as SSI (Standard Settlement Instructions), for example. The ACI Model Code provides industry best practices for settlements that covers continuous linked settlements (CLS) for forex trading, payments straight through processing (STP), compliance with Anti-Money Laundering (AML) and Combating Financing of Terrorism (CFT) laws in release of third party payments and more.
- The most important role of the back office is to verify the correctness of the transactions of traders against confirmation from the money broker or any other third parties independently. For foreign exchange and money market deals, this is usually done through Reuters, BARX, SWIFT, and other electronic trading and information systems. More sophisticated products like financial futures are matched online with the relevant exchange or regulatory body within the prescribed period. The ACI Model Code stipulates that back office broker trade confirmation should be received within two hours of a trade.
- After it is satisfied with the correctness of the trade, the back office authorises payment within the prescribed period. It also tracks payments to the bank by counterparties.
- The back office also takes care of several reconciliation processes, among them squaring of overnight positions with the bank's own accounts and brokerage accounts, margin calls, and custody accounts in securities trading. It then investigates and reconciles unmatched items.

Reconciliation

While forecasts can be used to minimize risk, the treasury function is also responsible for reconciliations at the end of every business days. The electronic payment processing systems that we considered in the previous chapter make this process much easier but the pressure for banks is greater, as there is little leeway as to when the reconciliation will be done. Another factor to consider is that there are also likely to be international transactions that have to be reconciled outside of regular business hours. On a daily basis, banks have to reconcile the operations of various functions such as trading, liquidity positions, and cash accounts.

The upside of daily and accurate reconciliation is that it can help minimize both errors and fraud. In broad strokes, the process of reconciliation starts with the expected position at the end of the previous reconciliation period (depending on what is being reconciled this can range widely from the previous day to the previous two hours). Then data for balances and float values for the period are added. In most cases, there will be some automated reconciliation done, so unmatched transactions have to be reconciled before reconciling actual to forecast transactions. The resulting cash position should match the closing position reported. Whenever a float is provided, the value of the float should be updated. Items that did not happen should be placed back in the forecast.

When dealing with hundreds of thousands or millions of transactions per day, this process is often layered and heavily dependent on technology. Nevertheless, understanding the basic mechanics can help prevent risk and better manage cash flows in each function, within each business unit of the bank.

Operations Process Control

The question of who does what and when should not be a question at all. From Barings Bank to Société Générale,[18] there are far too many case studies of banks that floundered or lost billions of dollars as a result of weak operations process controls. This is an area that is handled by the back office and is part of the operational risk management approach of the bank.

Usually it is up to the back office to grant and monitor access rights to accounts and trading duties. Access rights are often set by a clear delineation of responsibility that is well documented and typically rise with increased responsibility.

The concept of access rights is often associated with IT management, which grants a certain level of access to each user of the system within the bank. This is a large part of access rights, although this modern system of access is loosely based on the more traditional notion of access to specific information. In other words, who should have access to what?

Two issues come into play. One is privacy. There are clearly set rules about what customer information bank staff can access or divulge, even to spouses or business partners. Another is risk management. The wrong level of access to the wrong staff can expose the bank to a number of operational risks, from regulatory risks to actual fraud.

The back office also grants and monitors authorization levels. Traders, for example, are typically authorized to trade up to a certain amount and often require the countersignature of supervisors. Desks likely have their own limits as do divisions and so on. Checks and balances are usually put in place to make sure authorization levels are not exceeded and these checks are usually within the back office functions.

Basel rules pay particular attention to the importance of "strong control environments" in banks and financial institutions to better deal with risk. They note that banks "should have a strong control environment that utilizes policies, processes and systems; appropriate internal controls; and appropriate risk mitigation and/or transfer strategies."

---

[18] The French bank lost as much as EUR4.9 billion in 2007 and 2008 as a result of trades done by a single trader, Jérôme Kerviel, who exceeded almost every limit placed on him with virtually no oversight.

The HKMA, in its own *Supervisory Policy Manual for Operational Risk Management,* deals with risk control and mitigation in this regard, making it clear that AIs should have policies, processes, and procedures to control and mitigate risk and "documented" internal policies.[19] These policies should be developed so that they can adapt to the growth of the bank, changes in business activitie, or new developments in the market. This can be particularly important for Hong Kong banks, many of which are either developing new operations in Mainland China or are expanding their operations there.

A strong internal control system that includes authorization levels is key because, when well designed and enforced it can help protect the resources of an institution and improve compliance with existing rules and regulations. At the same time, says the HKMA, "sound internal controls will also reduce the possibility of significant human errors and irregularities in internal processes and systems, and will assist in their timely detection when they occur."

Finally, the back office is also responsible for rectifying errors or reversing transactions that may have already been processed. It is important that this function be independent of the traders. One way Jérôme Kerviel managed to avoid detection of his activities at SocGen for more than a year was by reversing transactions and taking them off the books, even after they had happened.

Summary

- The front office is responsible for planning, decision making, initiating and executing transactions, funding operations, investments, risk management, and interfacing with stakeholders.
- Interbank transfers are a responsibility of the front office. This includes executing trades between banks, to fulfill client mandates or on behalf of the bank's own positioning. Interbank transfers in Hong Kong can be denominated in HKD, EUR, RMB, and USD, and run through a series of Real Time Gross Settlement (RTGS) systems operated by the Hong Kong Interbank Clearing Limited (HKICL). There are RTGS systems for each of the four currencies. The systems are also known as the Clearing House Automated Transfer System (CHATS).
- The front office is also responsible for proprietary trading. This is done by traders and dealers who specialize in foreign exchange, money market products, debt security instruments, and financial derivatives.
- The corporate treasury focuses on maximizing the holdings of the bank or financial institution by maximizing liquidity and minimizing risk. Banks typically have entire

---

[19] Hong Kong Monetary Authority; "Supervisory Policy Manual: Operational Risk Management"; November 2005; Pg. 24 – Section 7.4.

departments dedicated to treasury management. The structure can vary but there are typically desks focused on fixed income or money markets, foreign exchange, capital markets or equities, and a proprietary trading desk. The corporate treasury has to deal with regulators, exchanges, other banks, rating agencies, other institutions, technology firms, and service providers.

- In regards to treasury management, the middle office typically deals with controls, valuations, reconciliation of trades, performance evaluations, model validation, monitoring risk, and monitoring limits.

- The Hong Kong Financial Reporting Standards (HKFRS) provide direction on how to deal with issues of accounting and finance. This includes the valuation and revaluation of assets. The HKFRS were developed on the basis of the International Financial Reporting Standards (IFRS).

- In general, the difference between HKFRS and IFRS are small. One exception is that of HKAS 39, which deals with the recognition and measurement of financial instruments. The Hong Kong version does not allow for its retrospective application.

- A key function of the middle office is ensuring regulatory compliance. Relatively high oversight make this a more predictable but demanding function.

- The middle office is also responsible for internal audits, which are typically driven by an independent internal audit function (IAF). The IAF has five key attributes: independence, authority and standing, objectivity and impartiality, resources and competence, and continuity.

- The back office is responsible for processing transactions, confirming transactions, settlement of transactions, reconciliation, and accounting entries.

- Cash management includes forecasting and controlling the financial assets of the institution while putting in place protections against fraud, errors, or loss.

- The back office also processes payments and settlements, including completing transactions, verifying their accuracy, granting authorization for payments, and reconciling processes.

- The importance of strong processes is outlined in the Basel accords, issued by the Basel Committee on Banking Supervision, which link "strong control environments" to effective operational risk management.

Key Terms

Back office	Corporate treasury
Banking Ordinance	Debt security instruments
Basel Accords	Exchange Fund Ordinance
Cash management	Financial derivatives
Clearing House Automated Transfer System (CHATS)	Foreign exchange
	Front office

Hong Kong Financial Reporting Standards (HKFRS)

Hong Kong Interbank Clearing Limited (HKICL)

Hong Kong Monetary Authority (HKMA)

Interbank transfers

Internal audit

Internal audit function (IAF)

International Financial Reporting Standards (IFRS)

Jérôme Kerviel

Middle office

Money market products

Monitoring

Operational risk

Proprietary trading

Real Time Gross Settlement (RTGS)

Reconcilement

Regulatory compliance

Risk management

Société Générale

Supervisory Policy Manual

Study Guide

1. Hong Kong Accounting Standard (HKAS) 39, part of the Hong Kong Financial Reporting Standards, differs from its equivalent on the International Financial Reporting Standards (IFRS) on one key feature. What is it? Why is this significant?
2. Explain the key features of an Internal Audit Function (IAF). Why is the IAF important? Where does it fit within the treasury and the bank or financial institution? Does the regulator in Hong Kong offer any insight into how to structure it and what its responsibilities are?
3. Explain what cash management is. How is it related to liquidity risk? What guidelines has the HKMA put in place that deal with both?

Further Reading

HKAS 39 at http://app1.hkicpa.org.hk/hksaebk/HKSA_Members_Handbook_Master/volumeII/hkas39.pdf.

> http://www.hkma.gov.hk/eng/key-functions/banking-stability/supervisory-policy-manual.shtml.

Banking Ordinance: http://www.legislation.gov.hk/blis_pdf.nsf/6799165D2FEE3FA9 4825755E0033E532/5A827AA51F496D08482575EE004568 BC/$FILE/ CAP_155_e_b5.pdf.

7

Market Risk and Other Risk Measures

After studying this chapter, you should be able to:

1 Explain the concepts of country risk, counter-party risk, market risk, and settlement credit risk.

2 Understand how mark-to-market, value-at-risk (VaR), and basis point value can be used to calculate market risk.

3 Discuss how an AI can best manage financial risks.

Introduction

For banks and other financial institutions, risk is an inherent potential, while conducting business, often resulting from losses or fluctuations in future income that are triggered by events or ongoing trends. Assessing and managing market risk is an important function of the treasury. Since risks are myriad, this can be a complex undertaking and one that should not be taken lightly. However, it is important to remember that risk is not the same as loss. A risk factor may never turn into a risk event. Risk assessment should not be paralyzing but empowering. The aim of risk management is to accomplish goals in the most effective manner possible. If the goal is more certainty in revenues, lower risk exposures may be called for. If the goal is faster growth, an institution may decide to take on more risk.

This chapter examines various facets of market risk, starting with some discussion of the considerations of risk that the treasury should undertake and brief discussions of country risk and market risk. The HKMA defines market risk as the "risk to an AI's financial condition resulting from adverse movements in market rates or prices such as foreign exchange rates, commodity or equity prices."

We then consider how to assess value-at-risk (VaR) and discuss basis point value and how to hedge market risk before discussing counterparty risk, issues of mark-to-market, operational risk, and payment and settlement risk. Finally, we spend some time considering how best to manage financial risk.

Risk Considerations

There is no shortage of risk considerations for the treasury function of any bank or financial institution. Every activity carries its own level of risk. Identifying risk, assessing it and putting processes in place to minimize exposures and unexpected impacts are key roles of the treasury. Risk assessment is a way to determine priorities and risk controls for an organization. The list of potential risk areas is quite large. For example, the treasury function has to consider interest rate risk on an almost daily basis but this particular risk can then be subdivided into more specific risks such as those associated with the absolute interest rate, yield curve, reinvestment or refunding, or embedded options. Another example of such subdivisions of risk can be found with foreign exchange that can be linked to transaction risk, translation risk, and strategic risk.[1]

Here we will focus on five broad risk areas: country risk, market risk, counterparty risk, operational risk and payment and settlement risk. But this discussion is merely a start. In depth discussions of each risk, and methods to tackle them can be found elsewhere in this book and in other volumes in this series.[2] It is important, however, to consider these

---

[1] Horcher, Karen. "Essentials of Managing Treasury". New Jersey. John Wiley & Sons. 2006. Print. P 138.
[2] "Operational Risk Management", another title in this series, explores risk exposures and controls in greater details.

risks in any discussion of treasury management. Not considering them can expose the bank to losses or liabilities that can be prevented with some planning.

Although there are several different kinds of risk, three factors are worth considering. The first is that risk refers to uncertainty and not necessarily losses. A risk factor may turn into a loss event or it may not. An unexpected windfall is, by definition, also a risk. The idea behind managing risk is to try to predict it and, should a risk turn into an actual event, minimize any losses. A second factor is that perceived risks are not always actual risks. A perceived risk can be intellectually contemplated and dealt with. An actual risk may freeze an organization from taking action. When taking an airplane, for example, the actual risk is the uncertainty of surviving the trip but the perceived risk is flying. A third factor is that managing risk is not necessarily about lowering it. Managing risk is about identifying risk and reaching a state in which the goals of the organization can be reached. If higher revenues are the objective, raising the level of risk may be one way of achieving it. If the goal is greater certainty, lowering risk may help. Sometimes, managing risk requires raising the level of risk to meet an objective.[3]

In managing risk, the bank has to set up a risk management organization and risk management processes that can deal with all types of risk factors. This module covers the types of risks facing a treasury operation, and how to measure such risks, and provides tools to understand how to hedge and manage different kinds of risks. The *Bank Asset and Liability Management* book in this series, covers other risk related topics including risk tolerance, risk base capital planning under Basel rules, and risk budgeting.

Country Risk

One risk that should be at the top of the list for banks in Hong Kong, which are prone to operate across borders, is country risk. Country risk can create a significant exposure for banks and financial institutions. The nature of country risk and how it develops into various forms of market risk should be well understood by the treasury operation.

Country risk is the amount of exposure an institution has to developments in a particular country, including the rules and discretion of that country's government and regulators. These changes can impact both the operational and transactional environments. Country risk includes legal, regulatory, political, economic, and business risks and can have a particularly significant impact on deals across borders and the international flow of funds. Country risk has become increasingly important as more complex legislation covering everything from competition to corruption has emerged around the world. Increasingly, for example, national laws such as pieces of legislation to tackle corruption in any one country can affect the operations of a bank or financial institution in another country.

---

[3] Rajendra, Rajiv. "The Handbook of Global Corporate Treasury". John Wiley & Sons: Singapore, 2013.

As with other types of risk, the HKMA offers guidance on how to deal with country risk in its *Supervisory Policy Manual*. The Hong Kong regulator says country risk is the primary factor differentiating international and domestic lending and "encompasses all uncertainties that arise from the economic, social, and political conditions of a country that may cause borrowers in that country to be unable or unwilling to fulfill their external obligations."[4]

The different types of country risk include:

- **Sovereign risk:** Which refers to the capacity or willingness of a foreign government to repay direct and indirect foreign currency obligations.
- **Transfer risk:** It emerges when a borrower is not able to access the foreign exchange necessary to service its debt. This type of risk was particularly visible during the Asian Financial Crisis of 1997. Further afield, it could be seen in Argentina during its own crisis in 2001.
- **Contagion risk:** Contagion risk can be seen when negative developments in one country can lead to a downgrade in a credit rating or a credit squeeze in neighboring countries or countries with deep ties. Contagion risk was a primary concern during the European debt crisis through 2011 and 2012.
- **Currency risk:** Is the risk that the domestic currency holdings or cash flow is not enough to pay for obligations in foreign currency. For example, if a loan is denominated in dollars but made to an entity that earns revenues in a domestic currency and that domestic currency drops in value against the dollar, it would be more difficult for the borrower to pay back its USD-denominated debt.
- **Indirect country risk:** It emerges when weakening economic conditions in a country impact the ability of a borrower to pay back a loan or meet other obligations, such as a foreign currency or interest rate swap.
- **Macroeconomic risk:** This type of risk is particularly significant at times of high inflation or when interest rates are rising, as it refers to the ability of a borrower to meet its obligations amidst a challenging macroeconomic environment.

Banks and financial institutions need to have clearly defined policies to deal with country risk. What's more, they should review their policies and operations in foreign countries on a regular basis to address any changes to country risk environments. When assessing country risk, organizations should consider both the size and scope of its activities as well as the profile of any customer or counterparty. Factors such as the quality of policy-making come into play along with social, political, and institutional stability and the quality of the legal and regulatory environment of a country.

Country risk can originate from a cross border loan in the banking book. It can also result from the trading book taking exposure from assets in foreign countries. During the Global Financial Crisis, domestic banks investing in U.S. collateral debt obligation

---

[4] HKMA. "Supervisory Policy Manual: Country Risk Management". 23 November 2011. P 2.

products incurred realized and unrealized losses due to such cross border exposure. Treasury holdings of bonds issued by European banks were impacted by the euro crisis in 2011. Therefore, market risk and country risk are closely related.

Market Risk

The HKMA defines market risk as the risk to the financial condition of an authorized institution (AI) resulting from adverse movements in market rates or prices, including foreign exchange rates, and commodity or equity prices.[5] A key factor is the volatility of a particular market because of the financial instruments traded on it or the quality of regulations, oversight, and market players. Risk may be less difficult to assess in developing or frontier markets.

In assessing inherent market risk, a bank has to consider the interaction between market volatility and business strategy, says the HKMA. For example, a trading strategy that focuses on intermediation between end-users could result in less market risk than a proprietary strategy.

The Basel accords recognize different forms of market risk,[6] from changes in equity prices, to interest rate risk related to fixed-income instruments, currency risk, and commodities price risk. The financial instruments we have discussed in the previous chapters, such as bonds, forward rate agreements, futures and options, swaps, and credit derivatives, all expose the bank to market risk.

AIs in Hong Kong and indeed around the world are required to maintain adequate capital to protect against market risk. According to the guidelines of the 2004 Basel II Accord and the updated rules of the 2011 Basel III accords, introduced to Hong Kong in stages from Jan. 1, 2013, banks have certain limits for various pools of capital and capital charges that must be met under the various categories of risk. There are different approaches to calculate the risk and capital ratios. The amendments introduced through the BAR 2013 have been adequately met by the capital positions of the various banks, most of which had already been working towards implementing Basel III requirements ahead of its introduction in Hong Kong.

In the standardised approach, the amount of capital to be set aside is calculated using the additive approach according to the four market risks: changes in interest rates (at different maturities), exchange rates, equity prices, and commodity prices. In every risk category, all derivatives (e.g., options, swaps, forward, futures) are converted into spot equivalents. Once the capital charge related to each of these risks is determined, they are added up to produce the market risk charge. The standardised approach takes into account notional amounts and market characteristics, but the computation does not allow for any correlation between the four market risk categories, assets, and portfolios. In other words,

---

[5] Hong Kong Monetary Authority, "Supervisory Manual: Risk Based Supervisory Approach." Pg. 19. Refer to "Further Reading" at the end of this chapter on how to download this pdf file.
[6] Shellagh Heffernan, *Modern Banking* (Chichester: John Wiley & Sons, 2005), 186–187.

portfolio diversification cannot be used to justify reducing the amount of capital to be set aside for market risk.

In the internal model approach introduced in Hong Kong[7] banks are permitted to use their own internal models to calculate the market risk charge, provided they have the approval of the national regulator. A bank must demonstrate that it has a sound risk management system integrated into management decisions, that it conducts regular stress tests, that it has an independent risk control unit, and that it undergoes external audits.

The internal model to be used must satisfy the following Basel II requirements:

- Value-at-Risk (VaR) must be computed daily.
- The risk factors to be monitored must be interest rates (for different term structures/maturities), exchange rates, equity prices, and commodity prices.
- One-tailed 99% confidence interval must be used, i.e., the loss level is at 99% and the loss should occur once in 100 days, or two to three days a year.
- The holding period should be 10 trading days or two calendar weeks.
- Non-linearities arising from option positions should be taken into account and the model must be built on at least a year's worth of historical data that must be updated at least once a quarter.

Unlike the standardised approach, the internal model approach recognises portfolio correlations in broad categories (e.g., fixed income) and across categories (e.g., fixed income products and currencies). The general market risk charge should be set at the higher of the previous day's VaR or the average VaR over the last 60 business days times a "multiplicative" factor k. The exact value of this factor is to be determined by local regulators, subject to an absolute floor of 3.

Value-at-Risk

Another important consideration of market risk is value-at-risk (VaR), which is a step closer to calculating the potential impact not of a risk but of a risk event. Basel II requires that banks allowed by their national regulator to use the internal model approach to calculate the market risk charge must use a model that computes the VaR of their holdings on a daily basis. Basel III, which Hong Kong started introducing in 2013 in a process expected to last several years, overhauls the trading-book rules and starts moving away from VaR, having identified a series of weaknesses in the traditional approach.

VaR is a measure of the worst expected loss that a bank may suffer over a specific period of time, under normal market conditions and a specified level of confidence.

---

[7] HKMA. "Supervisory Manual: Use of Internal Models Approach to Calculate Market Risk" (CA G-3) Web. 11 October 2012. This version superseded an earlier version published on 31 January 2007.

Another way of looking at VaR is that it is the expected loss of a portfolio over a specified time period for a set level of probability. For example, if a daily VaR is stated as $100,000 to a 95% level of confidence, this means that during the day there is only a 5% chance that the loss the next day will be greater than $100,000. The most commonly used VaR models assume that the prices of assets in the financial markets follow a normal distribution.

In his book *Measuring Market Risk*, Kevin Dowd enumerates the advantages of the VaR approach[8]:

- It lets senior management set the overall risk target of the firm and all other related matters down the line.
- It is applied to determine risk capital allocation from the firm level down to the individual investment decision. (A higher risk capital is allocated to a riskier project.)
- It is useful for reporting and disclosing purposes. VaR-based decision rules can guide investment, hedging, and trading.
- VaR information can be used to implement portfolio-wide hedging strategies that are otherwise rarely possible.
- It can be used to evaluate the performance of assets and individuals.

But Dowd also discusses the disadvantages:

- It does not give a consistent method for measuring risk. Different VaR models will give different numbers.
- It only measures risks that can be captured through quantitative techniques. It does not measure political risk, liquidity risk, personnel risk, regulatory risk, or operational risk.
- If a tail event does occur, we can expect to lose more than the VaR, but the VaR figure itself gives us no indication of how much that loss might be (tail loss effect).

The concept of fat-tailed distribution becomes relevant in the context of the disadvantages of VaR. Value at risk assumes normal distribution, which says that five or more standard deviations from the mean are rare and 10 or more are virtually impossible. In contrast, fat tail distribution posits that the standard deviations from the mean are practically infinite. Banks must be wary of a limitation of VaR that could lead understating market risk and could mean inadequate allocation of capital to guard against risk.

Basel III attempts to address these concerns, having learnt some lessons from the Global Financial Crisis. The new iteration of the accords creates a series of backstops in the way banks calculate their VaR. For starters, banks that use their own models to put a value on their trading book should also use a standardized approach as a backstop. Basel III also brings in tougher boundaries between trading books and banking books to prevent banks and AIs from moving assets between books to lower their capital requirements.

---

[8] Dowd, Kevin. "Measuring Market Risk". Chichester: John Wiley & Sons, 2005. Pg. 10–30.

FIGURE 7.1   Fat-tailed distribution

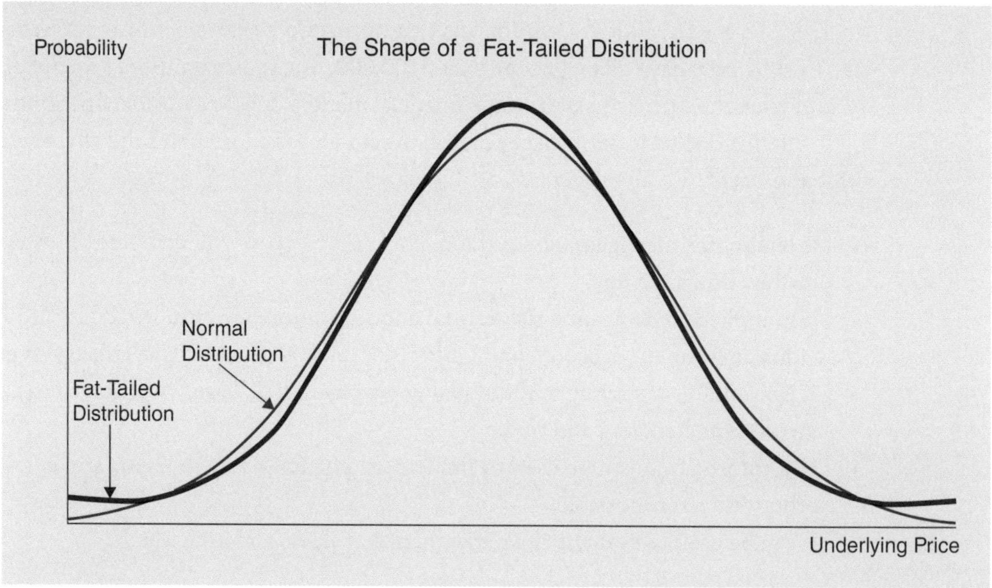

Source: HKIB

More significantly, however, Basel III starts moving away form relying on VaR to measure quantitative risk, in large part because of its inability to measure tail risk. Instead, the BIS is moving towards alternative risk metrics.

One prominent example of such a metric is an expected shortfall (ES) approach, which considers a wider range of possible outcomes and also takes into account the "riskiness" of a particular instrument given its size and the likelihood of losses.

Basel III also starts the process of introducing market conditions in internal models to calculate risk. This includes not only prevalent market movements but also market liquidity conditions that can have significant impact on the actual price of an asset.[9]

Basis Point Value and Hedging Market Risk

Basis point value is another way to calculate the potential impact of risk. Basis point value considers how much a position gains or loses for every 0.01% parallel move in the yield curve for a particular product. As such, it can help calculate market risk.

---

[9] Bank for International Settlements. "Second Consultative Document: Fundamental Review of the Trading Book". October 2013.

Banks can restructure their balance sheets to alter undesired fluctuations of earnings or portfolio net worth. The most transparent ways involve making direct changes in the repricing or cash flow characteristics of conventional (cash) asset and liability instruments. On the occasions when traditional cash instruments cannot be used feasibly to alter the risk characteristics of balance-sheet portfolios, hedging provides a non-traditional alternative.

A bank's overall hedging policy considers risk exposure, existing risk limits, and the use of hedging instruments, including derivatives such as futures, options, securitised assets, and interest rate swaps. Hedging policy takes into account the levels of cash book revenue and current market volatility, as well as the overall cost of hedging. On occasion, however, certain exposures may be left unhedged because hedging costs would be prohibitive.

For example, interest rate swaps are used to artificially hedge an asset/liability interest-sensitivity or duration position. Assume we have only one position on the book, a five-year sterling swap of £5 million notional, in which we pay a fixed rate and receive floating-rate interest.

As the maturity of the swap is longer than that of the longest interest rate futures contract, which is three years, we decide to hedge the position using a UK government bond, or gilt. As we have "borrowed" funds, the hedge action must be to "lend" funds. Therefore, we need to buy gilt in order to hedge the swap, as below:

Swap position	Hedge
Pay fixed	Receive fixed (buy bond)
Receive fixed	Pay fixed (sell bond)

To decide how much nominal of the gilt to buy, the hedge ratio needs to be established. This is done using each instrument's basis point value or BPV. To establish the nominal amount of the gilt required, the basic calculation is:

$$(\text{BPV swap} / \text{BPV gilt}) \times 10,000$$

In our example, we would need to calculate the BPV for the five-year swap. One way to do this is to view the swap as a strip of futures contracts, whose BPV is known with certainty. The short sterling future traded on the London International Futures and Options Exchange (LIFFE) is a standard contract with a BPV or "tick value" of £12.50. As our swap is a sterling swap, it will pay semi-annually, while short sterling futures mature every quarter. The calculations are:

Convert swap nominal to futures:	$5m \times 2$	$= £10m$
Futures periods:	4×5 years	$= 20$ contracts
Less "fixing" of first period of swap:	-2	$= 18$ contracts
(if a quarterly paying swap, this is -1)		
BPV:	$18 \times 12.5 \times 10$	$= £2250.$

Let us look at interest rate swaps, whose structure basically is an exchange of fixed- versus floating-rate interest payments on a specified notional principal. The floating leg may be on any required basis, but is usually reset on a semi-annual or quarterly basis.

As an example, a five-year swap that paid fixed and received quarterly floating payments would require the floating rate to be reset 20 times during its life, once when the swap was transacted and every three months thereafter. The swap therefore may be viewed conceptually the same as the sum of 20 separate segments, with the value of each segment dependent on the fixed rate of the swap, and on the market's expectation of the floating rate on the quarterly reset date.

The BPV of a swap is given as

$$BPV = 0.00001 \times \frac{d}{B} \times M$$

where

d is the number of days in the floating period

B is the year day-base (360 or 365)

M is the notional principal of the swap.

The BPV is the amount by which the swap changes value for every basis point that the closing day's same-maturity swap rate fixes above or below the swap fixed rate. A change in value given by a change in market rates is not realised on the day however but on the maturity of the swap.

The BPV of a futures contract is fixed, however, irrespective of the maturity of the contract, and is the "tick value" of the contract itself. For example, a Eurodollar futures contract could have a BPV of USD25, while the short sterling contract on LIFFE has a tick value of £6.25. In a combined position, therefore, consisting of an interest rate swap hedged with futures contracts, both instruments are sensitive to the same change in interest rates.

If we wish to compare the effects of a change in the value of both instruments, the most straightforward way to do this is to use the present value for both price changes. As futures contracts are settled on a daily basis, the present value of its basis point value is unchanged, so this is USD25 in the case of the Eurodollar contract. The present value of the BPV of an interest rate swap can be determined using a set of futures rates from a strip of similar maturity.

Counterparty Risk

Counterparty risk emerges when the performance of one or more counterparties in a contractual arrangement, such as an investment in a derivative or a foreign exchange trade, comes into question. There is counterparty risk during the presettlement and settlement periods of a deal. A key risk that both market participants and regulators have worked hard to limit or eliminate (as much as possible) is settlement risk.

This particular risk can also be found in the presettlement stage of a deal. Credit migration or deterioration of the credit rating of the counterparty during the presettlement stage will increase the risk profile of the transaction to the bank. The BCBS is in the process of finalizing the capital charge for such risks for OTC derivatives.

In February 2013, the BIS provided some guidance on how to manage settlement risk associated with foreign exchange transactions.[10] The forex market grew rapidly after 2000 and, in general, the market has gone a long way to reduce risks but some remain and the sheer number and size of the transactions that now occur make these risks greater. Worthy of particular consideration, says the BIS, are principal risk, replacement cost risk, and other forex settlement-related risks. To address these concerns, the BIS provides a series of seven guidelines on governance, principal risk, replacement cost risk, liquidity risk, operational risk, legal risk, and risks associated with capital for forex transactions such as spot transactions, forwards, swaps, deliverable forex options, and currency swaps.[11] Although the BIS recommendations are larger in scope, they emphasize four main points:

- Banks should ensure the management of settlement-related risks in forex transactions and put in place practices consistent with the management of counterparty exposures of similar size and duration.
- As much as possible, banks should reduce their principal risk by settling forex transactions through institutions that provide PvP arrangements or take care to identify, measure, control, and reduce the size and duration of principal risk.
- In analyzing their capital needs, banks should consider all the risks associated with the settlement of forex transactions and ensure there is sufficient capital in hand to deal with potential exposures.
- Where legally enforceable, banks should use netting and collateral arrangements to minimize replacement cost risk and fully collateralize mark-to-market exposure on physically settling forex swaps and forwards financial institutions or systemically important non-financial entities.

Similarly, during the settlement of a deal, counterparty risk is particularly important. Settlement risk emerges when the payments associated with a contract are made. The risk is particularly significant when it comes to cross-payments between two parties (or even more). Settlement risk can be potentially quite large because the entire payment could potentially be at risk if one party fails to keep up its end of the contract.[12]

As with country risk and almost every other type of risk that banks deal with, the HKMA provides guidance on how to identify and manage counterparty credit risks (CCR). The latter, says the HKMA, is a major source of credit risk for AIs engaged in

---

[10] Bank for International Settlements. "Supervisory guidance for managing risks associated with the settlement of foreign exchange transactions." February 2013.

[11] See Chapter 9 and the case study on the failure of Bankhaus Herstatt in 1974 to better understand the importance and potential implications of settlement risk in the forex market.

[12] Horcher, Karen. "Essentials of Managing Treasury". New Jersey. John Wiley & Sons. 2006. Print. P 138.

trading or capital market transactions such as OTC derivative, or products with long settlement dates.[13]

The approach to capitalizing counterparty risk has long varied from country to country and this has created an uneven playing field, particularly between banks operating in stricter regulatory environments and those in a more fluid one.

Basel III introduces a series of changes[14] that Hong Kong adopted through the Banking [Amendment] Ordinance 2012 (BAO 2012) and the Banking [Capital] Amendment Rules 2012 (BCAR 2012). The changes introduced through Basel III are quite elaborate, but what is most significant is the attitude towards risk that Basel III introduces and the new approach to measuring risk. The banking book, for example, is treated as a more plain vanilla book while new and more complicated rules are introduced to the trading book, and assign capital liquidity rules to the various categories of trades. This division remains a work in progress.

Nevertheless, through the BCAR 2012, the HKMA introduced a series of internal model calculations as an alternative to calculate counterparty credit risk exposures, particularly from over-the-counter derivatives transactions that proved to be a source of systemic risk during the Global Financial Crisis. If the HKMA approves, banks can now use and internal model calculation approach rather than a current exposure method to calculate their capital adequacy.

Mark-to-Market

Defining risk is only the beginning of the process of measuring it, managing it and, if necessary, minimizing the impact of any risk events. The economic and financial crisis that started in 2007 underscored a series of weaknesses in banks and financial institutions. A couple of years later, regulators through the Group of Twenty (G20) nations launched a series of reforms to reduce systemic risk, particularly in the trade of OTC derivatives. The reforms focused on trading OTC derivatives on exchanges or electronic platforms, clearing trades through central counterparties (CCPs), reporting of OTC derivative contracts to trade repositories, and subjecting non-centrally cleared derivatives contracts to higher capital requirements. By 2013, the International Organizations of Securities Commissions (IOSCO) developed a series of margin requirements to minimize these risks.[15] These requirements were developed alongside the BIS. One key change as of December 2015 is the use of variation margin. A schedule of initial margin requirements is included in Table 7.1.

The push to better analyze and prepare for risk inherent in these recommended margin requirements has been a feature of much of the regulatory guidance issued in the

---

[13] HKMA. "Supervisory Policy Manual: Counterparty Credit Risk Management". 3 June 2009. Pg. 4.

[14] These are discussed at length in other books in this series, including Credit Risk Management.

[15] International Organizations of Securities Commissions. "Margin requirements for non-centrally cleared derivatives". September 2013. Through Bank for International Settlements. Web. March 2014.

TABLE 7.1 Standardised initial margin schedule

Asset class	Initial margin requirement (% of notional exposure)
Credit: 0–2 year duration	2
Credit: 2–5 year duration	5
Credit: 5 + year duration	10
Commodity	15
Equity	15
Foreign exchange	6
Interest rate: 0–2 year duration	1
Interest rate: 2–5 year duration	2
Interest rate: 5+ year duration	4
Other	15

years after the Global Financial Crisis of 2007 and 2008. The ultimate objectives of these efforts were the reduction of systemic risk and the promotion of central clearing. These efforts included a series of haircuts for various products, which are included in Table 7.2. At the heart of these efforts was an understanding that capital and margin have important and complementary functions in mitigating risk but are different in various ways. Margin protects parties in a transaction by absorbing losses, ideally through collateral rather than capital. Capital, while necessary, is shared by an entire institution and may be more easily depleted in times of stress.

TABLE 7.2 Standardised haircut schedule

Asset class	Haircut (% of market value)
Cash in same currency	0
High-quality government and central bank securities: residual maturity less than one years	0.5
High-quality government and central bank securities: residual maturity between one and five years	2
High-quality government and central bank securities: residual maturity greater than five years	4
High-quality corporate\covered bonds: residual maturity less than one year	1
High-quality corporate\covered bonds: residual maturity greater than one year and less than five years	4
High-quality corporate\covered bonds: residual maturity greater than five years	8
Equities included in major stock indices	15
Gold	15
Addtitional (additive) haircut on asset in which the currency of the derivatives obligation differs from that of the collateral assets	8

Analyzing and determining risk remains a key function of the treasury. One approach to analysing risk is the use of mark-to-market accounting, also known as fair value accounting. Mark-to-market (MTM) accounting is based on the current market price of an asset or liability or some other fair value. When it comes to managing risk, the most obvious benefit of MTM is that it makes it easier to track values on balance sheets as market conditions change. By comparison, historical cost accounting, which is based on the historical value of transactions, is more stable but may actually hide market conditions.

MTM is an important objective for credit analytics. In an ideal world where every security was traded in a liquid market, the need to use models for MTM would become less important. However, at the present time MTM is only mark-to-market in the very best cases, and more often than not, it actually refers to mark-to-model. Reduced-form models, which start by identifying relationships between variables, fill an important need in this MTM context. By contrast, structural models that start out with deductive theories often diverge from current prices, particularly during times of market stress. Thus, structural models are less useful in MTM. One way to think about reduced-form models is that they offer a sophisticated way to interpolate and extrapolate between and beyond observed market prices while enforcing constraints implied by financial economic theory. The result of this extrapolation is often referred to as a *credit curve*—a relationship between tenor and spread that also controls for loss given default (LGD).

But before any actual estimation can take place, a good deal of work goes into pooling data that have been scrubbed and filtered for quality issues. In developing cohorts from the cleaned data, it is useful to focus on the usual suspects as dimensions for pooling: country or region, industry or sector, size, or credit rating. These dimensions define "homogeneous" pools of data within which the credit curves can be estimated. It is also important to note that, subject to the properties of the markets, the characteristics used to build cohorts can be modified to match the desired categories for the curves.

All this is useful to assess and tackle market risk as a a modeller might experiment with cohorts such as the following:

- **Regions:** Asia ex-Japan, Europe, Japan, Latin America, Middle East and Africa, North America.
- **Ratings:** Either agency ratings or market-based default probabilities from a structural model. At the very least, it is important to segment issuers into investment grade and sub–investment grade. A better option is to move to broad rating groupings such as the following: Aaa and Aa, A, Baa, Ba, B, all else in the lowest rating grades.
- **Sectors:** Banks, nonbank financial institutions, non-service businesses, service businesses and utilities.
- **Size:** Revenue less than 1 billion USD, revenue greater than 1 billion USD.

Another important consideration in the construction of these analytical curves is tenor. The final curve will be expressed in terms of spreads as a function of tenor for each cohort. Ideally, we want tenors from six months up to 30 years. Rarely is there enough information to match this ideal, however, so it is more likely that tenors will be 1 year, 2 years, 3 years, 5 years, 7 years, 10 years, 20 years, and 30 years.

Once the cohorts have been created, it is useful to take some time to evaluate various descriptive statistics for each cohort—in other words, produce a statistical analysis of risk. Though the data have presumably already been scrubbed well, this additional analysis provides guidance as to whether there are outliers that may have been masked in a more heterogeneous sample. Data visualisation techniques, combined with traditional statistical methods for outlier detection, constitute a useful way to find such outliers.

Despite its attractiveness, estimating parameters using this framework can still be difficult. Improper specification of the initial parameter values may cause an estimation algorithm to fail. As with many reduced-form techniques, these algorithms need a fair amount of supervision by analysts in order to avoid incoherent estimates. It is helpful to address this problem by adding parameter bounds for input to the estimation routine. Some manual smoothing at the end may also become necessary to achieve monotonically increasing curves across credit quality groups.

Operational Risk

Operational risk arises not only from a company's operations, but also from any disturbance in its operational processes. The disruption may come from events such as rogue trading or terrorist attacks to landmark legal settlement and systems breakdowns. Because the triggers are so varied, it is difficult to come up with an exact definition of operational risk. This has led to two extreme categorisations. A "narrow" view sees operational risk as stemming from failure within a company's back office or operations area. A "wide" view sees operational risk as a quantitative residual—the variance in net earnings not explained by other risks.

Most regulators adopt definitions that fall somewhere between the two and focus on the risk of failures in technology, controls and staff. The U.S. Federal Reserve Board's *Trading and Capital-Market Activities Manual* defines operations and systems risk as "the risk of human error or fraud or the risk that systems will fail to adequately record, monitor, and account for transactions or positions." The U.S. *Office of the Comptroller of the Currency (1989)* described operational risk as including system failure, system disruption, and system compromises. The BCBS defines operational risk in its Basel II guidelines "as the risk of loss resulting from inadequate or failed internal processes, people and systems or from external events. This definition includes legal risk, but excludes strategic and reputational risk." The HKMA follows the Basel II definition. In its *Supervisory Policy Manual for Operational Risk Management*, it defines operational risk as "risk of direct or indirect loss resulting from inadequate or failed internal processes, staff, and systems or from external events."[16]

---

[16] HKMA Supervisory Policy Manual, Risk-based Supervisory Approach (HKMA, 11 October 2001).

Payment and Settlement Systems and Risk

Interbank transfers are key components of the financial infrastructure of the city. A robust payment and settlement system is essential to support the very high volume of payments that Hong Kong's banking system and capital markets deal with. As such, it is key to minimizing payment and settlement risks. Payment systems in use allow for interbank transfers denominated in HKD, EUR, RMB, and USD. Hong Kong Interbank Clearing Limited (HKICL) operates payment systems in Hong Kong and provides banks with interbank clearing and settlement services. There are four main interbank transfer systems in use in Hong Kong.[17]

Since 1996, a number of Real Time Gross Settlement (RTGS) systems have been created to deal with payments among banks in multiple currencies. Before 1996, banks settled payments among one another through position netting, but such position netting was not obligatory and was not supported by Hong Kong legal framework. Position netting involved receiving or paying the net difference between the transfers payable or receivable to or from other banks at the end of each business day. This was not the safest way of tackling these transactions as it exposed banks to forex settlement risk or "Hestatt risk" should one bank fail to pay the amount due at the end of the day, and such a failure could trigger a chain of defaults.

RTGS operates on a deal-by-deal basis and requires banks to have more liquidity through the day. Hong Kong banks can obtain interest-free intraday liquidity through repo agreements with the HKMA using Exchange Fund Bills or Notes but this approach is generally seen as a contingency option as the market has sufficient liquidity and can use market mechanisms for liquidity arrangements.

A couple of factors come into play when banks use the various RTGS systems. The first is the payment-versus-payment mechanism through which foreign exchange transactions are settled simultaneously, which improves settlement efficiency and eliminates risk. The second is a series of improvements introduced over the years to make the system more efficient. This includes a number of optimizers that speed up the system through, for example, bulk settlement of cheques or periodic multilateral offsetting of payment instructions—done at 30 minute intervals through the RTGS Liquidity Optimizer.

RTGS Systems

Since 1996, the HKD-based RTGS system has allowed banks to settle interbank payments denominated in Hong Kong dollars. Also known as the Hong Kong dollar Clearing House Automated Transfer System (CHATS), the system settles payments continuously on a deal-by-deal basis across members without netting. See Table 7.3 for an illustration of the

---

[17] HKMA. "Payment Systems". Web. 5 May 2013. At: http://www.hkma.gov.hk/eng/key-functions/international-financial-centre/infrastructure/payment-systems.shtml.

TABLE 7.3

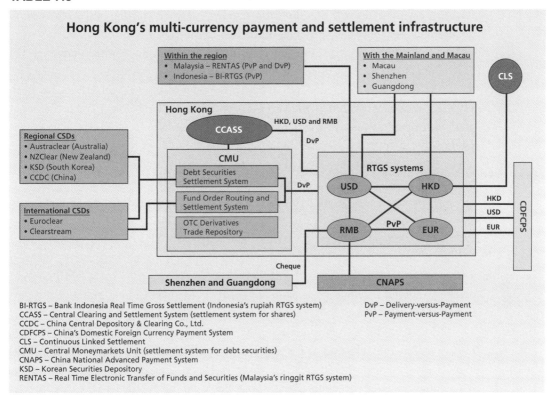

Hong Kong's multi-currency payment and settlement infrastructure

BI-RTGS – Bank Indonesia Real Time Gross Settlement (Indonesia's rupiah RTGS system)
CCASS – Central Clearing and Settlement System (settlement system for shares)
CCDC – China Central Depository & Clearing Co., Ltd.
CDFCPS – China's Domestic Foreign Currency Payment System
CLS – Continuous Linked Settlement
CMU – Central Moneymarkets Unit (settlement system for debt securities)
CNAPS – China National Advanced Payment System
KSD – Korean Securities Depository
RENTAS – Real Time Electronic Transfer of Funds and Securities (Malaysia's ringgit RTGS system)

DvP – Delivery-versus-Payment
PvP – Payment-versus-Payment

connectivity of the various payment and settlement systems in Hong Kong. The system handles both large payments between banks and the bulk clearing and settlement of cheques, payments related to the stock market, and other bulk electronic payments that are small in value, such as those made through the city's popular Electronic Payment System (EPS), auto-credit and auto-debit transaction or transfers made at automated tellers. Payments made as a result of the HKMA's monetary operations are also done through the HKD RTGS system.

From a legal standpoint, the system is based on the Exchange Fund Ordinance and has a single-tier membership structure that gives all licensed banks in Hong Kong access. In turn, banks are required to join the system and are expected to keep HKD settlement accounts with the HKMA. Banks with restricted licences may also join the system, depending on whether they meet a series of criteria.[18] Since 2004, the CLS Bank International has limited access to the system to facilitate foreign exchange trades through the Continuous Linked Settlement (CLS) system, which operates on a payment-versus-payment basis.

An RTGS system that operates in USD is also in use across Hong Kong since August 2000. The system, also known as USD CHATS, uses the Hongkong and Shanghai

---

[18] The criteria is set out in a couple of documents issued in 1999 and 2000 known as the "Access to the Real Time Gross Settlement System" and available through the HKMA website.

Banking Corporation as the settlement institution. The system handles USD-denominated interbank payments in real time but also handles the bulk clearing and settlement of cheques and stock-market payments, much like the HKD-denominated system. Banks in Hong Kong can access this system and can apply for direct membership, although the HKMA and HSBC approve memberships on an individual basis.

The Euro-denominated RTGS System, also known as the Euro CHATS, has been in operation since April 2003. Standard Chartered Bank (Hong Kong) Ltd is the designated settlement institution. As with the USD CHATS, banks in Hong Kong can access the system and can apply for membership through Standard Chartered or indirect membership by settling euro payments with direct members. The HKMA and Standard Chartered approve the participation of other financial institutions on a case-by-case basis.

The latest RTGS system in use in Hong Kong is denominated in RMB and is also known as renminbi CHATS. It first took effect in June 2007 when it evolved from the Renminbi Settlement System. The clearing bank is Bank of China (Hong Kong) Ltd. Bank of China maintains a settlement account with the People's Bank of China and is a member of China's National Advanced Payment System (CNAPS). In many ways, RMB CHATS can be considered a technical extension of CNAPS in Mainland China, although it is governed by Hong Kong law.

RMB CHATS is used to process RMB-denominated interbank payments in real time as well as bulk clearing of payments for items like cheques, much like the HKD CHATS does. As with the other RTGS systems, Hong Kong banks can join the system by opening settlement accounts directly with Bank of China. Other banks can apply to Bank of China to access the system but approvals are granted by the bank and HKMA on a case-by-case basis.[19]

Managing Financial Risk

Clear risk processes and organisational structures exist to measure, analyse and manage financial risks. So, while calculating risk can be complicated, it is important to keep one's proverbial eye on the ball. In other words, calculating the potential loss from a hypothetical risk event in only a tool towards the more significant goal of managing risk. This is because financial assets have well-defined mark-to-market values, and financial institutions can estimate the risks of these assets. Moreover, financial instruments such as swaps, options, and futures are readily available to offset these risks. Tools such as stress testing and VaR have been used in this task. The most important has been the adoption of an integrated set of risk processes and an organisational structure to handle risk.

---

[19] See Chapter 3 for more information on the operations of the Central Moneymarkets Unit and its role in relation to Hong Kong's RTGS systems. See Chapter 8 for a more detailed discussion of the offshore RMB payment and settlement systems.

Stress testing has emerged as a popular and almost universally used tool. Regulators increasingly rely on stress testing to assess the strength of banking systems. Basel III requires more banks to carry out stress tests. By 2016, banks have to meet a minimum of 60% liquidity coverage ratio moving gradually to 100% by 2019.

The HKMA's *Supervisory Policy Manual* includes a section on stress testing that was updated in 2012.[20] The HKMA says stress testing is the use of techniques to "assess a financial institution's potential vulnerability" in terms of profitability, liquidity, and capital adequacy in the face of extreme market movements or crises. Regulators increasingly rely on stress tests having learnt banks' risk systems are not always adequate to deal with severe market shocks when regular market conditions no longer hold true, new concentrations of risks or links between different risks emerge, shocks are amplified, or economic conditions deteriorate suddenly and credit markets freeze.

The main functions of stress testing include:

- Alert banks and other institutions of potentially unexpected outcomes associated with risks;
- Provide forward-looking assessments of risk exposures under stressed conditions;
- Improve understanding of risk profiles and monitor changes to that profile;
- Match an institution's risk exposures and risk tolerance;
- Supplement statistical risk control measures and quantify tail risk;
- Evaluate vulnerabilities;
- Strengthen capital and liquidity planning and strategic decision making.

Stress tests can be done under a variety of scenarios such as sharp declines in interest income (at times when rates drop unexpectedly), changes in the rates between major currencies (which can happen should a country devaluate its currency), or a decline in the value of a financial instrument (as was evident during the Global Financial Crisis). In the past few years, banks in the U.S. and Europe have used stress testing to shore up their risk control measures. One of the earliest implementers of this method was Citibank, which has expanded the use of stress testing around its international operations. The HKMA is not clear regarding what conditions banks have to consider in their stress tests but the BIS has provided some guidance.

Accounting control systems are designed to ensure that a business operates in line with strategies developed by senior management. Diagnostic controls, as well as a series of limits and sanctions, help ensure that operations are conducted as they should. Internal and external audits focus on confirming the existence of assets and liabilities for which the firm is responsible and accountable. To do this, auditors traditionally use a series of interviews and checklists to confirm operational integrity.

Another approach is to use reliability engineering, a body of statistical and analytical techniques concerned with the reliability, safety, and efficient operation of engineering

[20] Hong Kong Monetary Authority. Supervisory Policy Manual: Stress-testing. IC-5. September 5, 2012.

systems. Reliability engineering focuses on systems maintenance and reducing operational uncertainty by setting and meeting realistic operating specifications for process output. Operational risk management, for example, has derived techniques from reliability engineering to use in safety-sensitive fields such as nuclear plant safety, aircraft maintenance, and medical informatics. Moreover, the systematic gathering, categorising, analysing, and prioritising of data used in the engineering disciplines help to develop rigorous operational risk management methodology.

There are certain clear differences between engineering and risk management. Reliability engineering approaches tend to be very data-intensive and to focus on the evolving reliability of complex multi-component hardware systems. By contrast, the organisational systems that comprise ongoing operations are data-poor and involve people. This makes gathering data and predicting the systems' failure patterns much more challenging than that for hardware systems.

Another difference is focus. Engineers concentrate on reliability (the likelihood of a system functioning correctly), while operational risk managers focus on the financial impact of down-time and estimate potential costs of the next period.

Summary

- Risk assessment is a way to determine risk priorities and controls. The HKMA considers market risk as one of the eight inherent risks that face AIs in Hong Kong.
- Country risk refers to the amount of exposure an institution has to developments in a given country, including the rules and discretion of that country's government and regulators. Country risk can impact both the operational and transactional environment. Country risk includes legal, regulatory, economic, and business risks.
- VaR is a measure of the worst expected loss that a bank may suffer over a period of time that has been specified by the user, under normal market conditions and a specified level of confidence. This measure may be obtained in a number of ways, using a statistical model or by computer simulation.
- In measuring the VaR of a portfolio, we can use either the non-parametric or the parametric approach. In a non-parametric approach, the historical data is put into a histogram according to the payoff and frequency of occurrence. VaR is the α% tail of the return distribution. In the parametric approach, the distribution of the returns is assumed to be normal, an assumption that is empirically sound when the portfolio is large and well-diversified.
- Counterparty risk emerges when a bank undertakes a transaction with one or more outside parties. This risk is always present. It is particularly significant during the pre-settlment and settlement periods of a deal.
- Mark-to-market accounting is an accounting method that uses the current value of an asset or liability and is more reflective of market conditions than historical accounting, which is more stable.

- Another way to calculate the potential impact of risk is to use basis point value, which looks at how much a position gains or loses for every 0.01% parallel move in the yield curve for a particular product.
- Both Basel and the HKMA recognize market risk, which is the risk to the financial condition of an AI resulting from adverse movements in market rates or prices. This is broad ranging, as it can include anything from changes in foreign exchange rates to interest rates related to fixed-income products and commodity prices. Banks are required to keep a market risk charge that can be calculated using either the standardized approach or the internal model approach.
- Operational risk may be the broadest of all risks. It arises both from operation but also from operational processes. Operational risk is difficult to define but it can be seen through a "narrow" view or a "wide" view. The HKMA defines operational risk as "risk of direct or indirect loss resulting from inadequate or failed internal processes, staff and systems or from external events."
- Authorised institutions in Hong Kong and the rest of the world are required to maintain adequate capital to protect against market risk.
- A number of approaches are available to manage financial risk. These include accounting control systems and reliability engineering, which can be adapted to manage risk.

Key Terms

Accounting control systems

Reliability engineering

Financial risk

Basis point value

Monte Carlo simulation

Historical simulation

Delta normal method

Value-at-risk (VaR)

Fat-tailed distribution

Basel II

Mark-to-market (MTM)

Operational risk

Risk factors

Standardised approach

Internal model approach

Market risk

Counterparty risk

Counterparty credit risk (CCR)

Macroeconomic risk

Indirect country risk

Currency risk

Contagion risk

Transfer risk

Sovereign risk

Country risk

Supervisory Policy Manual

Study Guide

1. Country risk is one of the most frequent types of risk that AIs in Hong Kong face. List and discuss the six different types of country risk.

2. Your bank is considering launching a new product in a neighbouring Asian country that has recently instituted democracy and market reform. What approach would you take to analyse the country risk associated with your bank's new products?

3. Why are mark-to-market approaches more effective to calculate risk than historical accounting?

4. What is value-at-risk? How can it be calculated? List three advantages and three disadvantages of using VaR to calculate risk.

Further Reading

Butler, Cormac. Mastering Value at Risk: A Step-by-Step Guide to Understanding and Applying VAR. (Financial Times/Prentice Hall, 1999. Print.

Choudhry, Moorad. Bank Asset and Liability Management: Strategy, Trading, Analysis. Singapore: John Wiley & Sons (Asia) Pte Ltd, 2007. Print.

Dowd, Kevin. Measuring Market Risk. Chichester: John Wiley & Sons, 2005. Print.

Hong Kong Monetary Authority. "Risk Based Supervisory Approach," in Supervisory Manual. Web. 15 May 2010. <http://www.info.gov.hk/hkma/eng/bank/spma/attach/SA-1.pdf>.

Heffernan, Shellagh. Modern Banking. Chichester: John Wiley & Sons, 2005. Print.

8

RMB Payments and Settlements

Learning objectives

After studying this chapter, you should be able to:

1 Understand and explain the evolution of the use of the Renminbi in trade end investment in Hong Kong.

2 Discuss the operations of the RMB Real Time Gross Settlement (RTGS) system and how it has evolved.

3 Explain the role of Hong Kong as a gateway for the RMB on international markets.

Introduction

After adopting a managed floating exchange rate regime in 2005, China is taking significant steps to internationalize its currency: the renminbi. Hong Kong has emerged as the beachhead of this push to turn the RMB from a heavily controlled and strictly domestic currency into one used in international trade. At the end of 2012, there were more than 7,000 enterprises from Mainland China and overseas that leveraged the city's unique connection to Mainland China to streamline their businesses. Almost a third of China's trade is intermediated through Hong Kong as offshore trade or re-exports.

Although at the time of writing the RMB still accounts for a small fraction of international trade, the growth in the use of the RMB is nothing short of spectacular, one that matches China's economic growth. China's GDP jumped from USD400 billion in 1990 to more than USD7 trillion in 2011. By 2017, China should account for about a third of total global economic growth, according to the International Monetary Fund. So the RMB is increasingly used in trade and investment on the international stage, this even as China maintains relatively strict currency controls.

By virtue of their location, banks in Hong Kong have a significant amount of exposure to the RMB. As an international financial center with a very open approach to currency and strong institutions that have solid links with other financial centers around the world, Hong Kong is an ideal place from which to expand the internationalization of the RMB. On the one had, companies from Mainland China are prone to use Hong Kong as the jumping off point for international expansion. Conversely, global companies are likely to set up in Hong Kong as part of their approach to China.

RMB Clearing and Settlement

The use of RMB in international trade and investment started in November 2005, when the People's Bank of China (PBoC) said it would expand the RMB banking business in Hong Kong as a prelude to the internationalization of the RMB. As table 8.1 shows, the volume of RMB clearing is experiencing ongoing and significant growth.

The RMB business in Hong Kong became a serious consideration in 2009, when the government in Beijing launched a pilot scheme for RMB trade settlement that was rapidly expanded to incorporate all provinces and cities in the country, all of which are now allowed to use RMB to settle trade transactions anywhere in the world. As a result, the amount of China's total trade settled in RMB has risen steadily. Through 2010, just 2% of China's total international trade was settled in RMB and that figured had jumped to as much as 9% in the first half of 2012. Since January 2011, the Chinese government has also allowed the use of the RMB for international investments while foreign direct investment into China can be made in RMB under rules promulgated in October 2011. Much of this trade and investment moves through Hong Kong.

TABLE 8.1

Average daily turnover in cross-boundary arrangements with the Mainland

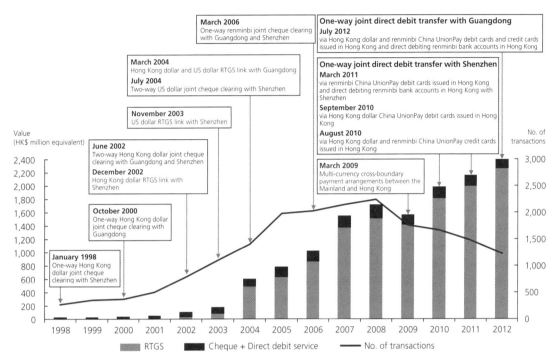

In 2010, the number of trade transactions settled in RMB through Hong Kong banks averaged RMB31 billion per month. In the first 10 months of 2012, that number had jumped seven-fold to RMB213 billion. Between January and October 2012, Hong Kong banks dealt with RMB2,125 billion worth of RMB-denominated trade settlements. To put this in perspective, this is compared to a total = of RMB2,284 billion worth of external trade settled in RMB. In other words, about half of China's external trade denominated in RMB is settled in Hong Kong. This is not, by a long shot, all of China's trade. As with most countries, China has to conduct much of its international trade in dollars or Euros but the growth has still been remarkable.

This is important for the treasury management of banks and other financial institutions because the growth of the RMB trade has opened a whole other avenue for cash and asset management, although it has also opened up more risks that have to be considered—risks that we discussed in the earlier chapter.

Hong Kong was the pioneer offshore market for RMB-denominated business. Thanks to its ties to Mainland China, Hong Kong started doing business in RMB as far back as 2004. China's 12th Five Year Plan for Economic and Social Development (2011–2015) further cemented the city's position by expressing explicit support for the development of Hong Kong as an offshore RMB business center and reinforcing the city's status as an international financial center. As a result, since August 2011, a number of measures have helped expand the geographical scope of the RMB trade settlement scheme to the entire country, promulgate administrative arrangements for RMB-denominated foreign direct investment, and introduced an RMB Qualified Foreign Institution Investors scheme.

RMB trade settlement has the following features[1]:

- Trade and current account transactions between Mainland China and other parts of the world can be settled in RMB.
- Offshore companies can make RMB payments through banks in Hong Kong to trade counterparts in Mainland China for the purchase of goods. The RMB necessary to settle payments can be bought in Hong Kong if necessary.
- Offshore companies can also receive payments, through banks in Hong Kong, from trade counterparts in Mainland China. These RMB proceeds can be deposited in Hong Kong banks and invested in a range of financial products or converted to other currencies.
- Offshore banks can convert or borrow RMB from other banks in Hong Kong, the clearing bank, or a correspondent bank in Mainland China.

The use of RMB for direct investments in Mainland China, in turn, can be done with the following conditions:

- With approval for the investment from authorities in Mainland China, an offshore company can both insert capital and carry out other relevant transactions in RMB instead of using other currencies.
- Hong Kong banks are allowed to provide a full range of RMB-denominated services, from remitting funds to arranging financing in RMB through bank loans or RMB-denominated bonds known as "dim-sum" bonds.

RMB in Hong Kong

Step-by-step, regulators in Mainland China and Hong Kong have expanded the scope of business that can be done in RMB. At the time of this writing in 2014, there was little that could not be done in RMB, at least in Hong Kong, to meet the needs of Chinese and international businesses. Although the RMB is still far from being a truly international currency in the way the USD, EUR, or the GBP are, it is an increasingly important currency as far as business with some kind of link to China.

Hong Kong now has the largest pools of RMB in the world outside of Mainland China. Customer deposits and certificates of deposit issued by Hong Kong banks topped RMB1 trillion by 2013. Corporations hold as much as 70% of these deposits and as many as one in six of these corporations are from overseas. According to projections by one international bank, RMB deposits will reach 40% of Hong Kong's total deposits by 2024 compared to 12% today.

At the same time, Hong Kong is the largest market outside of Mainland China for RMB-denominated bonds or dim-sum bonds. Between 2010 and 2012, 175 issuers put out RMB246 billion in these bonds. Whereas once the Ministry of Finance of China

---

[1] HKMA. "Hong Kong: The Premier Offshore Renminbi Business Centre". December 2012. Online at www .hkma.gov.hk. 10 May 2013.

or Mainland China banks were the only issuers of RMB bonds, the range of issuers has diversified considerably so that financial institutions and companies from around the world now issue such bonds to meet their financing needs in China. The amount of RMB-denominated loans made in Hong Kong has also climbed rapidly and now tops RMB116 billion.[2] Companies as varied as Hopewell, McDonald's, Volkswagen, Fonterra, Axiata and Emirates NDB all have issued dim-sum bonds to commercial and private banks, insurance companies, investment funds, and corporations.

Just opening up the market for the issuance of bonds is not enough, however. Hong Kong increasingly has a number of financial products that allow corporate treasuries to manage their pools or RMB funds. These products include currency futures, investments, funds, and insurance policies. There are products that give investors access to the bond and equity markets in Mainland China. Offshore banks can now access China's interbank bond market or the RMB Qualified Foreign Institutional Investor (RQFII) scheme.

In terms of retain and corporate banking the products available in Hong Kong for offshore RMB-denominated business include:

- Conventional and structured deposit and certificates of deposit;
- Currency exchange;
- Cheques;
- Bank cards;
- Remittances;
- Trade financing, loans, and advances;
- Wealth management products.

The RMB has also become an increasingly important presence in the capital markets. In this regard, banks already have the ability to offer a series of products that include:

- Debt origination;
- Investment funds with access to onshore and offshore markets;
- Commodity-linked products;
- Real estate investment trusts;
- Exchange-traded funds;
- Equity financing.

Finally, the RMB is also growing in importance within the money markets, forex markets, and even insurance. In this regard, the products available include:

- Spot FX trading;
- Deliverable forwards and futures;
- Non-deliverable forwards;
- FX options;
- Insurance plans and products.

---

[2] As of October 2012.

Clearing and Settlement

RMB-denominated business in Hong Kong is typically settled between banks using the Renminbi Real Time Gross Settlement (RTGS) system, which is also known as the RMB Clearing House Automated Transfer System (CHATS). The system allows banks from all over the world to make RMB payments. By the end of 2012, some 202 banks were participants of the RMB clearing platform in Hong Kong, according to the HKMA. Of these, 179 were branches or subsidiaries of foreign banks that have a presence in China. Because all of these banks can handle RMB transactions between Mainland China and countries in which they have operations, the RMB payment network now expands to more than 30 countries. The network is helped by some 1,300 correspondent banking accounts that overseas banks maintain with banks in Hong Kong. These accounts help overseas banks meet increasing demand for offshore RMB business. This increasing demand is visible in the daily turnover of the RMB RTGS system, which was virtually zero in 2009 but is now almost RMB200 billion.

We explored some of the features of the RMB RTGS system in Chapter 7, but it is worth exploring this system further not only for its relevance to treasury managers at a wide cross section of banks in Hong Kong, but also because this may be the most used RMB clearing and settlement system in the world.

The current RMB RTGS[3] system is an upgrade from the Renminbi Settlement System, which was discontinued in June 2007. To operate the system, the Bank of China maintains an account with the People's Bank of China—the central bank in the Mainland. The RTGS system operates daily from 8:30 am to 23:30 Hong Kong time. One of its main features is that it is linked up to the China National Advanced Payment System (CNAPS), the large-value RMB payment system in China. The system is based on the SWIFT protocols and provides a seamless interface with CNAPS. It also allows for links with similar RTGS systems in Hong Kong for trade in HKD, USD, and EUR. Significantly, it also provides an interface with securities clearing and settlement systems in Hong Kong such as the Central Moneymarkets Unit and the Central Clearing and Settlement System.

The liquidity of the RMB RTGS System comes from a range of sources including Hong Kong's growing RMB deposit base, the interbank money markets, issues of RMB securities, financing provided by the clearing bank, and liquidity facilities from the HKMA that uses a currency swap arrangement between the HKMA and the People's Bank of China.

Another significant feature of the system is that it is backed by the relatively strong legal and regulatory infrastructure of Hong Kong. In this particular case, the Clearing and Settlement Systems Ordinance of Hong Kong is the main piece of legislation.[4]

The operator of the RMB RTGS system (and the other currency RTGS systems) is Hong Kong Internbank Clearing Ltd (HKICL), owned by the HKMA and the Hong Kong Association of Banks. HKICL was set up in May 1995 to handle clearing functions that

---

[3] A list of RMB clearing members of Hong Kong Interbank Clearing can be found here: http://www.hkicl.com.hk/clientbrowse.do?docID=7198&lang=en.
[4] http://www.legco.gov.hk/yr03-04/english/ord/ord020-04-e.pdf.

had earlier been handled by the Hongkong and Shanghai Banking Corporation Ltd., the former management bank of the Clearing House. The HKICL provides interbank clearing and settlement services to banks in Hong Kong and operates a central clearing and settlement system for both public and private debt securities on behalf of the HKMA.[5]

The RMB RTGS system provides a number of services that include:

- RMB interbank funds transfers;
- RMB local cheque clearing and settlement;
- RMB cross-border joint cheque clearing;
- Delivery versus payment for RMB bonds through a link to the Central Moneymarekets Unit;
- Automated remittances of RMB funds from RMB bond issuances;
- Electronic clearing and settlement of RMB Central Clearing and Settlement System items, RMB investor accounts, and special items like money settlement instructions;
- Electronic clearing and settlement of RMB items done through the Electronic Payment System (EPS), both on the same day and next day;
- Electronic clearing and settlement of RMB autodebit items and autocredit items.

The system has emerged as a major gateway of liquidity. In January 2010, for example, HKICL processed just 54 RMB-denominated cheques and 518 transfers of funds through the RTGS system for a total of 522 transactions. By the last month of that year, the number of transactions had jumped to 1,042 cheques and 6,327 transfers for a total of 7,369 transactions. A year later, the number of total transactions in December was 92,450 (including 75,760 transfers). In December 2012, the system processed 115,269 transactions and the numbers continued to climb. In April 2013 the system processed 139,971 transactions.

Perhaps even more impressive is the total value of the transactions, which jumped from RMB 3 billion in January 2010 to RMB 255 billion in December 2010 to RMB 2,340 billion a year later and RMB 4,346 billion in December 2012. By April 2013, the total figure transacted for the month was RMB 5,794 billion.[6]

International Linkages

The RMB RTGS system is linked, in Hong Kong, to other similar systems for HKD, USD, and EUR clearances but the links of the RMB clearing system go much further afield. The combination of Hong Kong's four real time systems create a multi-currency clearing and settlement platform that allows for foreign exchange transactions to be settled in a payment-vs-payment (PvP) basis. The use of PvP makes the system more efficient while eliminating settlement risk associated with time lags or time zone gaps. Banks can trade and settle forex transactions that involve the RMB using a number of electronic trading platforms, such as

---

[5] Hong Kong Interbank Clearing Limited website at www.hkicl.com.hk.
[6] http://www.hkicl.com.hk/clientbrowse.do?docID=7237&lang=en.

the one provided by Reuters. The system supports the settlement of USD/RMB foreign exchange trades in Asian time zones while facilitating liquidity management.

The RMB RTGS system is almost identical to the HKD RTGS system. The clearing bank, in this case Bank of China, is a commercial bank. Participants open and maintain settlement accounts with Bank of China, through which all transactions are settled. The system is used for large-value transactions and small-value bulk clearing items. When transactions are settled, they are considered to be final and irrevocable. The system supports a real-time and end-of-day delivery-vs-payment (DvP) facility for RMB debt securities lodged with the CMU. Participants can arrange for DvP of RMB-denominated shares traded on the Stock Exchange of Hong Kong.

A couple of mechanisms have made the RMB RTGS system smoother. One is the RTGS Liquidity Optimiser. Another is a DvP function to support the listing of RMB-denominated securities on the stock exchange. Ultimately, the goal is to make the RMB RTGS system as functional as the much larger HKD RTGS system.

Banks in Hong Kong or around the world can participate in the RMB RTGS system by opening an account with the Bank of China in Hong Kong, which is the clearing bank for RMB trades. Banks around the world can also join the system indirectly through a correspondent bank in Hong Kong.

In June 2012, for example, the HKMA singed agreements with Euroclear Bank and J.P. Morgan Worldwide Securities Services to deliver cross-border collateral management, allowing international financial institutions to use securities held with either institution as collateral in triparty repo transactions with institutions that are members of the HKMA's Central Moneymarkets Unit[7] (CMU), to access liquidity in Hong Kong. Hong Kong's RMB trade is a particular focus of this agreement. Both Euroclear Bank and JP Morgan would act as collateral management agents for repo transactions, which would ensure that a number of obligations such as valuations, eligibility, haircuts, and substitutions are done automatically.[8] Six months later, UBS AG and HSBC took advantage of Euroclear's "Collateral Highway" to carry out the first RMB triparty repo ever, which used Euroclear Bank and the HKMA to manage collateral.[9]

In announcing this one repo deal, HSBC noted that by the end of 2015 the number of RMB deposits in Hong Kong would increase to as much as 30% of all Hong Kong deposits, up from 9% at the end of 2012. To manage these deposits firms would necessarily look to international repo markets to optimize cash balances. According to the HKMA, RMB cross-border settlements grew from RMB50 billion in August 2010 to RMB200 billion in October 2012.

The practicalities of that agreement and the first transaction was not lost on the markets. The links to Euroclear (and JP Morgan) that the HKMA fostered allows more banks

---

[7] See Chapter 3 for more details and a list of participants.
[8] HKMA. "Press Releases: Hong Kong Monetary Authority, Euroclear Bank and J.P. Morgan open cross-border liquidity and secured lending channels in Hong Kong". June 20, 2012. Online at http://www.info.gov.hk/gia/general/201206/20/P201206200545.htm. May 10, 2013.
[9] Euroclear. "UBS and HSBC choose Euroclear Bank and HKMA for first cross-border RMB Repo." December 5, 2012. Online at http://www.finextra.com/news/announcement.aspx?pressreleaseid=47674. May 10, 2013.

that earlier had limited acess to RMB liquidity to access funds in the Chinese currency to settle trades and finance projects. Conversely, Hong Kong banks would face lower risks in working with offshore banks to cover RMB payments thanks to the access to mutually acceptable collateral.[10]

The original focus of the HKICL was the provision of clearing services denominated in HKD but its role has evolved to operate foreign currency payment systems, including the RMB RTGS. The HKICL also operates the IT system of the Central Moneymarkets Unit (CMU), which is a central clearing and settlement system for public and private debt securities. The CMU, first set up in 1990, provides clearing and settlement facilities for Exchange Fund Bills and Notes and other HKD debt securities. Debt instruments cleared through the CMU are immobilized or dematerialized. Transfer of title is done through a computer book-entry form.

Summary

- The use of the RMB in international trade and investment has been expanding steadily since the People's Bank of China started a push to the international trade in 2005.
- In 2009, the Chinese government launched a pilot scheme to allow the settlement of international trade in RMB. By 2010, the scheme had expanded to cover every province and city in the country and allowed for trade to be settled in RMB through Hong Kong. From 2011, the Chinese government started to allow the settlement of investments in RMB.
- Hong Kong was the pioneer offshore market for RMB-denominated business. The 12th Five Year Plan for Economic and Social Development cemented the city's position in this regard.
- RMB trade settlement includes trade and current account transactions between China and other parts of the world, RMB payments through banks, receipt of payments through Hong Kong banks, and the purchase or borrowing of RMB among banks.
- The use of RMB for direct investment in Mainland China requires approval from authorities to insert capital or carry out transactions in RMB. Hong Kong banks are allowed to provide a range of RMB services related to investment in Mainland China.
- Hong Kong is the largest offshore market for RMB-denominated dim-sum bonds. Some 175 institutions issued RMB246 billion in these bonds between 2010 and 2012.
- RMB-denominated services through Hong Kong are settled using the RMB Real Time Gross Settlement (RTGS) system, also known as the Clearing House Automated Transfer System (CHATS). The system allows banks from a network of 30 countries to make RMB payments.
- The operator of the RMB RTGS system is the Hong Kong Interbank Clearing Ltd. (HKICL), which is owned by the HKMA and the Hong Kong Association of Banks.

---

[10] Lee, Georgina. "HKMA launches RMB cross-border repo." Asian Investor. June 21, 2012. Online at www.asianinvestor.net. 10 May 2013.

The system provides a range of services from interbank transfers to cheque clearing and payment processing.

- The RMB RTGS system is linked to similar systems to trade USD or EUR. It is also linked to international networks through a network of agreements aimed at allowing banks to better manage their RMB liquidity needs.

Key Terms

12th Five Year Plan for Economic and
    Social Development
Bank of China
Central Moneymarkets Unit (CMU)
Cheques
China National Advanced Payment System
    (CNAPS)
Clearing House Automated Transfer
    System (CHATS)
Delivery vs payment (DVP)
Dim-sum bonds
Electronic clearing
Euroclear Bank
Hong Kong Interbank Clearing Limited
    (HKICL)

Interbank transfers
JP Morgan
People's Bank of China
Real Time Gross Settlement (RTGS)
    system
Renminbi (RMB)
Repo deals
RMB Central Clearing and Settlement
    System
RMB Qualified Foreign Institutional
    Investor (RQFII) scheme
Settlement
Trade settlement

Study Guide

1. Explain the ongoing internationalization of the Renminbi. How can the Chinese currency be used by banks doing business in China?
2. What is the RMB RTGS system? How does it work? What requirements does a bank have to meet to take advantage of it?
3. What tools can an offshore bank with limited presence in Hong Kong use to access RMB liquidity?

Further Reading

Clearing and Settlment Systems Ordinance available through the Hong Kong government website at http://www.legco.gov.hk/yr03-04/english/ord/ord020-04-e.pdf.

PART 3

CASE STUDIES

9

Case Studies

After studying this chapter, you should be able to:

1 Understand and explain specific examples of risk including risks associated with segregation of duties, settlement risk, liquidity risk, and concentration risk.

2 Know and discuss the events that led to the failure of Barings Bank, Herstatt Bank, Metallgesellschaft AG and Lehman Brothers, and Long-Term Capital Management.

3 Explain what went wrong at Metallgesellschaft AG and how the company managed to come back from the brink of bankruptcy.

Introduction

Theoretical discussions of risk are useful exercises but they are not, in and of themselves, of much use if they do not help institutions prevent or mitigate risk. It is often up to the treasury to translate these theoretical discussions into practical terms and implement the strategies needed to limit it. This chapter examines four instances in which the treasury failed to do that.

The first case study may be the freshest in people's minds and probably the most famous. It is the failure of Barings Bank. This is also maybe the most spectacular of all the case studies. Weak management and confused lines of reporting combined together to bring down a venerable institution. From the time management discovered something was amiss, it took less than 72 hours for Barings Bank to be declared insolvent ending more than two centuries of history.

The second case is very well known among bankers as it led directly to the creation of the current set of international banking regulatory accords. The term Herstatt Risk was coined after the failure of Germany's Bankhaus Herstatt, not a large bank but one with great significance in international finance because it was involved in foreign currency transactions globally. When it failed, it did so without paying some USD620 million in foreign exchange contracts.

The third case did not end in corporate tragedy, but it almost did do away with Metallgesellschaft AG, a giant German energy conglomerate. Short of cash after a round of acquisitions, the company entered the U.S. market where it sought to leverage oil futures into healthy profits. But it did not take its own financial position into full account and was almost caught out when it could not cover billions in losses.

The fourth case, possibly the most famous failure of a financial institution in history, is that of Lehman Brothers. After more than a century and a half of successful and profitable operations, that historied institutions failed due to weak controls and reckless risk-taking.

Segregation of Duties: Barings Bank

Barings Bank was founded in London in 1762. It grew rapidly thanks to growing international trade. It soon started lending to foreign governments, including France and the United States. Relatively small compared to most clearing banks, Barings was still considered a pre-eminent financial institution. By the time a single trader named Nick Leeson was done with a set of unauthorized derivative trades, Barings Bank was no longer.[1]

A number of factors came together to bring down the bank but, with the exception of some tragically bad luck, all of them can be traced back to weak controls within the treasury. Even the fraud that Leeson managed to carry out could have been prevented with stronger controls, more careful oversight, and clear segregation of duties—specifically trading and supervision.

---

[1]Bernard, Alicia. "The Barings Collapse (A): Breakdowns in Organizational Culture & Management". International Institute for Management Development. 1995.

Leeson was a star. He joined Barings Securities Ltd in 1989, at the age of 22 after doing a similar job at Morgan Stanley. He was sent to Hong Kong and Jakarta as a settlement officer. When he applied for a job in Singapore, heading up settlements and accounting, the bank was glad to give it to him. He was good at his job. A year later, he was appointed assistant director and general manager at Barings Futures (Singapore) Pte Ltd (BFS). By then, he had already secured a trading license in Singapore but, partly due to conflicts within the organization and partly due to rapid growth, it was unclear whom Leeson reported to. That fact that Leeson was in charge both of his trades and of authorizing his own activities escaped notice.

This confusion allowed Leeson to undertake two lines of secret and dangerous activities. On the one hand, he boosted reported profits by trading between actual accounts and a now infamous secret account—account number 88888—in such a way that profits were credited to the secret account. On the other, he started taking open positions that amounted to bets on which way the market would go, acting against the clear policy of Barings.

By the end of 1994, he had GBP200 million in disguised losses from trades on Japanese derivative products. At this point, Leeson might have been able to bring it back into the black, but bad luck came into play. On 17 January 1995, a massive earthquake hit Kobe, Japan, and the bottom fell out of the market. At that particular time, Leeson had a small short on Nikkei 225 futures contracts and many outstanding options contracts under a straddle strategy that would have paid off had the market continued to trade within a narrow range. Leeson responded to the earthquake by building a large long position on Nikkei 225 futures, on the expectation that the market would recover quickly. A little more than a month later, his position was so large that he was losing GBP20 million for every 100 point drop in the Nikkei—which fell 2,000 points between the day the earthquake hit and February 27.

In the first two months of 1995, Leeson amassed losses of GBP638 million. In the end, total losses added up to GBP843 million. The Bank of England (B of E) worked on putting together a rescue package and got as far as getting commitments worth GBP600 million but because it was impossible to quantify the losses at the time, no rescue was forthcoming.

Barings, that venerable institution and cornerstone of the global financial system, fell.

Chronology

The events surrounding the fall of Barings evolved as follows:

- **1989:** Nick Leeson joins the settlements department at Barings Securities Ltd.
- **1992:** Leeson applies for post in Singapore as head of the settlements and accounting departments of Baring Futures (Singapore) Pte Ltd, a new company.
- **1992, April:** Leeson arrives in Singapore. His job includes heading up the company's floor operations at the Singapore International Monetary Exchange (SIMEX).

- **1992, July 1:** BFS starts trading on SIMEX as a clearing member, basically on equity derivatives on behalf of clients.
- **1992, July:** Leeson secures a trader's license in Singapore. He had not been able to get a similar license in the UK due to an outstanding county court judgment over a personal debt. He creates account 88888.
- **1993:** Leeson appointed Assistant Director and General Manager at BFS.
- **1995, January 17:** Massive earthquake hits Kobe, Japan. More than 6,000 people around Osaka and Kobe are killed. The bottom falls out of the market. Leeson had built a large position on contracts predicated on the market moving within a narrow range.
- **1995, Feb. 23:** Leeson and his wife fly from Singapore to Kuala Lumpur. Leeson faxes in his resignation for health reasons. Tony Hawes, a treasury executive at Barings, discovers account 88888.
- **1995, Feb. 24:** 7:15 am: Peter Baring hears of the losses in Singapore from Peter Norris.
  8 am: Barings management meets to consider the crisis.
  12 pm: Peter Baring asks Bank of England for a bailout.
  5 pm: Bank of England hosts meeting of other UK bankers and asks them to consider joint response.
  Japanese market continues to fall, dropping by 645 points in one day alone. The total drop since the earthquake was more than 2,000 points.
- **1995, Feb. 25:** Through the day, bankers consider recapitalization plans.
- **1995, Feb. 26:** Temporary bailout plan agreed upon in the morning but ultimately cannot be done. A judge signs an administration order in the evening and by 10:10 pm the Bank of England announces Barings has failed.
- **1995, Feb. 27:** With losses of more than USD1.4 billion, Barings Bank is declared insolvent.
- **1995, March 1:** Leeson and wife book flight to Bangkok via Dubai.
- **1995, March 2:** Leeson and wife detained in Frankfurt, Germany.
- **1995, March 2:** Internationale Nederlanden Groep N.V. (ING) buys the assets and liabilities of Barings Group for GBP1.
- **1995, July 1995:** Board of Banking Supervision issues report on the collapse.
- **1995, September:** Singapore Minister of Finance publishes its own report, which is more critical.
- **1995, November 23:** Leeson extradited from Germany to the UK.
- **1995, December 1:** Leeson pleads guilty to two charges of fraud and forgery. Prosecutors drop nine other charges. He is eventually sentenced to six-and-a-half years in jail.

Response and Management

Rumors that something was amiss at Barings were already surfacing in the market before the earthquake struck. Already, the positions that Leeson was taking up were too large to go unnoticed. At one point, the BIS called Barings to confirm that the bank had enough funds to meet obligations with SIMEX. Unfortunately, London did not investigate, thinking the SIMEX was aware of the bank's practice of taking equal and opposite positions from another exchange, a practice that Leeson was not actually following.

In early February 1995, staff from the treasury and settlements departments—Tony Hawes and Tony Railton—visited Singapore to follow up on the lack of information sent to London in support of margin requests. It did not take long for them to discover that something was wrong, but fraud was not yet on the table.

By Friday, February 24, 1995, it had become obvious that something had gone terribly wrong in Singapore. Peter Norris, head of investment banking, had received a phone call 24 hours earlier from James Bax, the Singapore-based managing director of Baring Securities, to inform him that Leeson had disappeared. After spending 24 hours sorting out exactly how bad the situation was, Norris called Chairman Peter Baring. By the time management discovered the bank was liable for contracts worth USD27 billion that were, by then, worth a fraction of that, it was too late to try to figure out the reason. The only thing that remained was to find a solution.[2]

The first question that management sought to answer was whether, given the extent of the damage, the bank could stay open. With an affirmative response from the lawyers, Barings stayed open one more day.

The second step was to look for a bailout from the B of E. Management estimated the losses at GBP400 million, a cautious estimate that fell far short of reality. The B of E then summoned more than a dozen CEOs or chairmen from clearing and merchant banks for a meeting that afternoon. Because the problem was not systemic but one specific to Barings, the B of E was not about to put its own money in.

At first, other British banks considered the possibility of setting up a "lifeboat" of funds, if the exposure to the derivatives could be capped—in other words, Barings had to stop the bleeding. At one point, the Sultan of Brunei, then the richest man in the world, considered capping the lifeboat. In the end, however, there was simply no telling how deep the losses would go on the unsettled futures, so no deal was forthcoming. By 8:36 pm on Saturday night, less than 72 hours after Peter Baring first had a whiff of a problem, Barings was bankrupt.

Analysis

The management at Barings thought the Singapore futures trading operation was a safe profit generator. In theory, what the unit did was buy Nikkei futures in one market and sell them at a higher price in another. The operation was based on the fact that, at the time, there were two main markets for Nikkei 225 futures: the Osaka Stock Exchange and

---

[2] Martin, Peter. "Death Came Sudden and Swift for Barings". Financial Times. 4 March 1995.

SIMEX. The idea was to leverage temporary differences that appeared between the prices quoted at one exchange or the other. If a dealer has links to both exchanges at the same time, risk-free profits are possible. Long positions should have balanced out short positions and the bank should have had no exposure to the movement of the Japanese stock market. But what was supposed to happen and what did happen are two different things.

What Leeson had done was to build huge long positions in two different Nikkei contracts based on the same basket of stocks. He had also a big short position in Japanese interest rate futures. The futures contracts committed Barings to buying USD7 billion worth of Japanese equities and USD20 billion (or more) of interest rate futures. Since the Kobe earthquake a month earlier, Japanese equities had fallen steadily and the contracts were worth a fraction of what Leeson had paid.

A few factors came together to confuse the picture and allow Leeson to operate unchecked long enough for his position to become untenable.

First was a lack of management clarity. It was unclear who was directly responsible for his activities. Unfortunately, nobody really was keeping tables on him. Barings Bank managed its business using a matrix system. Traders reported to product and local managers. Product managers had responsibility over profits while local managers handled operational and administrative matters. Back office staff reported to the local managers and filed reports to the head office in London. While in theory all this was easy enough, Leeson held several roles and it was unclear whom he reported to. This confusion was created by the rapid growth of Barings' operations in Asia and the conflicts that existed among the various groups. Top-level supervisors in London and Asia thought the other group was responsible for Leeson's activities. Similar confusion existed in regards to reporting associated with products and profits. Later, some supervisors who should have direct control over business activities said they did not actually feel in control.

Locally, Leeson should have reported to Simon Jones, who was chief operating officer of Baring Securities (Singapore), and to James Bax, who was managing director, as well as to directors of Barings Futures (Singapore). But Bax thought Leeson had a direct line to London and Jones had little involvement with Barings Futures, although London thought he was actively involved. Another line of reporting, on the product side, was even more convoluted, but the upshot was that, here again, everyone thought Jones was keeping tabs.

In the back office, things were no better. Local management in Singapore gave up operational control but there was confusion about who in London held all the strings. In theory, Tony Gamby, the settlements director at Barings, was responsible for all futures and options settlements from early 1994. All companies reported to him except for Barings Futures (Singapore). Barings Futures (Singapore) reported to Brenda Granger, the manager of futures and options settlements, but it was unclear whom she reported to. Bad personal relations among management made problems even less likely to be identified.

A second factor was little, if any, questioning of how Leeson was making profits that were clearly out of sync with what he was authorized to do. BFS started trading on the SIMEX in July 2013, basically in three types of derivatives that included 10-year Japanese government bond futures, Nikkei 225 futures, and 3-month Euroyen contracts.

There was no OTC dealing permitted but the company was allowed to take an intra-day position that had to be matched or closed by the end of each business day. Marked by a low-risk philosophy, BFS only had authority to take position on behalf of clients. Leeson could not take bets on the market beyond some small intra-day limits. One profitable line of business was "switching," which took advantage of arbitrage opportunities among different exchanges, such as leveraging the open outcry system used by SIMEX with the computer-based systems in Toronto or Oslo. Even though this business was supposed to be very low risk, it still generated GBP30 million in revenue in 1994 and earned Leeson a bonus of GBP450,000.

A third factor was that Leeson, thanks to a combination of independence and wide areas of responsibility, could operate virtually unchecked by his supervisors while those who reported to him did not question what he was doing. There were daily reports of trades sent to London but Account 88888 was not on a master list of accounts because it was intended as an error account, so it was put in a suspense file. False journal entries helped hide month end balances on this account. Leeson also created false trades, which allowed him to alter the position sheet sent daily to SIMEX—this position sheet was used to calculate the daily margin call. Because much of the information on the position sheet was fictional, the margin requirements were much lower than they should have been.

Lessons Learnt

The industry derived a number of lessons from the failure of Barings, even if they have not always been heeded:

- The main lesson for the industry of the downfall of Barings is the importance of clearly segregating duties and, in turn, setting clear reporting lines. Had these theoretically simple things been done, Barings would arguably be very much alive today. The fact that front and back office operations were not segregated allowed Leeson to remain in charge of both at Baring Futures (Singapore) and, in effect, approve his own false positions.
- A system of checks and balance for operational risk failed at Barings. Not only was management not on top of what the Singapore Futures unit did, there was no reconciliation between client records and the funding that Barings in London provided. As a result, false information was never verified. The collapse of the bank underlined in the strongest possible terms the importance of such checks and balances.
- After the collapse of Barings, both London and Singapore exchanges reviewed their regulatory rules and auditing, surveillance, and clearing practices to safeguard against settlement risk. An international advisory panel eventually recommended that SIMEX enhance customer protection, upgrade its clearing system and procedures to bring in real time settlement and more critical risk management systems, promote information sharing among exchanges, require clearing firms to register senior officers, strengthen

market surveillances and enhance the large trade reporting system. In the end, not only did Barings fail to protect itself but the exchanges themselves failed to communicate adequately enough to spot large discrepancies in reported positions.

- Finally, ongoing reviews of operational procedures are important. There was almost nothing in what Leeson was doing that upper level management would not have been able to spot with relative ease in a review of internal controls.

Settlement Risk: Herstatt Bank

Settlement risk is the risk that a counterparty does not deliver a security or its value in cash, as per an agreement through which the security was traded even after the other party or parties deliver the security in question or the cash value. In other words, settlement risk is the risk that one party in a trade does not pay up. Three decades ago, Germany's Bankhaus Herstatt (Herstatt Bank) provided a prime example of what can go wrong and how, if unattended, settlement risk can be a significant concern. When regulators closed Herstatt in 1974, the bank left the dollars it owned on foreign-exchange deals unpaid.[3] Banks around the world were left with losses of about USD620 million.[4] Even decades after the collapse, the failure of Herstatt remains the prime industry example of settlement risk and counterparties not being paid.

The Herstatt failure remains significant to this day, even if similar impact would be unlikely today due to developments in technology. Still, it was the failure of this bank that led a group of 11 developed economies to work with the BIS to create the BCBS, which in turn would develop the regulatory standards for banks around the world. In other words, the Herstatt failure may have changed the face of banking around the world.

Among the 2,500 or so credit institutions in the German banking system, there are banks, cooperatives, and commercial banks. All three operate along broadly similar lines. Germany's banking system is highly stable by international standards. And yet, even in Germany there have been bank failures, including the 1974 fall of Herstatt, the "largest and most spectacular failure in German banking history since 1945."[5]

Despite this rather grandiose statement from the BIS, the reality was that Herstatt was not a large bank—even by the standards of the day—but it was systemically important because it played a role in processing foreign exchange orders. Founded in 1956 in Cologne, Herstatt grew to have assets of DM2.07 billion and become the thirty-fifth largest in the country. The trouble at Herstatt had to do with a large foreign exchange

---

[3] Basel Committee on Banking Supervision. "Working Paper No. 13: Bank Failures in Mature Economies." Bank for International Settlements. April 2004.

[4] Koleva, Gergana. "'Icon of Systemic Risk' Haunds Industry After Demise". American Banker. 23 June 2011.

[5] Ibid, pg 5.

business that also proved to be rather risky. When the U.S. dollar started to appreciate unexpectedly and rapidly in the early 1970 s, Herstatt got in trouble. By September 1973, the bank had far too much debt and suffered losses that added up to four times its capital.

Herstatt did not adapt quickly enough to the changing dollar, although it did change its strategy in late 1973 to try and capitalize on the rising dollar. And the change worked until mid-January 1974, when the dollar changed direction. By March 1974, Herstatt had open exchange positions of DM2 billion, eighty times larger than the bank's limit and three times as large as the amount of capital the bank held. By the time the seriousness of the problem became obvious, the bank had no choice but to close its position and it was too late to avoid a failure. In June, the Federal Banking Supervisory Office (BAKred) took away Herstatt's licence. The bank had assets of DM1 billion and liabilities of DM2.2 billion.

Chronology

The events surrounding the fall of Herstatt evolved as follows:

- **1973, March:** Bretton Woods System collapses and currencies start floating freely as gold peg is done away with.
- **1973, September:** Dollar appreciates rapidly.
- **1974, January:** Dollar shifts direction and starts depreciating.
- **1974, March:** Special audit approved by the Federal Banking Supervisory Office finds Herstatt's open positions added up to DM2 billion, eighty times larger than the bank's limit of DM25 million.
- **1974, June:** Herstatt forced to close foreign exchange positions, leading to losses of DM470 million.
- **1974, June 26:** Federal Banking Supervisory Office withdraws Herstatt's banking licence. The bank had assets of DM1 billion but liabilities of DM2.2 billion.

Response and Management

There was little Hestatt could do to save itself when BAKred took away its licence on June 26, 1974 and forced it into liquidation.

After the Second World War, the Bretton Woods System had kept currencies stable by pegging the dollar to gold and other currencies to the dollar. When Bretton Woods collapsed in March 1973, currencies started to float freely. The general expectation was that the dollar would depreciate rather rapidly, opening the door for some risky bets on what was expected to be one-way movement. When these expectations proved wrong and the dollar started to gain value through 1973, Herstatt was caught going in the wrong direction. For Germany's regulators and other banks, the problem was not how to save Herstatt but how to avoid any kind of contagion. But the biggest three banks in Germany failed to organize a rescue.

Herstatt lost its licence in the afternoon in Germany, which was the morning in New York, where counterparties were expecting to get dollars for Deutsche marks. Those dollars never arrived. Chase Manhattan, Herstatt's clearing bank in New York, did not fulfill the orders. The result was a domino of defaults. The bank failed in the middle of the day, creating a fault line in the international currency exchange regime. At one point, the term "Herstatt risk" emerged in respect to the settlement risk associated with foreign currency transactions across different time zones—although today, the lag between delivery and payment seems old fashioned.[6] Although this would not happen today, the decision to simply stop operations meant banks elsewhere, from New York to Hong Kong, were not paid for foreign exchange transactions. The result was a domino effect that led to other bank failures.

After the Herstatt failure, which led to cross-jurisdictional implications, the members of the G-10 countries and Luxemburg created a standing committee under the BIS. This committee became known as the Basel Committee on Banking Supervision, which started to develop regulatory approaches that have been adopted globally.

Analysis

Herstatt Risk became a byword for settlement risk. Although this was not the cause of the collapse at Herstatt, which failed due to foreign exchange risk, the settlement risk associated with the bank turned into a significant loss event for those institutions for whom Herstatt was a counterparty. Herstatt represented significant operational risk for those other institutions.

The much more prevalent use of technology in the last four decades makes similar failure events associated with Settlement risk unlikely today but there are two issues that remain significant: transparency and risk control.

There was a possibility that Herstatt could have been rescued but when Germany's biggest banks considered a bailout, they were held back by the simple fact that they did not know the actual size of the losses. This lack of transparency made it impossible for any of them to step up.

Another issue was one of risk control. Herstatt did not exercise such control with any degree of efficacy. From the moment that Bretton Woods ended, Herstatt adopted a faulty strategy in its proprietary trading of foreign currency. The movement of the dollar, which moved in exactly the opposite direction from what Herstatt expected, is seen as a major reason behind the fall of the bank. At the time of the failure, the bank's foreign exchange risk was about three times as large as the amount of capital it held.

---

[6] Koleva, Gergana. "'Icon of Systemic Risk' Haunds Industry After Demise". American Banker. 23 June 2011.

Lessons Learnt

The industry derived a number of lessons from the failure of Herstatt in 1974. These included:

- The failure underlined the importance of introducing risk limits. Following the failures, regulators introduced limits to how much risk a bank could take on their foreign exchange operations. In 1976, a Second Amendment to the Banking Act limited risks in credit business and tightened controls of the Federal Banking Supervisory Office. Perhaps the biggest after-effect of the failure was that regulations were introduced to deal with large credits and a principle of dual control was introduced. Of even greater long-term impact for depositors was the Association of German Banks introduced a deposit protection scheme.[7]
- Herstatt Risk thus became a byword for the risk of the counterparty financial institution in a foreign exchange deal fails to deliver. In other words, Herstatt Risk is settlement risk. The main lesson for banks was the importance of minimizing this risk that arises in the time lag of the delivery between two major currencies. Technology has changed this situation drastically but settlement risk remains a consideration on longer trades. In 2002, the Continuous Linked Settlement system was instituted and operated by CLS Group Holding AG. The largest banks in the world created the system to settle foreign exchange flows. The system operates with gross-value instructions and multi lateral net funding. Real time gross settlement (RTGS) systems have also become common, as they ensure transactions are settled quickly and in succession, limiting risk. Another new development is the use of central bank payment and settlement services for cross-border and multi-currency transactions, which work on delivery-versus-payment systems. Another avenue to minimize Herstatt Risk is the use of over the counter (OTC) bilateral contracts done by computer or phone.

Liquidity Risk in Position Hedging: Metallgesellschaft AG

Metallgesellschaft AG was a commodity sales and engineering conglomerate with 46,000 employees and turnover of more than USD15 billion in 1993. It had 251 subsidiaries in Germany and abroad and provided trade and financial as well as engineering services. Deutsche Bank and Dresdner Bank were the principal owners. In the early 1990s, the company was caught unawares in a financial crisis when it lost more than USD1.3 billion following speculation in oil futures. While the company should have been able to absorb

---

[7]Basel Committee on Banking Supervision. "Working Paper No. 13: Bank Failures in Mature Economies." Bank for International Settlements. April 2004. Pg 6.

the losses, the timing was unfortunate in that they happened at a time when it was short on cash and funding following a spate of acquisitions. Without enough cash on hand to meet its obligations, the giant conglomerate was brought to the brink of bankruptcy and was saved only by some quick support from banks and massive divestitures.

Metallgesellschaft AG did not fail. In 1999, the group acquired GEA AG and a year later it shifted its focus towards specialist mechanical engineering. In 2005, it renamed itself as GEA Group Aktiengesellschaft. Nevertheless, for a few years there in the early 1990s, it was touch and go for the storied German conglomerate, which found itself on the brink of bankruptcy.

In 1992, the New York arm of the company shifted its energy activities from traditional trading into integrated risk management under the name MG Energy.[8] MG Energy sold gasoline, heating oil, and diesel to wholesale and retail customers on fixed-price and long-term contracts as it sought to profit from low oil prices after the end of the Gulf War in 1991. With oil prices at a low point, customers sought to lock in some savings. Two years later, MG had outstanding supply obligations of 160 million barrels of oil over ten years.[9]

That was only part of the story, however. In the early 1990s, following a reorganization of the conglomerate from the headquarters in Frankfurt, Metallgesellschaft undertook a series of acquisitions, including buying the nonpaper division of Dynamit Nobel AG for USD706 million. Twice the company raised capital. By 1991, it had 52,000 employees. The entry into the U.S. energy market was a direct result of weakness in metal prices in Europe. The company had large operations focused on the sale of recycled metals.

MG's approach to hedging was to buy oil futures but the company could not match the maturity dates with its obligations. What it did instead was to buy shorter futures and roll them over immediately after selling them. When, in November 1993, OPEC decided to keep production level, the spot oil price of oil dropped by about USD5 to below USD14.50 per barrel but long-term prices remained stable. This wiped out about 20% of the value of MG's futures. By January 1994, Metallgesellschaft AG had operating losses of DM1.8 billion (USD1.03 billion) for the year 1993. On top of that, potential losses on futures positions could add up to DM1.5 billion (USD857 million) over two to three years.[10] When incoming chairman Ronaldo H. Schmitz called off the derivatives strategy, the company had debt of USD4.9 billion.

Chronology

The events surrounding the fall of LTCM evolved as follows:

- **1881, May 17:** Metallgesellschaft founded.
- **1991:** Gulf War ends and oil prices drop.

---

[8] Hawkins, David F and Wyns, Guy. "Metallgesellschaft AG". Harvard Business Review. 194-097. 19 May 1995.
[9] The Economist. January 15, 1994.
[10] Hawkins, David F and Wyns, Guy. "Metallgesellschaft AG". Harvard Business Review. 194-097. 19 May 1995.

- **1991, June:** Metallgesellschaft acquires nonpaper division of Dynamit Nobel AG for USD706 million.
- **1991, December:** Acquisitions through the year amount to USD2 billion.
- **1992:** Metallgesellschaft Corp in New York shifts energy activities from trading to risk management as MG Energy.
- **1993, February:** Chairman Heinz Schimmelsbusch launches divestment program to raise USD600 million in cash.
- **1993, July:** MG has outstanding supply obligations of 160 million barrels of oil over 10 years.
- **1993, November:** OPEC decides to keep production stable and spot oil prices drop. Long-term prices remain stable.
- **1993, December:** Metallgesellschaft Corp accumulates trading losses of USD660 million.
- **1994, January:** Metallgesellschaft Corp announces operating loss of USD1.03 billion for fiscal 1993 and future losses of up to USD857 million over two to three years.
- **1994:** Bank bailout of USD2.06 billion sought along with cuts in staff, inventory, and materials, and divestiture of non-core business.
- **1995, January:** Metallgesellschaft announces another huge loss of DM 2.63 billion for fiscal year 1994.
- **1996, January:** Metallgesellschaft announces profits of DM118 billion on revenue of DM17.64 billion. Most of bank bailout is paid out.
- **1996:** Company completely exists U.S. market after abandoning fixed-priced contracts for oil.

Response and Management

The crisis at Metallgesellschaft was one of cash—it did not have enough of it. Shortly after taking over the company in 1993, Schmitz brought in four new board members, including Kajo Neukirchen, a corporate rescuer, as the company was close to enter the largest bankruptcy in history after the Second World War.

Management's first step to deal with the crisis was to raise money. Neukirchen put together a bank bailout worth USD2.06 billion and started to cut USD1.63 billion in costs, including cutting 7,500 jobs, inventory, and materials. He also started selling off noncore businesses to raise another USD600 million.

Analysis

Metallgesellschaft's 1992 annual report points out that "futures and options markets provide tools that enable seasoned market participants to manage those price risks and to benefit from significant business opportunities that risk and volatility make possible." Hubris? In this case, it seems so.

The company had entered the U.S. energy market to counter weakness in the European metals and the subsequent fall in liquidity there. This entry followed some significant acquisitions that left the company with little liquidity and large debts. Through 1991, Metallgesellschaft spent USD2 billion on acquisitions and had 52,000 employees spread around 258 companies.

The sales of fixed contracts for oil products was, at first, quite successful. In a paper on the failure of the company, John Digenan and other authors point out that at one time, profits topped USD5 per barrel. But the contracts were unique in that they included a clause that allowed a counterparty to terminate the contract if the related front-month New York Mercantile Exchange (NYMEX) futures contract was greater than the fixed prices at which MG was selling the oil. If the buyer exercised the option, MG would have to pay half of the difference between the futures price and the fixed price. While the option proved popular among customers, it left MG short of cash when spot prices for oil fell unexpectedly.[11]

Two things went wrong. One was that MG did not have enough funding to support immediate margin calls. The second was that the timing of cash flows made it impossible to maintain the company's hedging strategy on the price of oil. MG was caught in a cash crunch: classic liquidity risk. The company's strategy was good for market risk but it did not take into account funding risk and the positions they were taking were so large, that this risk was enormous.

There was another issue. The company made wrong assumptions of economies of scale. The company had such a great portion of open NYMEX contracts that liquidating contracts was an issue, so despite hedging the company thought it was left open to vulnerability in the event of rising oil prices—but what ultimately hurt the most was when prices fell and customers started cancelling the long term contracts, requiring the company to come up with cash.[12]

Lessons Learnt

The industry derived a number of lessons from the financial crisis at Metallgesellschaft in the 1990s. These included:

- The importance of considering liquidity risk in any hedging strategy. Even the best strategy can fail if the company does not have enough cash to meet its obligations.

---

[11] Digenan, John; Felson, Dan; Kelly, Robert; Wiemert, Ann. "Metallgesellschaft AG: A Case Study". Stuart School of Business. Illinois Institute of Technology. 2004.
[12] Digenan, John; Felson, Dan; Kelly, Robert; Wiemert, Ann. "Metallgesellschaft AG: A Case Study". Professional Risk Managers' International Association. 2004.

Perhaps the greatest lesson is that market movements have consequences that can be far reaching and companies, financial or otherwise, have to consider all the ramifications of market movements.

- The problems at Metallgesellschaft also underscored the importance of differentiating between hedging and speculating. The company was speculating under the guise of hedging. Had they been truly hedging, changes in the price of oil would not have mattered much to them.

- A final lesson is that it is important for companies to understand the details of their financial positions and how changes in their respective markets can affect those positions. Adequate financing is a tool like any other but without it, companies can go bankrupt.

Liquidity Risk: Lehman Brothers

The bankruptcy filing of Lehman Brothers Holdings Inc. is considered the largest in the history of the United States. Lehman Brothers started out as a small grocery store opened by Henry Lehman, a German immigrant, in Alabama in 1850. The business expanded enormously over more than a century and a half. It survived railroad bankruptcies, the Great Depression, two world wars, and a merger and a spin-off from American Express to become the fourth largest investment bank in the United States. In 2007, it celebrated its largest profit ever. In 2008, it went bankrupt.

Lehman did not survive the subprime mortgage crisis in the U.S. in 2008, as a chain reaction caused by poor risk control brought down the once-celebrated bank. Ultimately, the collapse was caused by the large positions in subprime and other lower-rated mortgage tranches that the company had taken when securitizing the underlying mortgages. In 2006, Lehman securitized USD146 billion in mortgages and 2007 was a golden year for the company. It reported record net income of USD4.2 billion even as it accumulated a mortgage-backed securities portfolio of $85 billion. Even after the housing market in the U.S. started to fray, Lehman held on to its enormous mortgage positions. The company did not budge when defaults on subprime mortgages rose to seven-year highs at the beginning of 2007.

The first signs of trouble at Lehman surfaced on March 16, 2008. JP Morgan Chase acquired Lehman's rival in underwriting mortgage-backed securities, Bear Stearns, through a stock swap that valued that the once lofty bank at $2 per share. The sale, or rescue, of Bear Stearns was a watershed moment in the Global Financial Crisis. It was not long before speculation spread that Lehman could become the next Bear Stearns, even as most observers thought Lehman was simply too blind to follow in the same path.

In a single day on March 17, Lehman's stock fell as much as 48% and it kept on dropping. The valuation of Lehman's huge mortgage portfolio was questioned even when things seemed to look up including when the company raised USD4 billion through an issue of preferred stock that was convertible into Lehman shares at a 32% premium to its price at the time.

But in June 2008, Lehman reported its first quarterly loss in the 14 years since it had become independent of American Express. The company lost USD2.8 billion but managed to raise USD6 billion from investors as one of the many measures to reverse the slide in its share value and its future prospects. Lehman said it had boosted its liquidity pool to an estimated USD45 billion, decreased gross assets by USD147 billion, and reduced its exposure to residential and commercial mortgages by 20% while cutting down leverage from a factor of 32 to about 25. This herculean effort was not enough.

Lehman's stock plunged 77% in the first week of September 2008 and continued falling the next week. It lost 45% on September 9, alone, dropping to USD7.79. Its prospects became even murkier when the Korea Development Bank backed out of a plan to buy the once-venerable institutions for USD4 billion, a fraction of what it was once worth. And then, Lehman's clients started pulling out en masse. For the third quarter of 2008, Lehman reported losses of USD3.9 billion. The business was hemorrhaging capital. On September 11, 2008, Lehman's stock plunged again, this time by 42%. Last ditch efforts to arrange for a takeover of the ailing investment bank by Barclays Plc and Bank of America were fruitless.

Lehman Brothers filed for bankruptcy with the United States Bankruptcy Court for the Southern District of New York on September 15, 2008. That day, the company's stock price hit a rock bottom of 21 cents per share. The failure of Lehman marked the beginning of the Global Financial Crisis that would last until 2012 and emerge as the worst financial crisis since the 1930 s.

Chronology

The failure of Lehman Brothers evolved over several years.

- **1850:** Henry, Emanuel, and Mayer Lehman set up Lehman Brothers.
- **2003:** Riding a housing boom in the United States, Lehman acquires five mortgage lenders including subprime lender BNC Mortgage.
- **2007, February:** Lehman's stock price hits a record high USD86.18, giving it a market capitalization of nearly USD60 billion.
- **2007:** Lehman's mortgage-backed securities portfolio grows to $85 billion, about four times the shareholders' equity.
- **2007, August:** The failure of two Bear Stearns hedge funds causes a sharp fall in the value of Lehman's stock. The company closes BNC Mortgage and lets 1,200 employees go.
- **2007, November:** Lehman's stock rebounds thanks to a temporary bloom in global equity markets, but the company fails to trim its mortgage portfolio.

- **2007, December:** Lehman reports record annual net income of USD4.2 billion on revenue of USD19.3 billion.
- **2008, March:** Lehman Brothers shares fall 48% following the near-collapse of Bear Stearns, the second largest underwriter of mortgage-backed securities that was taken over by JP Morgan Chase.
- **2008, June:** Lehman announces second-quarter losses of USD2.8 billion and is forced to sell US$6 billion worth of assets. It was the first quarterly loss for the company since it was spun-off from American Express in 1994.
- **2008, September 9:** South Korean state-owned Korea Development Bank refuses to back Lehman and sets the stage for the ultimate fall of the investment bank.
- **2008, September 10:** Lehman reports a loss of USD3.9 billion, a write-down of US$5.6 billion, and a business restructuring plan.
- **2008, September 13:** A takeover plan between Lehman, Barclays PLC, and Bank of America is unsuccessful.
- **2008, September 15:** Lehman files for bankruptcy along with its 22 affiliates. The company has USD639 billion in assets and USD619 billion in debt. Its stock drops 93% in a single day.
- **2008, September 20:** Barclays PLC's acquisition of Lehman's North American investment banking and capital markets business along with its New York headquarters and data centers for $1.35 billion is approved.
- **2008, October:** Nomura, a Japanese brokerage, acquires most of Lehman's Asia Pacific franchises and part of its Europe and Middle Eastern division for $225 million and $2, hiring over 8000 employees.

Response and Management

The crisis at Lehman spun out of control far too fast but at the core of the problem was an inability to consider the liquidity implications of switching from a brokerage model to an investment bank one. The switch required a massive increase in liquidity risk but also made it more difficult for the bank to borrow capital and hedge risks. These liquidity risks could have been avoided by carefully considering the demands of the new business lines it entered and, perhaps, to move more slowly into new business lines.

Still, when real estate prices in the United Stated started to crash in 2006 Lehman Brothers continued to pursue an aggressive expansion strategy. In early 2007, shortly after it reported its highest profits ever even as the prices of real estate were crumbling, the bank made it clear that the risks created by defaults in residential mortgages were contained and would not impact earnings at the firm. Speaking at a conference call after the company's earnings for 2007 were reported, Lehman's new Chief Financial Officer Erin Callan (who had been appointed at the end of 2007) said she did not expect the problems in the subprime market to spread to the rest of the housing market or hurting the broader U.S. economy.

That attitude underscores the lack of risk controls at the bank. At a time when most of their peers were reducing their exposure, Lehman decided to expand and acquire market share. It increased its credit risk, operational risk, and market risk. In 2007, Lehman backed more mortgage-backed securities than any other firm. In the fourth quarter of the year, global equity markets briefly rebounded and so did fixed-income assets but Lehman did not take this opportunity to cut down on its mortgage portfolio.

More careful market analysis in response to the crisis could have shed some light on the risks the bank was taking but a widespread culture of growth and pressure to expand at a rapid rate overcame any considerations of risk. A high leverage ratio only amplified the problems—Lehman had assets of USD691 billion but only $22.5 billion in shareholder equity, which meant its liabilities were about $668.5 or 30 times its equity. A negative return of 4% would, at any time, have wiped out the equity. During boom times, this was no problem. When the bust happened, it was unsustainable.

Analysis

In its annual report for 2007, Lehman had identified a series of risks that threatened the business. One was market risk inherent in potential changes to the value of the various financial instruments it invested in. A second was credit risk in the form of a counterparty that was unable to honor its debts. Third was operational risk in the event of losses caused from weak internal processes. Reputational risk was considered in the event that the public lost faith in the business. Liquidity risk was also considered as part of this exercise; Lehman's annual report thought it a possible risk that the bank would not be able to meet payment obligations, borrow funds in the market at a good price, fund commitments, or liquidate assets. These risks, the bank made it clear, had to be carefully managed and balanced to ensure the continuation of operations.[13]

To do well in the ultra-competitive investment banking business, Lehman Brothers needed to show as much as 15% growth in annual revenues. This required even faster growth in the total capital base. To achieve this level of growth, the management changed the business strategy of the bank. It switched from being a brokerage, which has lower risk, into an investment bank. Rather than make money from transaction fees it sought to make money from long-term investments, particularly in real estate, leveraged loans, and private equity. As part of this change, it got heavily involved in high-interest subprime loans and mortgages, which had proliferated thanks to a housing bubble through the first decade of the century.

---

[13] Lehman Brothers. "Lehman Brothers Annual Report 2007". 2008.

Lehman was not the only bank to get involved in subprime loans or on derivative products intended to limit the risk associated with them. As housing prices rose and defaults stayed in check, many banks did very well by originating loans, turning them into securities called Residential Mortgage Backed Securities, and selling those securities to other investors as profitable investments with little risk due to the independence of the loan takers and the rising real estate prices.

The structure started to crumble in 2006 when real estate prices burst and interest rates started to climb. Default rates began to rise and investors came to realize that these mortgage-backed securities had more risk than was originally thought. Rating agencies started to downgrade them. Suddenly, Lehman (and other banks) was stuck with assets they could not sell, backed by mortgages that were in default and guaranteed by real estate that was dropping in value. Lehman had invested aggressively in these securities, much more so than any other investment bank. In the first quarter of 2008, Lehman reported losses of USD2.5 billion and the losses and the fact that the bank now had a weak balance sheet with illiquid assets was a terrible combination. Suddenly, all the risks that it had earlier considered as part of its risk control exercise were coming to the forefront. And the key risk was liquidity risk—with its assets losing value and an inability to sell those assets, Lehman found itself short of cash. In the second quarter of 2008, Lehman reported another loss of USD3.9 billion. By then, the market had little faith in Lehman and it became very hard for the bank to borrow enough to manage daily operations.

Bankruptcy became one of the few likely options for the bank. Negotiations for a sale with other banks failed and the U.S. government chose to not intervene. On September 15, 2008, Lehman Brothers filed for bankruptcy after 158 years. It was the largest bankruptcy in history and turned a credit crunch into a full blown financial crisis.

Lessons Learnt

A number of key lessons emerged from the bankruptcy at Lehman Brothers:

- Rapid expansion at the expense of risk control can have disastrous effects. It is one thing to consider risks, and another to take those considerations into account when planning future activity. Risk measurement and control efforts done simply as an exercise without a direct line to the decision makers are useless.
- It is key for management to have accurate daily views of the liquidity positions, to be able to monitor them and react quickly to changes. In the case of Lehman, there were plenty of warning signs that liquidity was becoming a problem.
- It is key to understand where the risks lie. Mortgage backed securities were intended to disseminate risk but in Lehman's case they concentrated risk because the bank became the largest single participant in that particular market.

Summary

- A single trader brought down Barings Bank, founded in London in 1762. Nick Leeson built enormous—and unauthorized—derivative trading positions by faking signatures and taking advantage of a lack of management oversight. His downfall, in the end, was some very bad luck. He built enormous positions in Japanese Nikkei 225 futures, whose value dropped significantly following the massive earthquake in Kobe, Japan, in 1995. The losses to Barings added up to GBP843 million.

- Germany's Herstatt Bank built very large positions in foreign exchange following the end of the Bretton Woods System in 1973. The bank, Germany's thirty-fifth largest, bet that the USD would move in a different direction following the elimination of the gold peg. By March 1974, Herstatt had open exchange positions worth DM2 billion, about eighty times larger than its limit and three times as big as the capital it held. In June, Germany's regulator pulled its licence. The decision came down in the afternoon in Germany and the bank was not able to close off contracts with counterparties in other time zones.

- Metallgesellschaft AG was a large German conglomerate that was brought to the brink of bankruptcy by a shortage of liquidity. Following a series of large acquisitions and some weakness in its home market, the company made a decision to start trading in U.S. energy markets, selling long-term oil contracts and hedging on futures. The decision proved disastrous, particularly after oil spot prices dropped and the company had to start paying out contracts with cash it did not have.

- Lehman Brothers was the fourth largest investment bank in the United States when it declared bankruptcy in 2008, ending more than a century and a half of history. The bank was brought down by a combination of high-leverage, very little actual equity, and aggressive positions in risky securities that were not backed by sufficient risk control.

Key Terms

Account 88888

Arbitrage

Bailout

Bank for International Settlements (BIS)

Bank of England

Barings Bank

Basel Committee on Banking Supervision (BCBS)

Black Monday

Bretton Woods System

Chase Manhattan

Checks and balances

Concentration risk

Deposit protection scheme

Deutsche Bank

Dresdner Bank

Euroyen contracts

Federal Banking Supervisory Office
(BAKred)

Futures

Hedging

Herstatt Bank

Herstatt Risk

Kajo Neukirchen

Kobe

Lehman Brothers

Liquidity risk

Long-Term Capital Management (LTCM)

Metallgesellschaft AG

MG Energy

Residential mortgage backed securities

New York Mercantile Exchange (NYMEX)

Nick Leeson

Nikkei 225

Over the counter (OTC)

Risk control

Russian Financial Crisis

Salomon Brothers

Segregation of duties

Settlements

SIMEX

US Federal Reserve

Study Guide

1. Outline what went wrong at Barings Bank. In retrospect, what would have helped the bank avoid the crisis?
2. What is Herstatt Risk? Where does the term come from? Is this a significant risk today? Why?
3. From a standpoint of treasury management, what did Metallgesellschaft AG do wrong as it entered the U.S. market? Should it have entered the market at all? Why or why not?
4. Where markets justified in doubting Long Term Capital Management's investments? Imagine you are in charge of investments at a bank and some of those investments were held by the firm in 1998. Would you take your money out? Why?

Further Reading

Martin, Peter. "Death Came Sudden and Swift for Barings". *Financial Times*. 4 March 1995.

Nick Leeson. "Rogue Trader: How I Brought Down Barings Bank and Shook the Financial World."

Lowenstein, Roger. "When Genius Failed: The Rise and Fall of Long-Term Capital Management".

Basel Committee on Banking Supervision. "Working Paper No. 13: Bank Failures in Mature Economies". Bank for International Settlements. April 2004.

CMU Members

Below is a list of CMU members as of April 2013:

ABCI Securities Company Ltd.
ABN AMRO Bank N.V.
Agricultural Bank of China Ltd.
Allahabad Bank
Allied Banking Corporation (Hong Kong) Ltd.
Australia and New Zealand Banking Group Ltd.
Autoridade Monetaria de Macau
Axis Bank Ltd.
Banca Monte Dei Paschi Di Siena S.P.A.
Banco Bilbao Vizcaya Argentaria, S.A.
Banco De Oro Unibank, Inc.
Banco Santander S.A.
Bangkok Bank Public Company Ltd.
Bank Julius Baer and Co. Ltd.
Bank of America, National Association
Bank of Baroda
Bank of China (Hong Kong) Ltd.

Bank of China International Ltd.

Bank of China Ltd., Hong Kong Branch

Bank of Communications Co. Ltd.

Bank of East Asia, Limited (The)

Bank of India

Bank of New York Mellon

Bank of Nova Scotia (The)

Bank of Taiwan

Bank of Tokyo-Mitsubishi UFJ, Ltd. (The)

Bank Sarasin And Cie AG

Bank Sinopac, Hong Kong Branch

Banque Privee Edmond de Rothschild SA

Barclays Bank PLC

BNP Paribas Securities Services

BNP Paribas Wealth Management

BNP Paribas, Hong Kong

BOCI Securities Ltd.

BSI Ltd.

Canadian Imperial Bank of Commerce

Cathay Bank

Cathay United Bank Co. Ltd.

CCB International Securities Ltd.

Chang Hwa Commercial Bank, Ltd.

Chiba Bank, Ltd. (The)

China Central Depository and Clearing Co. Ltd.

China Citic Bank International Ltd.

China Construction Bank (Asia) Corporation Ltd.

China Construction Bank Corporation

China Development Bank Corporation

China Everbright Bank Co., Ltd.

China International Capital Corp HK Securities Ltd.

China Merchants Bank Co. Ltd.

China Minsheng Banking Corp. Ltd.

Chinatrust Commercial Bank Ltd.

Chiyu Banking Corporation Ltd.

Chong Kong Bank Ltd.

Chugoku Bank, Ltd. (The)

Citibank (Hong Kong) Ltd.

Citibank N.A.

Citic Capital Finance Ltd.

Citic Securities Brokerage (HK) Ltd

Citicorp International Ltd.

Commerzbank Ag
Commonwealth Bank of Australia
Cooperative Centrale Raiffeisen-Boerenleenbank BA
Coutts and Co. Ltd.
Credit Agricole (Suisse) SA
Credit Agricole Corporate and Investment Bank
Credit Suisse AG
Dah Sing Bank Ltd.
Daiwa Capital Maarkets Hong Kong
DBS Bank (Hogn Kong) Ltd.
DBS Bank Ltd., Hong Kong Branch
Deutsche Bank Aktiengesellschaft
DZ Bank AG Deutsche Zentral-Genossenschaftsbank
E. Sun Commercial Bank Ltd.
East West Bank
EFG Bank AG
Erste Group Bank AG
Falcon Private Bank Ltd.
Far Eastern International Bank
First Commercial Bank, Ltd.
Fubon Bank (Hong Kong) Ltd.
Guotai Junan Securities (Hong Kong) Ltd.
Hachijuni Bank, Ltd. (The)
Hang Seng Bank Ltd.
HKFE Clearing Corporation Ltd.
Hong Kong Note Printing Ltd.
Hogn Kong Securities Clearing Co. Ltd.
Hong Leong Bank Berhad, Hong Kong Branch
Hongkong and Shanghai Banking Corporation Ltd.
HSBC Bank USA, National Association
HSBC Broking Securities (Asia) Ltd.
HSBC Global Asset Mgt Hldgs (Bahamas) Ltd. Client A.C.
HSBC Nominees (Hong Kong) Ltd.
HSBC Nominees (Hong Kong) Ltd.—Euroclear Bank SA/NV
HSBC Private Bank (Suisse) SA
Hua Nan Commercial Bank, Ltd.
ICBC International Securities Ltd.
ICICI Bank Ltd., Hong Kong Branch
Indian Overseas Bank
Industrial and Commercial Bank of China (Asia) Ltd.
Industrial and Commercial Bank of China (Macau) Ltd.
Industrial and Commercial Bank of China Ltd.

Industrial Bank of Taiwan Co. Ltd.

ING Bank N.V.

Intesa Sanpaolo S.P.A.

J.P. Morgan Securities (Asia Pacific) Ltd.

JPMorgan Chase Bank, National Association

KBC Bank N.V., Hong Kong Branch

Korea Exchange Bank

Korea Securities Depository

Land Bank of Taiwan Co. Ltd.

LGT Bank AG

Lloyds TSB Bank PLC

Luso International Banking Ltd., Macau

Macquarie Bank Ltd.

Malayan Banking Berhad (TDG AS Maybank)

Mega International Commercial Bank Co. Ltd.

Melli Bank Plc, Hong Kong Branch

Mitsubishi UFJ Securities (HK), Ltd.

Mitsubishi UFJ Trust and Banking Corporation

Muzuho Corporate Bank, Ltd., HK Branch

Mizuho Securities Asia Ltd.

Morgan Stanley Asia Ltd.

Nanyang Commercial Bank Ltd.

National Australia Bank Ltd.

National Bank of Abu Dhabi

Natixis

Newedge Group

Oversea-Chinese Banking Corporation Ltd.

Philippine National Bank

Phillip Securities (Hong Kong) Ltd.

Portigon AG

Pt. Bank Negara Indonesia (Persero) Tbk.

Public Bank (Hong Kong) Ltd.

Punjab National Bank

Quam Securities Company Ltd.

RBC Capital Markets (Hong Kong)

Reserve Bank of New Zealand

Royal Bank of Canada, Hong Kong

Royal Bank of Scotland PLC, Hong Kong (The)

Shanghai Commercial Bank Ltd.

Shanghai Pudong Development Bank Co. Ltd.

Shiga Bank Limited (The)

Shinhan Asia Ltd.

Shizuoka Bank, Ltd. (The)
Sinpac Securities (Asia) Ltd.
Skandinaviska Enskilda Banken AB
Societe Generale
Societe Generale Bank and Trust
Standard Bank PLC
Standard Chartered Bank (Hong Kong) Ltd.
State Bank of India
State Street Bank and Trust Company
Sumitomo Mitsui Banking Corporation
Svenska Handelsbanken AB (Publ)
Tai Sang Bank Ltd.
Taipei Fubon Commercial Bank Co. Ltd.
Taishin International Bank Co. Ltd.
Taiwan Business Bank
Taiwan Cooperative Bank, Ltd.
Taiwan Depository and Clearing Corporation
Taiwan Shin Kong Commercial Bank Co., Ltd.
The Hong Kong Mortgage Corporation Ltd.
The Shanghai Commercial and Savings Bank, Ltd.
The Stock Exchange of Hong Kong Ltd.
Toronto Dominion Bank
UBS AG, Hong Kong
UCO Bank
Unicredit Bank AG
Union Bank of India
United Overseas Bank Ltd.
VC Capital Ltd.
Wells Fargo Bank N.A., Hong Kong Branch
Westpac Banking Corporation
Wing Hang Bank Ltd.
Wing Lung Bank Ltd.
Woori Bank, Hong Kong Branch

Bond Pricing

Return on Debt Securities

The yield on a debt security represents the return on the investor's investment. By yield, we mean the interest rate that can be earned on the bond, as currently quoted by the market or implied by the current market price.

The yield is not the same as the coupon paid by the issuer, which is based on the coupon rate and the face value of a bond. For example, a corporate bond with a par value of $1,000 may promise to pay a coupon rate of 5% annually for ten years, which comes to $50 a year. But if doubts arise about the issuer's ability to repay, nervous investors may sell the bond at a discount, say for only $900, for fear they will get nothing if the issuer defaults.[1]

If the issuer does default, then the bondholder will not earn any yield at all and could be forced to accept a steep discount on the $1,000 par value or lose the principal altogether. There could be a zero return on debt securities and even a wipe-out of the investment.

---

[1] The coupon rate will remain at 5% annually, but the yield will be 5.5%, because the market value has fallen to $900 ($50/$900 = 0.055 × 100 = 5.5%). This is a concept known as "convenient yield."

This example also illustrates the price-yield relationship in bonds. When a bond's price goes up, its yield goes down. When its price falls, its yield goes up. There will be buyers for the bond in either direction because, as discussed earlier, the various bond market players have different needs and purposes. Proprietary traders are primarily interested in price because their interest is to make money as soon as possible; long-term investors are mainly focused on yield because they have a long investing horizon.

The important thing is that each player knows how to measure the return on the various instruments in order to make the investing decision that is most appropriate to his or her situation.

Yield to Maturity

The yield to maturity (YTM) or gross redemption yield is the most frequently used measure of return from holding a bond. It is defined as the internal rate of return (IRR) of a bond given the bond price. YTM can also be defined as the rate of return that makes the sum of discounted cash flows equal to the market price when the bond is held to maturity. YTM takes into account the pattern of coupon payments, the bond's term to maturity, and the capital gain (or loss) arising over the remaining life of the bond.

One formula for YTM (there are others) is given below:

$$c(1 + r)^{-1} + c(1 + r)^{-2} + \ldots + c(1 + r)^{-Y} + B(1 + r)^{-Y} = P$$

where:

c = annual coupon payment
Y = number of years to maturity
B = par value
P = purchase price
r = discount rate of the cash flow

In the example of the corporate bond above, let us assume that the maturity date is two years away. We know that the purchase price is $900, the par value is $1,000, and the annual coupon payment is $50. So, plugging these numbers in, we get:

$$50(1 + r)^{-1} + 50(1 + r)^{-2} + 1,000(1 + r)^{-2} = 900$$

This is where it gets complicated. The only way to solve for the YTM is to use the process of numerical iteration, which involves estimating a value for r and calculating the price associated with that estimated yield. If the calculated price is higher than the price of the bond at the time, the yield estimate is lower than the actual yield, and so it must be adjusted until it converges to the level that corresponds with the bond price.

Fortunately, there are programmable calculators and online calculators that will crunch the numbers. The yield to maturity of the corporate bond above is 10.826%. You can estimate the YTM of various other bonds in this way and compile a list that will show you which ones have the highest yields to maturity and therefore are the best instruments to invest in, all other things being equal.

But while YTM is the most commonly used measure of yield, it has one major disadvantage: implicit in its calculation is the assumption that each coupon payment as it becomes due is reinvested as YTM. This is clearly unlikely, due to the fluctuations in interest rates over time. In practice, the measure itself will not equal the actual return from holding the bond, even if it is held to maturity. That said, the market standard is still to quote bond returns as YTMs, bearing the key assumptions behind the calculation in mind.

Note that YTM is different from the holding-period return or the actual/total return on the bond investment. The actual/total return will be the same as YTM only if the bond is held to maturity and all the coupons are invested at the same rate as YTM, following the concept of interest-on-interest in bond investment.

Credit Spread

As mentioned earlier, government bonds are regarded as virtually risk-free because the government can raise taxes, reduce spending, or simply print more money to redeem the bond at maturity. In comparison, corporate issues are much more risky because companies do not have the resources of governments. To compensate for this higher risk, corporate bonds have higher yields than government bonds.

The difference in yields between a corporate bond and the benchmark government bond in the market where they trade is the credit spread, which represents the return on the corporate issue. The higher the credit spread, the better the return on the bond—but the higher the risk of default as well. Junk bonds, for example, will typically have higher yields than bonds with investment grade quality in the market.

There may be times when the irrationality of the markets will make the credit spread of even a junk bond smaller than usual. Perhaps junk bond prices have surged as overconfident investors discount the risk and chase them (thus lowering their yields) even as they sell off safe government bonds at discounted prices (thus raising their yields).

Contrarian and value investors may want to take advantage of narrowing credit spreads in this situation and buy government bonds. If the opposite is the case—if a corporate bond's credit spread surges as overly pessimistic bondholders sell off the corporate issue in favour of government bonds, raising the yield on the corporate bond while decreasing the yield on government bonds—contrarian investors may choose to buy the corporate bond.

After the collapse of Lehman Brothers in 2008, investors realised that the spread between corporate yield and government bond yield may not be explained exclusively by the "chance of default" or credit spread, but also by the liquidity spread of the issue during abnormal times. Flight to quality might happen as a result of a widened spread overnight.

Z-Spread

The conventional approach for analysing an asset swap[2] uses the bond's YTM in calculating the spread. However, the assumptions implicit in the YTM calculation, which we discussed earlier, that each coupon payment as it becomes due is reinvested, make this spread problematic for relative value analysis, so market practitioners instead use what is termed the Z-spread, also known as ZSPRD, for this kind of analysis.

The conventional approach to compare the return of a corporate bond is to subtract the YTM of a government bond from the YTM of the bond with similar maturity. However, this approach might be problematic if the structure of cash flow of the government bond is different from the corporate bond, say a MBS that has a characteristic of reducing face value.

The Z-spread uses the zero coupon yield curve to calculate spread, so it is a more realistic, and effective, spread to use. The zero coupon curve used in the calculation is derived from the interest-rate swap curve.

The Z-spread is the basis point spread that would need to be added to the implied spot yield curve such that the discounted cash flows of a bond are equal to its present value (its current market price). Each bond cash flow is discounted by the relevant spot rate for its maturity term.

The Z-spread formula is shown below[3]:

$$P = \sum_{i=1}^{n} \left[\frac{C_i + M_i}{(1 + ((Z + S_i)/m))^i} \right]$$

where
n is the number of interest periods until maturity
P is the bond price
C_i is the coupon in period i
M_i is the redemption payment in period i (so bond cash flow is all C plus M)
S_i is the spot yield for period i
Z is the Z-spread
m is the frequency of coupon payments

---

[2] An asset swap is defined as an interest-rate swap or currency swap used in conjunction with an underlying asset such as a bond investment. The bond's YTM is the basis for calculating the spread on the assets being swapped.
[3] We do not take into account the semi-annual compounding approach to bond investment in the interest of simplification.

Bond Products

Let us now consider some bond products and their intricacies. One key instrument is the most vanilla product of all, which is the fixed rate bond. As its name indicates, this bond pays fixed interest annually until maturity, regardless of the swings in its market price or changes in market interest rates.

Investors who require fixed and stable cash flows are typically attracted to fixed rate bonds, particularly if they are local currency government bonds and are therefore virtually risk free. The downside is that these bondholders are vulnerable to inflation and interest-rate increases. The fixed amount they receive every year will be worth less if inflation is high and the price of their bond will fall if interest rates rise because there will be new fixed rate bonds that will offer higher coupon rates.

As a practical note, note and bond prices are quoted in dollars and fractions of a dollar. By market convention, the normal fraction used for Treasury security prices is 1/32. In Figure 4.1, the decimal point separates the full dollar portion of the price from the 32nds of a dollar, which are to the right of the decimal. Thus, the bid quote of 105.08 (:08, −08) means $105 plus 8/32 of a dollar, or $105.25, for each $100 face value of the note. The number "12" under "ask" further abbreviates the presentation of the price sought by a seller. It shows only the 32nds of a dollar; the full dollar portion of the price carries over from the bid price. In the example shown in Figure 4.1, "12" is shorthand for 105—the whole dollar amount of the bid price—and 12/32, or $105.375 per $100 par value.

Ask prices are always higher than bid prices for notes and bonds, but the figure shown in the "ask" column in Figure 4.1 may be lower. This indicates that the ask price has gone to the next higher whole dollar. If the price is quoted as 105 31-1, the ask price will be 106-1/32, that is, the next highest dollar amount above the bid price. Following the ask price is the "change"—the difference between the current trading day's bid price and the bid price of the preceding trading day. It, too, is a shorthand reference to 32nds of a point. In Figure 4.1, the change is shown to be an increase of 3/32, or 9 cents per $100 face value. Often, both the bid and ask quotes change by the same amount from the previous day's levels; that is, the "spread" between bid and ask is usually maintained. Some very active issues may be quoted in 64ths of a point. To reflect this in the quote, a plus sign (+) would follow the price. A quote of 104.07+ means 104 and 7/32 plus 1/64, or 104 and 15/64.

Cash Flow of a Fixed Rate Bond

Suppose you bought the U.S. Treasury note referred to in the market as "the 6 1/2s of August 2005" with a minimum size of $100. These particular securities are first identified by the interest rate established by the U.S. Treasury. In the case of Hong Kong the

HKMA sets the rates. The "6 ½" refers to the interest rate of the bonds or notes at the time of issue. U.S. Treasuries with a maturity of 10 years are notes and those with longer maturities are bonds.

The bid is the dollar price[4] a buyer is willing to pay and the ask is the price at which the seller is willing to sell. Both figures use numerical shorthand to express the prices and are quoted in dollars and fractions of a dollar; the fraction used in Treasury security prices is 1/32 (or 3.125 cents), by market convention. A bid of, for example, "105.08" means $105 and 8/32 of a dollar, or $105.25. The ask price would be listed using a similar convention.

Clean Price/Dirty Price

The clean price is the price of a debt security that excludes any interest that has accrued since issue or the most recent coupon payment. It is the original quotation given by the bond dealer. When an investor hits the price, the investor will pay the cash value of the clean price plus the accrual interest earned by the seller (the bond dealer) on the settlement date. (The accrual interest is calculated on simple interest.) This is called the dirty price—the price of the debt security includes the accrual interest.

Fixed rate bonds are usually quoted by their clean price. The general market practice is that the buyer of a debt security must pay the seller the accrual interest on the settlement date. The settlement price of a debt security transaction is therefore different from the clean price.

Suppose you sell the 6 1/2s of August 2005 in Figure 4.1 and the settlement date is 18 October 2003. The buyer will pay you the accrual interest and the clean price of the note. The day count convention of U.S. Treasury notes is ACT/ACT. The clean price is 105.375 (that is, 105 + 8/32). Therefore:

Number of days from the last coupon date to the settlement date = 10/18/03 – 8/15/03 = 64 days

Number of days from the last coupon date to the next coupon date = 02/15/04 – 8/15/03 = 184 days

Accrual interest on $10/18/03 = (6.5/2) \times (64/184) = 1.13$

Clean price = 105.375

Dirty price = 105.375 + 1.13 = 106.505

The formula for calculating dirty price is set out below:

Dirty price = Clean price + Accrual interest

---

[4] Bid and ask can also be quoted as a percent of the bond's face value and indicated with a colon. Thus, bid and ask in Figure 4.1 will be presented as 105:08 and 105:12. In the past, treasury bonds were quoted as small as 1/32 (one small pip). Today, the quote can be ¼ of a small pip.

Accrual Interest

Accrual interest is calculated on a 30-day month/360-day year for corporate bonds and municipal bonds, and on actual calendar days for government bonds. When calculating accrued interest on a bond that is being sold, it is conventional to consider the time period from the most recent payment up to, but not including, the date on which the bond sale is settled.

The two important steps in calculating accrual interest are thus the following:

- Determine the next coupon date and the last coupon date
- Determine the number of days according to the day count convention (ACT/ACT, 30/360, ACT/360, ACT/365)

Day Count Convention

This brings us to day count convention. The dirty price will differ on the same instrument being settled on the same day depending on the day count convention in use. Figure 4.3 summarises the day count conventions.[5]

For example, suppose a semi-annual 11% coupon bond due on 10 Jul 2011 is quoted at 95-16 and settles on 15 Mar 09.

- 95-16 is the clean price
  The last and the next coupon payment are 10 Jan 09 and 10 Jul 09 respectively.
  If the day count convention is **ACT/ACT:**
  Number of days between 10 Jan 99 and 15 Mar 99 is 64
  Number of days between 10 Jan 99 and 10 Jul 99 is 181
  Total accrued interest up to 15 Mar 99 is $(11/2) \times (64/181) = 1.94$
  The quoted price is 95-16 or 95 16/32 or 95.50
  Dirty price/cash price = 95.50 + 1.94 = 97.44
- If the day count convention is **ACT/360**:
  Number of days between 10 Jan 99 and 15 Mar 99 is 64
  Number of days between 10 Jan 99 and 10 Jul 99 is 181
  Total accrued interest up to 15 Mar 99 is $(11/2) \times 64/(360/2) = 1.95$
  Dirty price/cash price = 95.50 + 1.95 = 97.45
- If the day count convention is **30/360**:

  Formula: Number of days = $30 * N + \text{Max}(30 - D_1, 0) + \text{Min}(30, D_2)$

---

[5] The SWX Swiss Exchange paper "Accrued Interest & Yield Calculations and Determination of Holiday Calendars" is a useful resource on day count conventions. Refer to "Further Reading" at the end of this chapter on how to download this document.

TABLE B-1 Summary of day count conventions

ACT/365	Used for Japanese government bonds and some older Irish government bonds
ACT/ACT	Used for U.S. Treasury notes and bonds. The factor of N may be 181, 182, 183 or 184. The number of dates of full year may look like 362, 364, 366, or 368 (N × 2)
30(E)/360, 30/360 ICMA, 30s/360, Eurobond basis (ISDA 2006)	Used for euro bonds and Irish government bonds issued before 1999
30(A)/360, 30/360, 30/360 U.S., 360/360	Used for U.S. corporate bonds and many U.S. agency issues. It is most commonly referred to as "30/360," but the term "30/360" may also refer to any of the other conventions of this class, depending on the context.

Where:

N is the number of months in between

D_1 is the date of settlement

D_2 is the date of the upcoming coupon payment

Number of days between 10 Jan 99 and 31 Jan 99 is $Max(30 - 10,0)$ or 20.

Number of days for Feb 99 is 30×1 or 30 (30/360)

Number of days between 1 Mar 99 and 15 Mar 99 is $Min(30,15)$ or 15.

Therefore, 10 Jan 99 to 15 Mar 99 is $(20 + 30 + 15)$ or 65.

Total accrued interest up to 15 Mar 99 is $(11/2) \times 65/(360/2) = 1.99$

Dirty price/cash price = 95.50 + 1.99 = 97.49

Zero Coupon Bond

Zero coupon bonds[6] are bonds that do not pay interest. They are instead sold to investors at a deep discount from their par value, which is the amount the zero coupon bond will be worth when it comes due. When a zero coupon bond matures, the bondholder will receive one lump sum equal to the initial investment plus the imputed interest.

Zero bonds are similar to bills in that neither one has coupons, but the maturity of bills is less than one year at inception (zero coupon bonds have longer maturities) and bills are quoted in terms of the embedded discount rate, instead of the "bill price."

Investors can purchase different kinds of zero coupon bonds in the secondary market. These are issued by a variety of sources, including the U.S. Treasury, corporations, and local governments.

Zero coupon bonds may be created by a brokerage firm when it strips the coupons off a bond and sells the principal and the coupons separately. This technique is used frequently

---

[6] See the website of the U.S. Securities and Exchange Commission at http://www.sec.gov/answers/zero.htm.

with Treasury bonds. The resulting zero coupon issue is marketed under such names as CATS (Certificate of Accrual on Treasury Securities), Tiger (Treasury Investors Growth Receipt), or STRIPS (separate trading of registered interest and principal of securities).

Because zero coupon bonds pay no interest, they are the most volatile of all debt securities. When interest rates rise, for example, zero coupon bonds fall more dramatically than bonds paying out interest on a current basis. However, when interest rates fall, zero coupon bonds rise more rapidly in price than full-coupon bonds, because the zeros have locked in a particular rate of reinvestment that becomes more attractive the further rates fall.

The greater the number of years that a zero coupon bond has until maturity, the less an investor has to pay for it, and the more leverage is at work for him. For instance, a bond maturing in five years may double, but one maturing in 25 years may increase in value ten times, depending on the interest rate of the bond.

When a Treasury note or bond is stripped, each interest payment and the principal payment becomes a separate zero coupon security. Each component has its own identifying number and can be held or traded separately. For example, a Treasury note with 10 years remaining to maturity consists of a single principal payment at maturity and 20 interest payments, one every six months for 10 years. When this note is converted to STRIPS form, each of the 20 interest payments and the principal payment becomes a separate security.

The US Treasury does not issue or sell STRIPS directly to investors. STRIPS can be purchased and held only through financial institutions and government securities brokers and dealers.

Pricing a Zero Coupon Bond

There is only one cash flow at the maturity of the zero coupon bond, as shown in the formula below:[7]

$$\text{Zero bond price} = \frac{100}{(1 + \text{Discount rate})^t}$$

For example, suppose the face value of a zero coupon bond is $100, which you will receive one year later, the cash flow is virtually default free (because the bond is stripped from a U.S. Treasury note), and the discount rate is 10%. That $100 face value of a zero coupon bond should be priced at:

$$\text{Cash flow} = 100/(1 + 10\%) = 90.909$$

You are willing to pay no more than $90.909 for this cash flow.

---

[7] The superscript "t" is the period of time. When the model is on a semi-annual basis, "t" stands for half-year.

What if the cash flow is not default free, for example, because the issuer is a corporation, not the government? In this case, you will demand a higher return from the investment and will charge a higher discount rate for the cash flow, say at 20%.

$$\text{Zero coupon bond (risky)} = 100/(1 + 20\%) = \$83.33$$

What these two examples illustrate is that the pricing of a zero coupon bond depends on several factors. In the example above, the credit risk of the issue reflects the probability of default of the issuer. Other factors include liquidity risk and interest rate risk. As we learned in the previous chapters, investors can hedge interest rate risk by using an asset swap, for example, so that the fixed rate coupons are converted into floating rate coupons. However, it is difficult to isolate credit risk and liquidity risk.

Bootstrapping

We can also construct a zero coupon yield curve, which plots zero coupon yields against term to maturity. The resulting yield curve is often regarded as the true term structure of interest rates because there is no reinvestment involved; the stated yields are equal to the actual annual return. That is, the yield on a zero coupon bond of n years maturity is regarded as the true n-year interest rate.

However, there are only a limited number of zero coupon bonds in the market, so analysts use a method called **bootstrapping** to construct the zero coupon curve. The analyst starts at the front end of the yield curve with a known six-month Treasury bill and a known one-year government bond yield. By so doing, a forward rate is determined that can then be used to equate a one-year security with two six-month securities, one commencing today and maturing in six months, and the other starting in six months and maturing one year from today. The same iterative process is repeated over and over to construct a complete a zero coupon yield curve.

Why take the trouble to do this painstaking bootstrapping exercise? It is because the zero coupon yield curve is ideal to use when deriving implied forward rates and defining the term structure of interest rates. It is also the best curve to use when determining the *relative value*, whether cheap or expensive, of bonds trading in the market, especially zero coupon bonds, and in pricing new issues, irrespective of their coupons. However, it is not an absolutely accurate indicator of average market yields because most bonds are not zero coupon bonds. It is an invaluable tool if you are valuing the zero coupon bonds in your portfolio or are considering buying them.

Spot Rate and Forward Interest Rate

Suppose you invest \$1 at an annual rate of 6.60% for two years. Compounded yearly, you will get $\$1 \times (1 + 6.6\%)^2$ dollars at the end of two years. This interest rate is termed the *two-year spot rate* to emphasise the fact that it assumes an investment that begins immediately and lasts for two years.

A different type of interest rate involves an agreement made immediately for investment at a later date and repayment at an even later date. For example, one might agree to borrow $1 in a year and repay $1 plus a stated amount of interest one year later (i.e., two years hence). The interest rate in question is termed a *forward interest rate* to highlight the fact that it covers an interval that begins at a date forward (i.e., in the future).

By referring to the term structure, one can find the implied forward rate or the expected future spot rate of the coming period. The forward rate is a particularly important concept in the pricing of interest-sensitive products.

The general equation for forward interest rate is as follows:

$$\left(1 + R_{0,n+1}\right)^{n+1} = \left(1 + R_{0,n}\right)^{n} \cdot \left(1 + F_{n,n+1}\right)$$

Where
$R_{0,n+1}$ = spot rate from time 0 to $n + 1$
$R_{0,n}$ = spot rate from time 0 to n
$F_{n,n+1}$ = forward rate between time n and $n + 1$

Floating Rate Notes (FRNs)

Floating rate notes, which are also called *floaters,* are debt securities that do not pay a fixed coupon. Instead, they pay a variable coupon that changes in line with a specified reference rate, such as a money market reference rate like LIBOR or the federal funds rate. An FRN also pays a spread and this spread remains constant through the life of the bond.

Almost all FRNs have quarterly coupons, that is, they pay out interest every three months. Some FRNs are reset every six months. At the beginning of each coupon period, the coupon is calculated by taking the fixing of the reference rate for that day and adding the spread.

Some FRNs have special features such as maximum or minimum coupons; these are known as capped FRNs and floored FRNs, respectively. Those with both minimum and maximum coupons are called collared FRNs. Some FRNs are perpetual, having no stated maturity date. FRNs can also be obtained synthetically by the combination of a fixed rate bond and an interest rate swap. This combination is known as an asset swap.

Quotation

Suppose a new five-year FRN pays a coupon of 3 months LIBOR +0.10%, and is issued at par (100.00). In other words, it will pay interest on the par value at whatever the LIBOR rate is on the fixing day and specified time once every three months, plus a spread of +0.10% over that LIBOR rate. The quotation will follow this notation format: "3M LIBOR + 10."

If the perception of the creditworthiness of the issuer deteriorates, investors will demand a higher spread, say LIBOR +0.15%, when the FRN is reset at the beginning of the coupon period. Responding to the demand, a dealer will make a market of 17/15, meaning that he will buy the FRN at the equivalent of LIBOR +0.17%, and sell it at the equivalent of LIBOR +0.15%. If a trade is agreed, the price is calculated.

In this example, LIBOR +0.17% would be roughly equivalent to a price of 99.65. This can be calculated as par, minus the difference between the coupon and the price that was agreed (0.07%), multiplied by the maturity (five years).

Risk of Holding FRNs

FRNs actually carry little interest rate risk. Unlike a fixed rate bond, whose price declines when interest rates rise, the expected coupons of the FRN will increase in line with the increase in forward rates. This means that its price will remain constant no matter the quantum of the rate rise. The major risk of holding FRNs is the credit risk. If the credit of the issuer deteriorates, investors will demand a higher return from the issue and pressure the bond price lower than par value. As a result, the effective yield from the FRN will be higher and the spread will be widened even though the contracted spread remains unchanged.

Because FRNs are almost immune to interest rate risk, they are considered conservative investments for investors who believe market rates will go up. The risk that remains is credit risk, such as the possibility that the issuer may default on the FRN.

Valuation of FRNs

A three-year FRN carries a coupon of 6M LIBOR + 10. It is now trading at 17/15. What is the price of this floater? The valuation technique is to assume a constant LIBOR for the rest of the floater. Suppose 6M LIBOR is 5.5%. The semi-annual coupons will be 2.8% (5.5% + 0.10% = 5.6%/2), as shown in Table B-2.

TABLE B-2   Particulars of a three-year FRN

Period	LIBOR	Cash flow	DF	PV (CF)
1	5.50	2.80	0.9728	2.7237
2	5.50	2.80	0.9463	2.6495
3	5.50	2.80	0.9205	2.5774
4	5.50	2.80	0.8954	2.5072
5	5.50	2.80	0.8710	2.4389
6	5.50	102.80	0.8473	87.1033
Total =				100.0000

Source: HKIB

TABLE B-3 Particulars of a three-year FRN

Period	LIBOR	Cash flow	DF	PV (CF)
1	5.50	2.80	0.9719	2.7213
2	5.50	2.80	0.9446	2.6448
3	5.50	2.80	0.9180	2.5705
4	5.50	2.80	0.8922	2.4982
5	5.50	2.80	0.8671	2.4280
6	5.50	102.80	0.8428	86.6374
Total =				99.5003

Source: HKIB

- If the discount rate is set to 5.6%, the price of the floater will be at par (100).
  **
  $0.9728 = 1/(1 + 5.6\%/2)$
  $0.9463 = 1/(1 + 5.6\%/2)^2$
- If the discount rate is set to 5.67% (LIBOR + 17), the price of the floater will be at discount 99.8094.
  **
  $0.9724 = 1/(1 + 5.67\%/2)$
  $0.9456 = 1/(1 + 5.67\%/2)^2$
- If the price of the floater is at 99.50, the effective yield will be given as shown in Table 4.12. You simply reverse the previous process and work out the effective yield.
  **
  $0.9719 = 1/(1 + 5.78\%/2)$
  $0.9446 = 1/(1 + 5.78\%/2)^2$
- The spread is 28 (LIBOR + 28).

Pricing FRNs

Below are two models for pricing a floater:

- Continuous model

$$Bf = (L + K^*) \cdot e^{-r_1 t_1}$$

- Discrete model

$$Bf = \frac{(L + K^*)}{(1 + r_1 \cdot t_1)}$$

FIGURE B-1 **Pricing a floater**

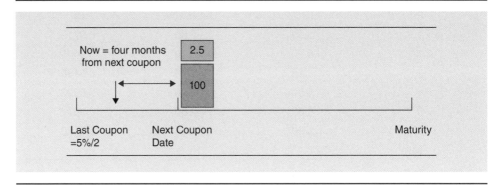

Source: HKIB

Where (for both models):

Bf is the price of the floater.

K* is the interest payment set in the previous reset day.

"r_1" is the effective interest rate at the moment to access the value of the note.

"t_1" is the length of time from the moment to access the note to the next reset day.

For example, the nominal amount of a six-month LIBOR floater is $10,000,000. The interest rate is fixed at 5% today. Two month later, the market interest rate is 4%. The value of the floater two months later is:

$$Bf = 10,000,000\,(1 + 5\%/2)/(1 + 4\% \times 4/12) = 10,115,132 \text{ or } 101.15132\%$$

Please note that *Bf* is worth 10,000,000 when it is valued on the reset day:

$$10,000,000\,(1 + 5\%/2)/(1 + 5\%*6/12) = 10,000,000 \text{ or } 100\%$$

The credit spread is assumed to remain unchanged. The remaining time to maturity of the FRN is disregarded because floaters involve little interest rate risk. A graphical representation of this example is shown in Figure B-1.

Inverse Floaters

An inverse floater, also known as a ***reverse floater*** and ***bear floater***, is an FRN whose coupon fluctuates inversely with its reference rate. The coupon increases when the reference rate decreases and decreases when the reference rate increases.

These notes are targeted at investors who want a high initial yield in an environment where the yield curve is upwardly sloped in order to make big gains when rates fall. There are many inverse floater variants. The step-up inverse floater, for example, features a step-up constant (7.5% minus three-month LIBOR for the first six months, 8.5% minus three-month LIBOR for the second six months, and so on) and also a fixed above-market first coupon followed by the inverse formula.

Inverse floaters earned an unsavoury reputation in the 1990s when money market bets using them went bad. Money market funds are typically restricted to investing in money market instruments with maturities under a year. But exceptions are made for floaters with maturities of more than a year. Some money market funds used this loophole to buy inverse floaters to bet on the direction of interest rates.

When their interest-rate expectations did not pan out, the funds lost money in volumes far higher than usual for money market funds. Several badly hit fund companies were forced to step in and make up for the losses of their investors with their own money, an expensive lesson that hopefully everyone in the money market industry has learned.

Basic Elements

With each coupon payment, the floating rate is reset for the next period according to the formula below:

$$\text{Floating rate} = \text{Fixed rate} - \text{Coupon leverage reference rate}$$

The multiplier is called the coupon leverage. Often, it is equal to 1, but this is not always the case. If the multiplier exceeds 1, the instrument is called a leveraged inverse floater.

A typical coupon is calculated as a fixed coupon minus the floating reference index for example, 7.5% minus three-month Euribor. Such notes combine an FRN and an interest rate swap of twice the notional size.

If LIBOR resets in a rising rate environment, this will cause the inverse floater to fall in value, not to reset its value to par. Investors typically also buy a cap with a strike price at the level of LIBOR, thus creating in effect a zero coupon—that is, it is struck at the fixed rate element. If rates rise beyond this strike, producing negative coupons, then the long cap will make up the difference back to zero. The coupons cannot become negative, at least.

Pricing Inverse Floaters

To learn about pricing an inverse floater, let us first examine the relationship between a floater and an inverse floater. The combination of a floater and an inverse floater actually equals the value of a fixed rate bond. It is therefore possible to construct a portfolio consisting of a floater and an inverse floater such that the cash flow will be identical to a fixed rate bond.

For example, a three-year $50 floater and a three-year $50 inverse floater can be put together so that the cash flow of the portfolio is identical to a 3-year fixed rate bond with a face value of $100. Suppose the coupons of the floaters are based on 6-month LIBOR and 12% minus 6-month LIBOR, respectively. The cash flow on the coupon date will be:

Floater receives = $50 \times$ LIBOR/2;
Inverse floater receives = $50 \times (0.12\text{-LIBOR})/2$
The portfolio receives = $50 \times 0.12/2$ or $100 \times 0.06/2$, which is a $100 fixed rate bond with a semi coupon of 6%.

Since we can easily measure the value of the fixed rate bond and the a floater, the value of the inverse floater is:

Inverse floater = 2 * Fixed rate bond − Floater
(Depending on the formula of inverse floater)

To illustrate, let us consider the example of an inverse floater that has a floating rate of 12% − 2 * LIBOR. What is the value of the inverse floater?

- Construct a portfolio consisting of a floater and an inverse floater, such that it is independent of the floating rate
- Construct a fixed bond that is equal to the portfolio of floating rates
- Inverse $(0.12 − 2 * L) + 2 *$ FRN $(L) = 3*$ Fixed rate bond

The portfolio represented on the left hand side of the equation will generate 0.12/2 coupon on each coupon date.
The fixed rate bond on the right hand side of the equation will generate 3 * F/2. Therefore, the coupon of the fixed rate bond in the portfolio is 0.04 or 4%:

Inverse $(12\% − 2 *$ LIBOR$) = 3 *$ Fixed rate $(4\%) − 2$ FRN $($LIBOR$)$

Risks of Holding an Inverse Floater

The experience of the money market fund managers mentioned earlier highlights the interest rate risk taken on by holders of inverse floaters. This is a risk, as we know, that holders of FRNs do not really face, since the coupons of FRNs float along with the reference rate. If you refer to the previous portfolio, it is not difficult to find that the risk of holding inverse floaters could be several times that of holding a fixed rate bond, depending on the multiplier of the coupon formula. In addition, investors in inverse floaters also face credit risk, in that the issuer of the instrument may default on its obligations.

Duration

Duration is an important concept in comparing the risk of holding various bonds, given the different coupon rate and maturity of bonds. One of the more objective approaches is

FIGURE B-2   Duration of a fixed rate bond

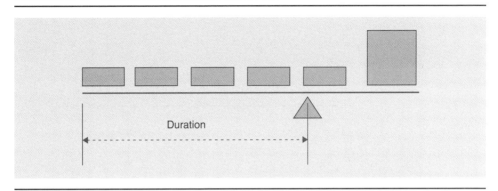

Duration

Source: HKIB

to bring them all into a similar scale—the equivalent risk of a zero coupon bond. And that is the meaning behind the duration.

The concept of duration as it applies to interest rate risk revolves around the notion that the volatility of a bond price can be measured by the "length" of the bond. The key ideas are:

- Duration is the weighted-average term-to-maturity of the bond's cash flows, the weights being the present value of each cash flow as a percentage of the bond's full price.
- It is also the weighted average time over which the cash flows from an investment are expected, where the weights are the relative time-adjusted present values of the cash flows.[8]
- For working purposes, duration can be defined as the approximate percentage change in price for a 100-basis-point change in yield.

A useful analogy is a series of tin cans spaced equally on a seesaw, as shown in Figure B-2. The size of each can represents the cash flow due, the contents of each can represent the present values of those cash flows, and the intervals between them represent the payment periods. In this graphical representation, duration is the distance to the fulcrum that would balance the seesaw.

The concept of duration is further explained by Figure 4.17, which looks at duration as it applies to a zero coupon debt security. As we know, the coupon is stripped from a zero coupon bond. This means that all the tin cans—all the weights—are at one end of the seesaw. Thus the duration—the distance to the fulcrum that would balance the seesaw—of a zero coupon is longer than the duration of the fixed rate bond depicted in Table 4.15.

The greater the duration of a bond is, the greater its percentage volatility. This is borne out in the markets. As previously noted, zero coupon bonds tend to be the most volatile of all debt securities. The phenomenon can be explained in part by their long duration.

---

[8] Gardner, Mona J.; Mills, Dixie I. and Cooperman, Elizabeth S. "Managing Financial Institutions: An Asset/Liability Approach", 4th Edition. South-Western College, 2004. Pg. 631.

FIGURE B-3   Duration of a zero coupon bond

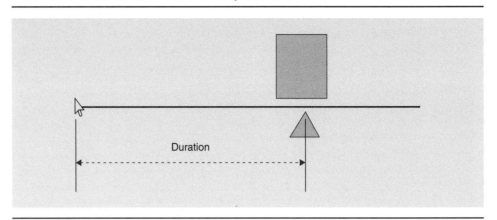

Duration

Source: HKIB

In general, duration rises with maturity and falls with the frequency of coupon payments. It also falls as the yield rises (the higher yield reduces the present values of the cash flows).

The duration of a security can be interpreted as the approximate percentage change in the price for a 100-basis point parallel shift in the yield curve.[9] Thus, as a measure of percentage of volatility, duration—or more strictly, "modified duration," because the concept originated by British economist Frederick Macaulay in 1938 has since been modified by others—is valid only for small changes in yield.

A duration of 5, for example, means that the price of the bond will change by approximately 5% for a 100-basis point change in yield. The formula for duration of a fixed rate bond is given below:

$$\text{Duration} = \frac{t_1 \cdot PV(CF_1) + t_2 \cdot PV(CF_2) + \ldots + tn \cdot PV(CFn)}{K \cdot PV(\text{Total Cash Flow})}$$

Where:
$PV(CF_t)$ = the present value of the cash flow in period t discounted at the yield-to-maturity
$PV(\text{Total cash flow})$ = the present value of the security
K = number of payments per year

The above formula applies to simple vanilla securities only. For bonds with complicated structures such as callable bonds, the "effective duration" formula is used, as shown below:

$$\text{Duration} = \frac{(V_- - V_+)}{2 \cdot V_0 \cdot \Delta y}$$

[9] Fabozzi, Frank J.; Martellini, Lionel and Philippe Priaulet. "Advanced Bond Portfolio Management." John Wiley & Sons: New Jersey, 2006. Pg. 276.

Where:

Δy = change in the yield of the security,

V_+ = the estimated value of the security if the yield is up by Δy,

V_- = the estimated value of the security if the yield is down by Δy,

V_0 = initial price of the security (per 100).

Let us take an example[10] of a bond with the following characteristics:

- Coupon rate = 8%
- Term = 5 years
- YTM = 8%
- Price = 100

t	CF_t	Discount factor	$PV(CF_t)$	$t \times PV(CF_t)$
1	4	0.9615	3.85	3.85
2	4	0.9246	3.70	7.40
3	4	0.8890	3.56	10.67
4	4	0.8548	3.42	13.68
5	4	0.8219	3.29	16.44
6	4	0.7903	3.16	18.97
7	4	0.7599	3.04	21.28
8	4	0.7307	2.92	23.38
9	4	0.7026	2.81	25.29
10	104	0.6756	70.26	702.59
Total			100.00	843.53

Macaulay duration = 843.53/(100 * 2) = 4.217666

Duration is a good measure of the interest rate risk of not only a security, but also a set of interest rate sensitive portfolios. The relationship between Macaulay duration[11] and the percentage change of a portfolio is given below:

$$\text{Percent change in bond price} = \frac{\Delta B}{B} = -MD \times (\Delta y)$$

$$\text{Percent change in bond price} = \frac{\Delta B}{B} = -\left(\frac{1}{1+\frac{y}{k}}\right) \times MacD \times (\Delta y)$$

---

[10] This example is adapted from "Price Volatility Characteristics of Fixed Income Securities" by Frank J Fabozzi, Mark Pitts and Ravi E. Dattatreya in "The Handbook of Fixed Income Securities", edited by Frank J Fabozzi and Steven V Mann (McGraw Hill Professional, 2005).

[11] This refers to the original formulation by Frederick Macaulay in 1938, and is so termed to distinguish it from modified duration, which is the result of later modifications to original equation.

where

ΔB = change of bond price

MD = modified duration

$MacD$ = Macaulay duration

Δy = change of yield to maturity

Alternatively, we can look at modified duration, as set out below:

$$\text{Modified duration} = \frac{\text{Macaulay duration}}{1 + \dfrac{y}{k}}$$

For example:

$$\text{Modified duration of the portfolio} = 4.2177/(1 + 0.08/2) = 4.0555$$

For a 1% increase in interest rate, the % change of the portfolio will be:

$$\text{Percentage change of the bond price} = -4.0555 * (+0.01) * 100 = -4.0555\%$$

or

$$\text{The new price} = 100 * (1 - 4.0555\%) = 95.94$$

Convexity

If duration applies only to a small change in yield, how do we measure a bigger change? For a larger yield change, volatility is measured by both the duration and an additional concept called convexity. This term is derived from the price-yield curve for a normal bond, which is convex in shape. In other words, the price is always falling at a slower rate as the yield increases. The more convexity a bond has, the better, because it means the bond's price will fall more slowly and will raise more quickly on a given movement in general interest rate levels.

As with duration, convexity, as it applies to straight bonds, increases with a lower coupon rate, lower yield, and longer maturity. Convexity measures the rate of change of duration, and for an option-free bond, it is always positive because changes in yield do not affect cash flows.

Figure B-4 shows the difference in measurement between duration and convexity of the same bond. When interest rates are increased from R0 to R1, the bond price is expected to decline from B0 to B1*, based on the estimation of duration. But in fact, the actual price is higher than B1*, because the price-yield relationship of a coupon bond is convex in shape.

When a bond has a call option, however, cash flows are affected. In that case, duration gets smaller as yield decreases, resulting in negative convexity.

One formula for convexity is given below:

$$\text{Convexity} = \frac{t_1 \cdot (1 + t_1) \cdot PV(CF_1) + t_2 \cdot (1 + t_2) \cdot PV(CF_2) + \ldots + tn(1 + tn) \cdot PV(CFn)}{K^2 \cdot PV\,(\text{Total Cash Flow}) \left(1 + \dfrac{yield}{k}\right)^2}$$

FIGURE B-4 Duration and convexity compared

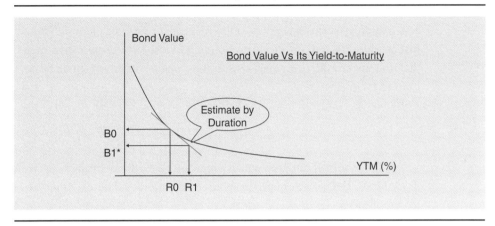

Source: HKIB

Convexity can also be expressed by this alternative formula, called "effective convexity":

$$\text{Convexity} = \frac{\left(V_- + V_+ - 2V_0\right)}{2 \cdot V_0 \cdot \Delta y^2}$$

The example below shows how convexity is applied.

t	CF$_t$	Discount factor	PV(CF$_t$)	t * PV(CF$_t$)	t(1 + t)PV(CF$_t$)
1	4	0.9615	3.85	3.85	7.69
2	4	0.9246	3.70	7.40	22.19
3	4	0.8890	3.56	10.67	42.67
4	4	0.8548	3.42	13.68	68.38
5	4	0.8219	3.29	16.44	98.63
6	4	0.7903	3.16	18.97	132.77
7	4	0.7599	3.04	21.28	170.22
8	4	0.7307	2.92	23.38	210.44
9	4	0.7026	2.81	25.29	252.93
10	104	0.6756	70.26	702.59	7,728.45
Total			100.00	843.53	8,734.39

$$\text{Convexity} = 8{,}734.39 / (1 + 8\%/2)^2 \times 2^2 \times 100 = 20.1886$$

Percentage change in price due to convexity = $1/2 \times \text{convexity} \times (\Delta y)^2 \times 100$
$$= 1/2 \times 20.1886 \times (0.01)^2 \times 100$$
$$= 0.1009\%$$

For those readers who are interested in the mathematical explanation, we give the details below.[12]

---

[12] The mathematical explanation is extracted from a note from Dr. Kenneth R. Stanton of Merrick School of Business at the University of Baltimore.

To explain the relationships between price changes, yields, and duration, we begin with the fundamental valuation formula. Let c_t represent the entire cash flow at time t generated by an asset that has yield r, and a maturity of T annual periods. (Basic texts, or texts that are not directed specifically to bonds, add some confusion when they fail to explain that they are considering *annual* yields and *annual* cash flows). In that case, the valuation formula is equal to:

$$P = \sum_{t=1}^{n} \frac{c_t}{(1+r)^t}$$

The modified duration equals *minus* 1.0 times the derivative of P with respect to r, divided by P. That is, we obtain the modified duration by differentiating the P with respect to r as follows:

$$\frac{\partial P}{\partial r} = \partial \frac{\sum_{t=1}^{n} \frac{c_t}{(1+r)^t}}{\partial r}$$

$$\frac{\partial P}{\partial r} = \sum_{t=1}^{n} \left(\frac{c_t}{(1+r)^{t+1}} \cdot -t \right)$$

$$\frac{\partial P}{\partial r} = \left(\frac{-1}{(1+r)} \right) \sum_{t=1}^{n} \frac{t \cdot c_t}{(1+r)^t}$$

When dealing with bonds, the semi-annual nature of the cash flows requires that we make some minor adjustments to the modified duration formula. We begin with the usual valuation formula, where c_t represents the entire cash flow at time t and the bond has a maturity of $2T$ semi-annual periods:

$$P = \sum_{t=1}^{n} \frac{c_t}{\left(1 + \frac{r}{2}\right)^t}$$

$$\frac{\partial P}{\partial r} = \sum_{t=1}^{n} \left(\frac{c_t}{\left(1 + \frac{r}{2}\right)^{t+1}} \cdot -\frac{t}{2} \right)$$

$$\frac{\partial P}{\partial r} = \left(\frac{-1}{2 \cdot \left(1 + \frac{r}{2}\right)} \right) \sum_{t=1}^{n} \frac{t \cdot c_t}{\left(1 + \frac{r}{2}\right)^t}$$

Portfolio Duration

A portfolio's duration can be obtained by calculating the weighted average of the duration of the bonds in the portfolio.

$$D_{portfolio} = w_1 D_1 + w_2 D_2 + \ldots + W_k D_k$$

Where:

Wj = Weighing of bond j in terms of its market value to the portfolio

Dj = modified duration of bond j

For example, given the portfolio below, which is comprised of three bonds (semi-annual; ACT/360), what is the modification duration of the portfolio?

Bond	Coupon Rate	Days from last CDate	Face Value	Price	YTM	Macaulay Duration
A	10%	50	1mio	120	8%	7.5
B	5%	60	2mio	70	7.5%	6.5
C	0%	n.a	3mio	50	8.5%	5.0

Procedure:

- Find the dirty price of the bonds and determine the value of the portfolio
- Determine the modified duration of each bond

Bond A:

Dirty price = Clean price + Accrual interest = $120 + 10^* 50/360 = 121.389$;

Modified duration = $7.5/ (1+0.08/2) = 7.21$

Bond	Price	Accrual Interest	Dirty Price	Face Value	Market Value	% to the portfolio	Modified Duration
A	120	1.389	121.389	1mio	1,213,890	29.39	7.21
B	70	0.83	70.83	2mio	1,416,600	34.30	6.30
C	50	0	50	3mio	1,500,000	36.31	4.80
					4,130,490	100.00	

Market value of the portfolio

= 121.389% * 1mio + 70.83% * 2mio + 50% * 3mio = 4,130,490

Modified duration of the portfolio

= 29.39% * 7.21 + 34.30% * 6.30 + 36.31% * 4.80 = 6.02

What happens to the portfolio when the overall interest rates have risen by 1%?

The value of the portfolio should have dropped by 6.02% (roughly) or 248,655 (4,130,490 * 6.02%).

Index